IMAGES
of America

TEHACHAPI

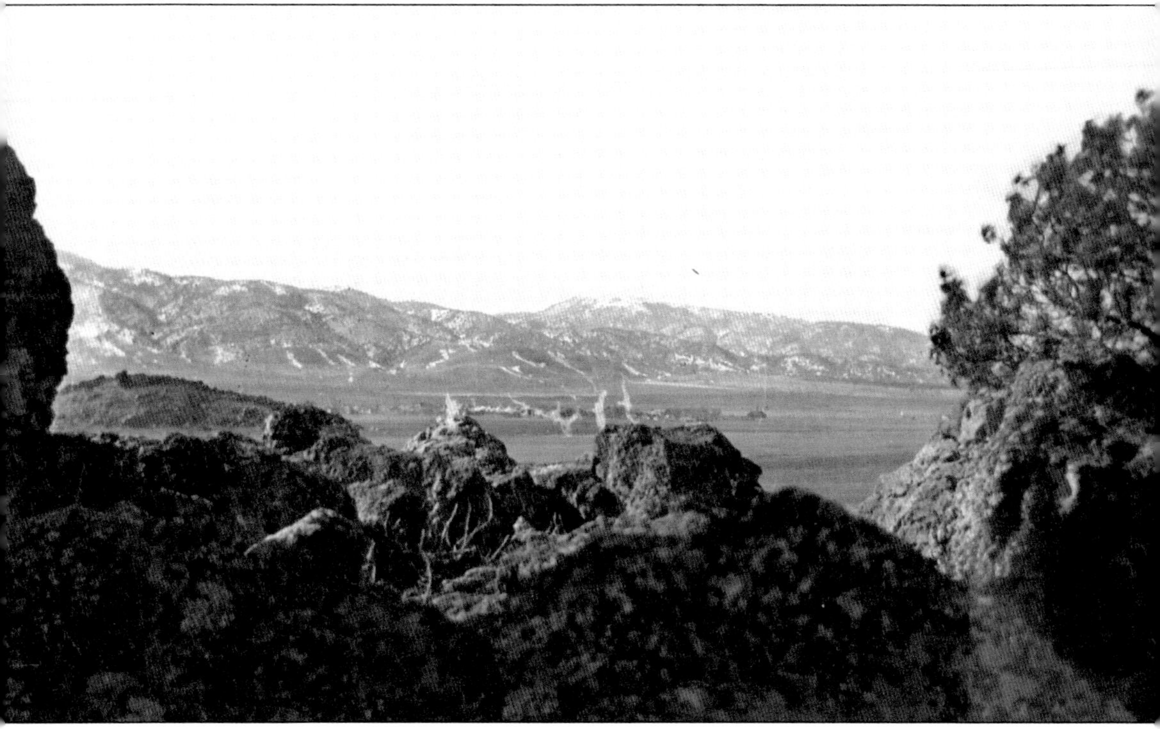

The Tehachapi Valley extends east to west for 10 miles. It is framed on the north by the Sierra Nevada and on the south by the Tehachapi Mountains, which then blend into the Coastal Range. When the first settlers arrived in 1854, little had changed since Jedediah Smith's journey here in 1827. (Tehachapi Museum.)

ON THE COVER: Time to celebrate! Railroad workers raise a toast to the completion of tracks over the Tehachapi Pass, a task many predicted was impossible to accomplish. Over 3,000 men with hand tools, brawn, and sweat created a rail system in 1876 that remains a marvel of engineering and human skill. Not shown are any of the Chinese laborers, 300 of whom lost their lives in blasting accidents. In the wake of such labor, a new town came into existence: Tehachapi. (Tehachapi Museum.)

IMAGES
of America

TEHACHAPI

Gloria Hine Gossard

ARCADIA
PUBLISHING

ISBN 978-0-7385-5560-7

Published by Arcadia Publishing
Charleston, South Carolina

Printed in the United States of America

Library of Congress Catalog Card Number: 2007928545

For all general information contact Arcadia Publishing at:
Telephone 843-853-2070
Fax 843-853-0044
E-mail sales@arcadiapublishing.com
For customer service and orders:
Toll-Free 1-888-313-2665

Visit us on the Internet at www.arcadiapublishing.com

CONTENTS

ACKNOWLEDGMENTS

This is a companion volume to *The Three Valleys of Tehachapi*, an Images of America book by Arcadia Publishing. Both works may be considered similar in that they give a historical account of the Tehachapi Valley, a dividing point between Central and Southern California. Whereas *The Three Valleys* covers the western portion of the Tehachapi Valley (settled in 1854), *Tehachapi* provides a pictorial account of the people and events that turned a frontier town into a city.

When the Southern Pacific Railroad arrived in the Tehachapi Valley in 1876, there were already two small towns: Williamsburg (1868) and Greenwich (1875). Both were founded by individuals. The railroad established Summit Station, but the people called it Tehachapi Summit. As the town grew (absorbing both Williamsburg and Greenwich), so did the role of its residents, and Tehachapi soon became the area's commercial center. Many names first introduced in *The Three Valleys* often reappear in this publication, as these early settlers were all civic-minded individuals whose influence guided the growth of a frontier town into the city of Tehachapi.

Due to the efforts of the Tehachapi Heritage League, much of the history of this area has been preserved through photographs and memories of descendants of these early pioneers. The cooperation and assistance of the following were invaluable in creating this book: the Tehachapi Heritage League, with special thanks to Jerrie Cowan, Del Troy, and Charles White; C. J. Brown and Nick Smirnoff for their computer skills; Judy Reynolds for proofreading; and Jerry Roberts of Arcadia. Unless otherwise noted, all photographs are from the archives of the Tehachapi Museum and represent the collections of the Cummings family, Herb and Ollie May Force, J. C. Jacobsen, Frank Nejedly, the Leiva/Kelcey family, Ed Wiggins, F. O. Wyman, the Southern Pacific Railroad, and the USDA/Tehachapi Resource Conservation District.

My sincere thanks to all, and to you, the reader.

—Gloria Hine Gossard

INTRODUCTION

This part of our county [Tehachapi] seldom receives any notice through the press. It is one of the best sections of our county. It is an agricultural, stock, lumber and mining country, and in about four years, eleven months, and twenty seven days the Southern Pacific will be completed to that point. . . . Then [it] will be the liveliest place in Kern County, if we are not mistaken in our figures.

—*The Havilah Miner*, October 11, 1873

This editor's enthusiasm for Tehachapi was a far cry from the opinion held by California's Spanish and Mexican authorities between their ruling years of 1772 and 1848. To them, it was just part of the vast land that lay east of the coastal valleys, a place they called *Tierra incognito*, or "the unknown land." Their colonization interests were concentrated on the coastal lands where ships with provisions from Alta California (Mexico) could set anchor and return with wine from mission vineyards, cattle hides, and tallow.

A Spanish padre, Francisco Garces, was considered the first to discover the Tehachapi Valley in 1776. His Yuma Indian guides led him from Arizona over a centuries-old inter-tribal trading route through the arid Mojave Desert and along the foothills of the Sierra Nevada and the riparian-riddled Central Valley. They called this valley *Ta-hacha-Pah-Na*, or "the place where the people of the acorns lived." Garces considered it suitable for agricultural purposes and described it as a "land having numerous oaks and other trees."

Authorities, however, remained uninterested. The land continued to be ignored and was ventured into only when pursuing deserting soldiers or mission Indian neophytes. This made the Tehachapi Valley an ideal route for those wishing to avoid detection and detention. Authorities were hostile to all intruders, and American fur trapper Jedediah Smith fell into this category. In 1827, Smith, who kept a daily journal and drew his own maps, retraced Garces's route into the streambeds of the Central Valley. Others soon followed. Among those who have since become familiar names in western history were Ewing Young, Kit Carson, and John C. Fremont. Carson would later describe the 10-mile-long Tehachapi Valley as "a beautiful, low pass."

Fremont was less frugal with words. A lieutenant with the U.S. Topographical Corps of Engineers, he was also an amateur botanist. His journals not only included geographical data, but detailed descriptions of various plants and other flora. He also injected his own feelings, such as "the air was filled with perfume, as if we were entering a highly cultivated garden." As an engineer, Fremont also noted the Tehachapi Valley could be used as a route for a north-to-south railroad. Bear in mind this was in 1844—a full six years before California would become part of the United States.

To all early travelers, the Tehachapi Valley was a 4,000-foot-high oasis between the desert sands and creosote bushes to the east and the tule-choked bogs and lakes to the west. Large groves of trees provided restful shade, and jaded horses and mules could replenish themselves on acres of lush forage. Game was abundant, and spring-fed creeks slackened one's thirst. The natives, though cautious of strangers, were peaceful and friendly. Yet even after statehood, when the valley became part of public domain and open to homestead, there was no rush of settlers. The only sign of activity was when the local natives were transferred to the newly established Sebastian Reservation in nearby Tejon Canyon. There they mingled with other mountain and valley tribes while Fort Tejon was constructed in the adjoining Canon de las Uvas (Grapevine Canyon).

The Tehachapi Valley continued to attract travelers. Most were on their way to the gold fields of Northern California or the Kern River. Others were survey parties. One such group, led by Lts. Robert S. Williamson, J. G. Parke, and George M. Anderson, was entrusted with the task of finding a suitable route for a railroad. Williamson's final report, issued to the U.S. House of Representatives in 1854, recommended the Tahachapa [*sic*] Pass as the most practical route, even though it would "present some difficulties."

Williamson's group may well have crossed paths with geologist H. S. Washburn, who was conducting a survey for the surveyor general of California. Washburn's report, released in 1854, provided the most complete, in-depth description of the Tehachapi Valley, which at this time was spelled Tachichipi, Teechapa, Teh-chapa, and Tahachapa. Along with soil analysis, he noted the abundance of springs and timber, and concluded that some five-sixths of the township was adapted to agricultural purposes, "one-half of which is good, first rate tillable land and the other half well adapted to the raising of stock."

Washburn mentioned finding some traces of gold and that a mining claim was even then in the process of being sold. The buyer was George Cummings, and the claim included such improvements as a "board house, smith's shop, and a ditch fence." Washburn also listed a homestead claim, newly filed by John Brite. Both Cummings and Brite would have a lasting influence on local history and lend their names to such geographical features as Brite's Valley, Brite's Canyon, Cummings Mountain, and Cummings Valley. Washburn concluded his report with the comment, "Nowhere in California have I seen greater inducements for the enterprising and hardy settler."

By 1855, the John Brite and William Wiggins families, George Cummings, Francois Chanac, Thomas Goodwin, and Grant Cuddeback had established themselves in this area. Five years later, the number of settlers was still less than two dozen. Perhaps the reason was that many of those coming west were attracted to a more salubrious climate. As a land of four seasons, Tehachapi often endured some deep freezing and heavy snowfall. By now, the name was often erroneously defined as "valley of wind" and "frozen land." It was also isolated, the nearest towns being Visalia and Los Angeles. The latter had yet to outgrow the image of a sleepy pueblo, and the former was still growing. As a town, Bakersfield was nonexistent, just a finger of dry land surrounded by marsh from the Kern River.

Its isolation made the Tehachapi Valley a prime area for outlaws and horse thieves. It was a perfect channel for driving horses stolen from the Central Valley into ready markets in Utah, New Mexico, and Mexico. Mounted dragoons from Fort Tejon began patrolling the area against action by those such as Joaquin Murietta and his brothers. (One of Tehachapi's beloved old-timers, Abelino Martinez, served as a courier to Murietta as a youngster.) Outlaw gangs, including Tiburcio Vasquez, Santos and Francisco Sotello, and the Mason and Henry Gang, found the surrounding canyons and mountains to be ideal hideouts and passages between Visalia and Los Angeles. Even years later, when a daily stagecoach began operating between San Pedro and Caliente, holdups became so numerous that a guard with a shotgun was assigned to each driver. It should be noted that lawlessness increased when the railroad arrived in Caliente and was instrumental in that town's reputation as just another hellhole of the West.

Despite these challenges and those of nature (including severe droughts), the valley offered great inducements for the "hardy and enterprising settler." Cattle and horses grew fat and multiplied, and fields of oats and barley thrived in the virgin soil. In time, other enterprises like gold, salt, lime, timber, and orchards proved profitable. In 1868, enough settlers had arrived for James Williams to create a thriving town called Williamsburg. (It even had a hotel with inside water faucets.) Locals, however, preferred to call the community Tahachapa.

One

The Beginning Years

The frontier reached by the Pacific railroad . . . moves forward at a swifter pace and in a different way than the frontier reached by the birch canoe or the pack horse.

—Frederick Jackson Turner, "The Significance of the Frontier," 1920

The Southern Pacific Railroad inched its way south through the San Joaquin Valley and, in early 1875, arrived at the base of Bear Mountain, establishing Caliente. The town soon became the area's center of commerce. Tehachapi farmers supplied the products that fed the freight teams trekking daily to the railroad with ore from mines in the Mojave Desert. That same year, Peter D. Greene started Greenwich, a town he considered in the best location to serve the railroad. For a while it flourished with a livery and stage relay station and an express and post office. (Letters were addressed to "Tahachapa" or "Tehachapa." Williamsburg thus became Old Tahachapa.)

The Southern Pacific ignored both Caliente and Greenwich, and plotted out its own town: Summit Station. Once again, residents used the name Tahachapa or Tehachapa, and Summit Station became Tehachapa Summit. The name *Tehachapi* was introduced by William Brewer in his book *Up and Down California*, an account of a four-year survey. Brewer referred to the area as "Tehachapi," adding "on your map Tahachapa." The name and spelling clicked with Southern Pacific officials, who changed their town to Tehachapi.

This is not the story of how a railroad established a thriving community and a city. In essence, it is the story of hardy and enterprising settlers creating three raw frontier towns that eventually became one incorporated city. Ironically, the final location and spelling came closest to the name used by the native people: *Ta-chip'i*, which means "the place."

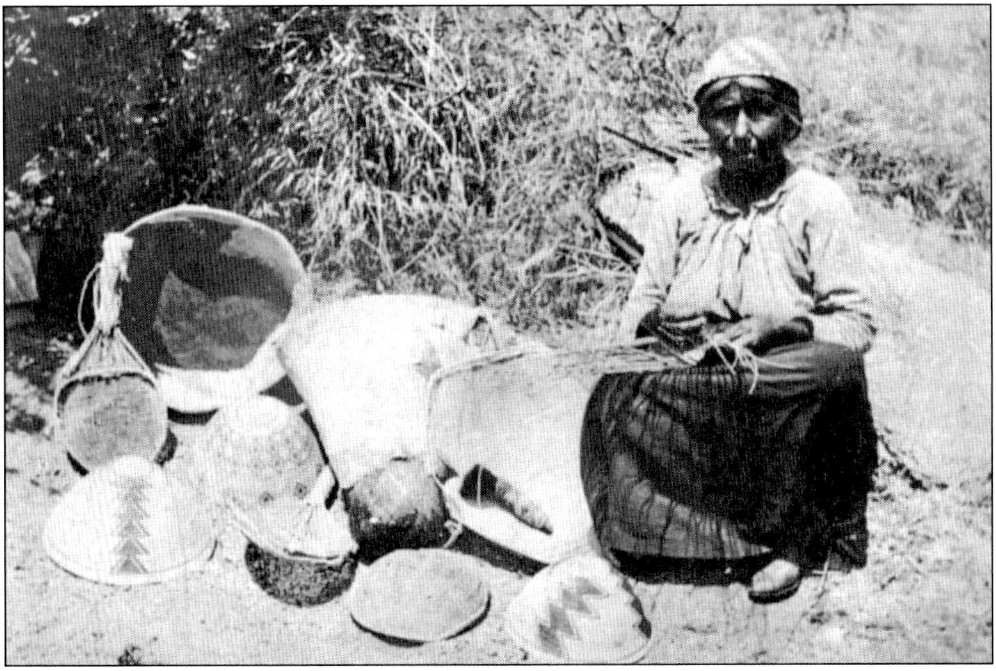

The native inhabitants described themselves as the *Noo-ah*, or "the people." In 1877, ethnographic researcher Stephen Powers wrote the following in his *Contributions to North American Ethnology, Volume III*: "In the famous Tahichapah Pass was a tribe called by themselves Ta-hi-cha-pah'na, by the Kern River Indians Te-hichp', and by the Yokuts Ka-wi-asuh."

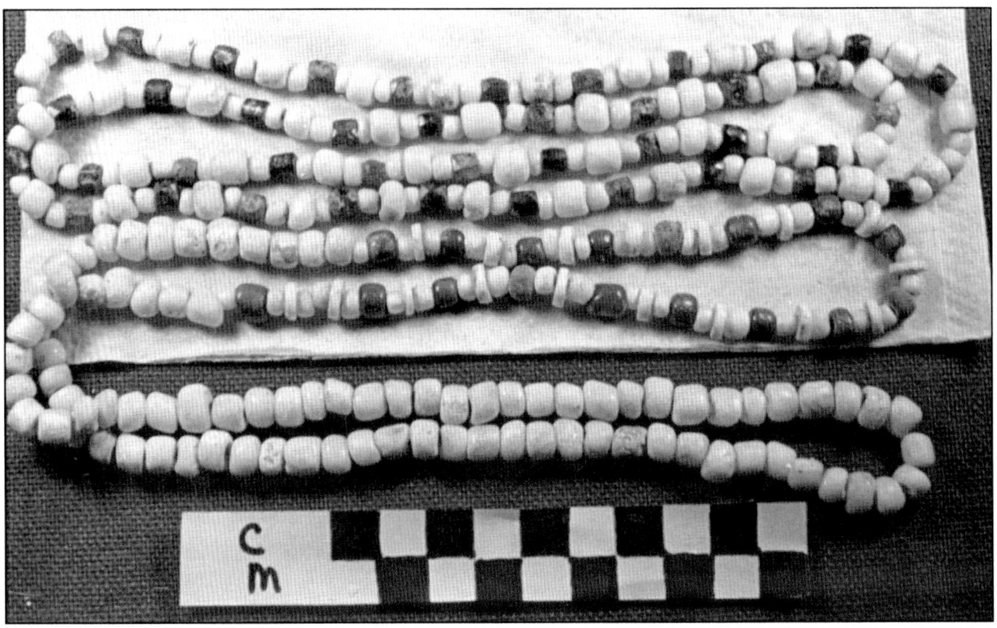

The trading beads displayed in the Tehachapi Museum may date back to the journey made by Padre Garces in 1776. Subsequent travels by American fur trappers and Hudson Bay Company workers could also have brought these and other items as offerings of friendship to the Native Americans they encountered.

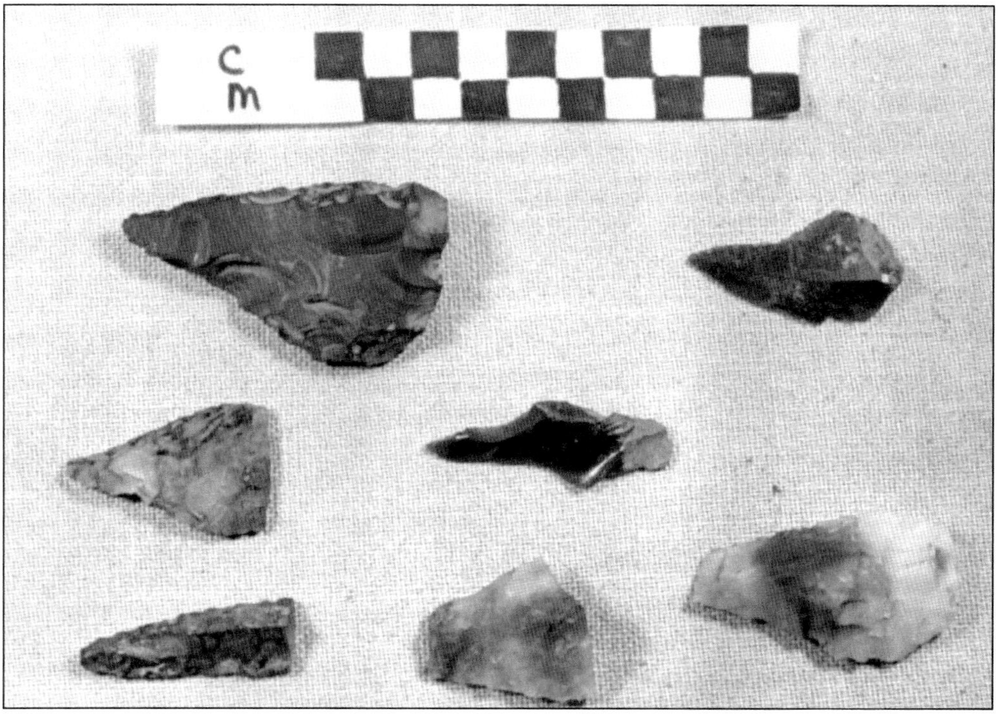

Local Native Americans used arrowheads to hunt small game and wildfowl. In order to make them, stone was chipped and beveled to a sharp point. The darker ones are obsidian, or volcanic rock, which could be found in the Owens Valley area. Trade between tribes living in different areas was quite common.

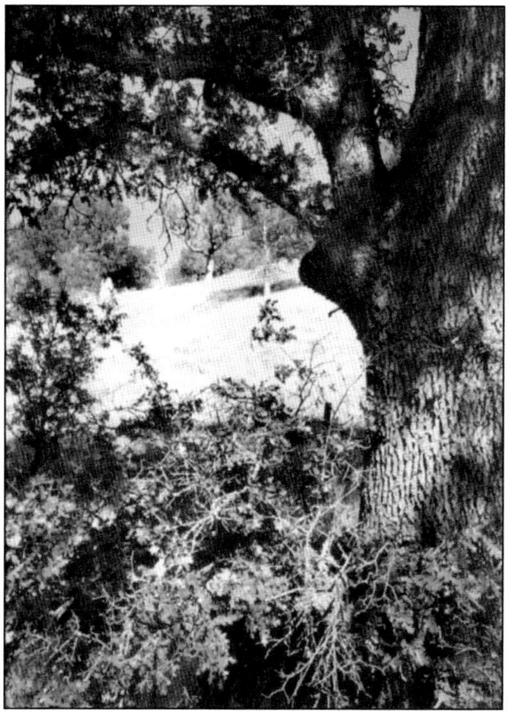

Tehachapa was said to mean 'Big Tree Valley' because of the large oak trees and was probably so named on account of the numerous white oak trees in which the country abounds, according to the *Kern County Gazette* of January 26, 1878. (Author's collection.)

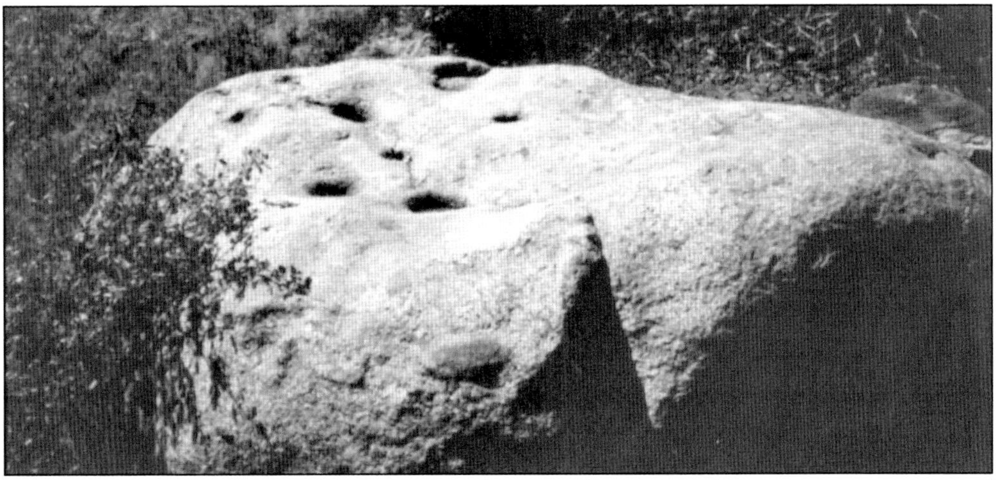

Mortar holes in large boulders are remnants of a time when Native American women gathered to grind acorns, their staple diet, into a coarse meal. These boulders, scattered throughout the valley, provided fodder for the once-common definition of Tehachapi as "the place where the people of the acorns live." (Author's collection.)

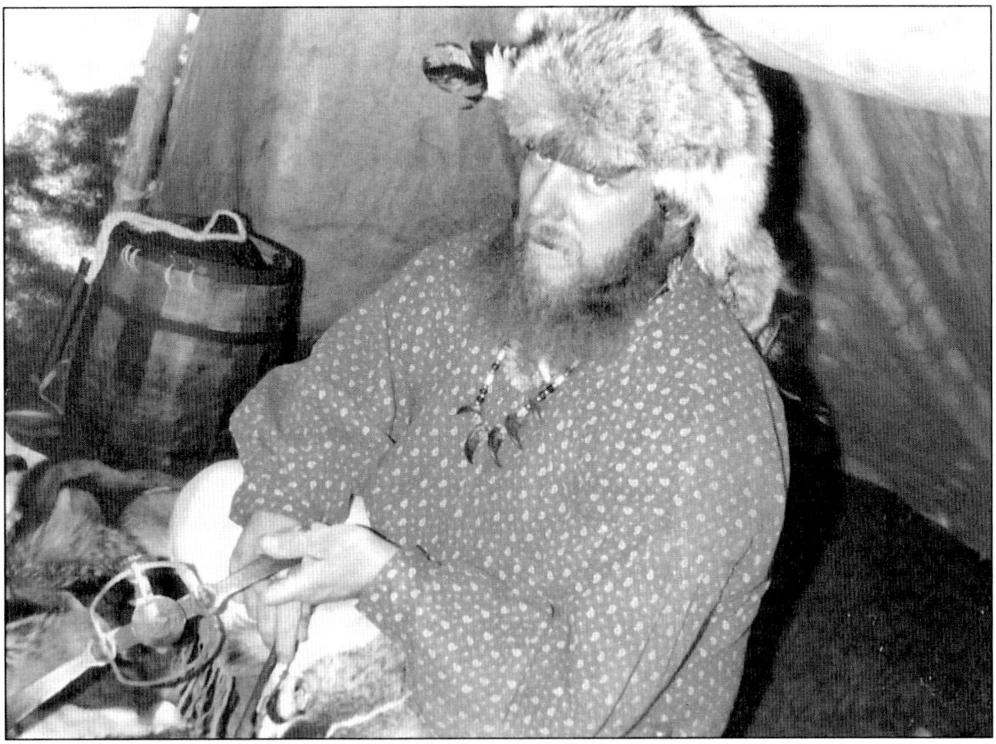

William Sasnett of Tehachapi displays a trap and the customary outfit of a typical early-1800s fur trapper. A re-enactor, Sasnett pays homage to mountain men such as Jedediah Smith, who played a brief but important role in the history of the West. His role in history has been eloquently depicted by historian/author Robert Glass Cleland in his *c.* 1950 *The Reckless Breed of Men*. Cleland writes of Smith, "He has traveled the first of the great transcontinental routes to California, made known the valleys of the San Joaquin and Sacramento to the American trapper and through them to American settlers."

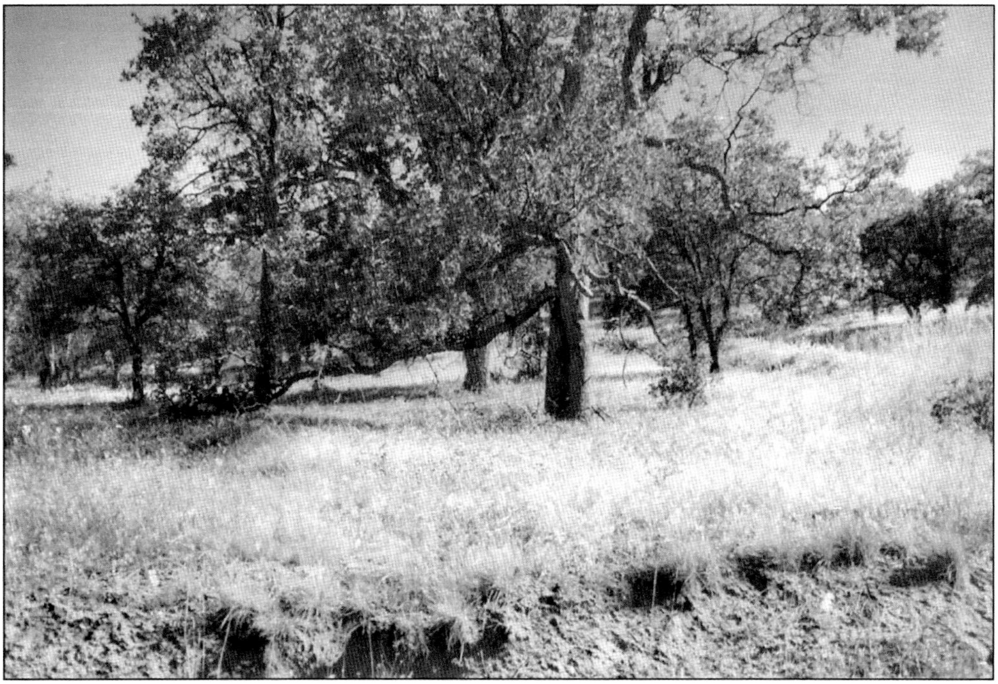

The oak-studded hillsides provided many definitions for the name *Tehachapi*. These included "land of many trees" and "land of the acorns." Padre Garces's Native American guide called the land *Tah-hee-chay- Pah'na*, or "land where the people of the acorns live." (Author's collection.)

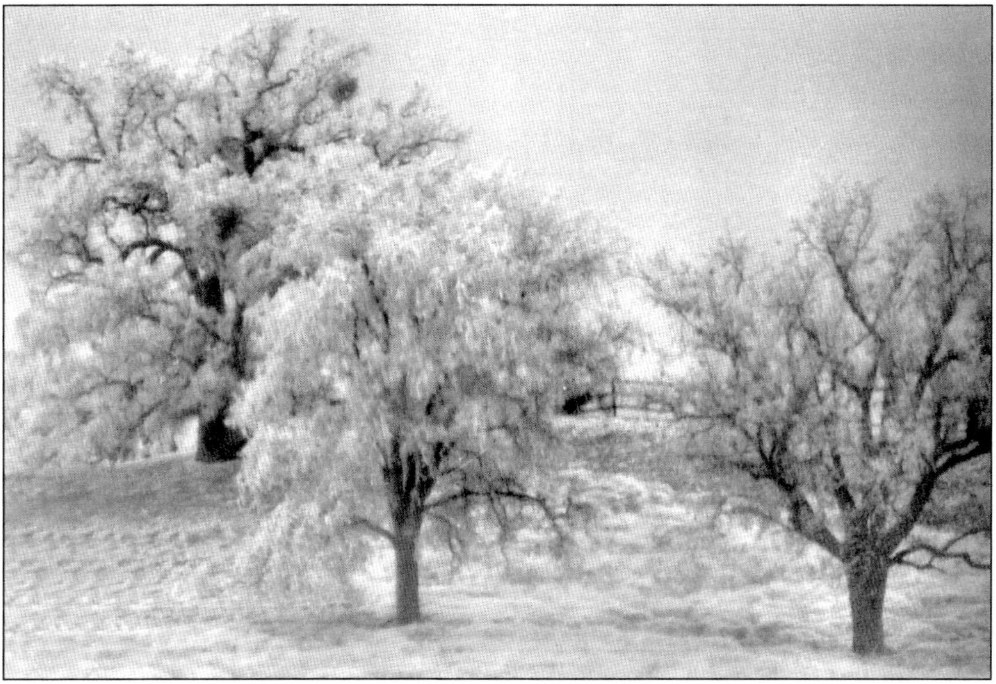

The name *Tehachapi* prompted many spellings, such as Tee-chapa, Tahachapa, and Te-cha-pana. There were also an equal number of definitions. Wintertime and frosted trees brought about such translations as "the land of wind and snow" and "frozen trees." (Author's collection.)

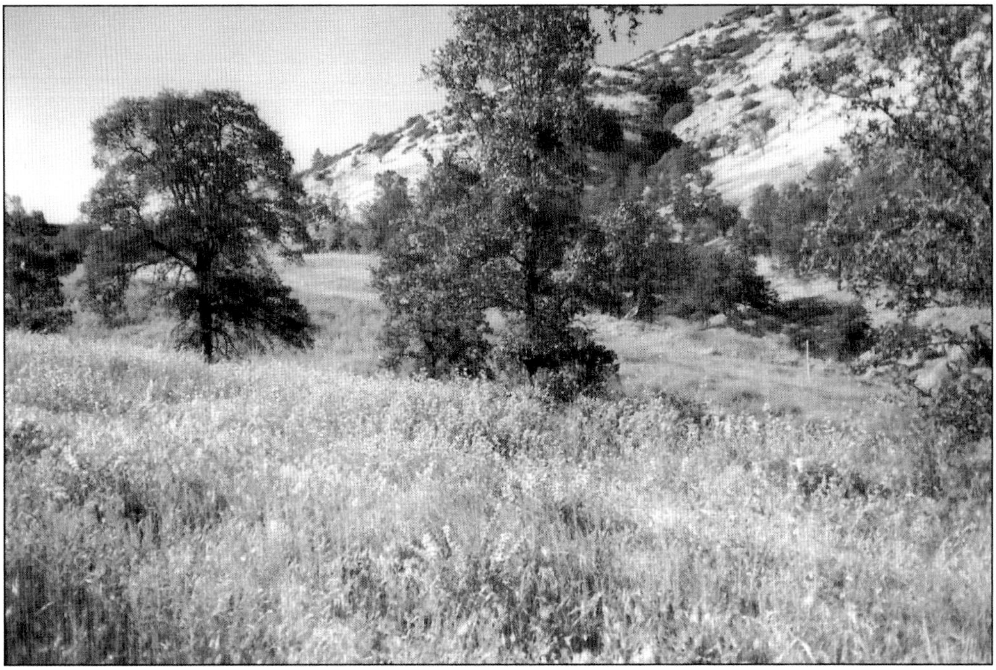

"We crossed where the Coast Range and the Sierra Nevada join together—a beautiful, low pass." Christopher "Kit" Carson gave this description of the Tehachapi Valley following his journey with Lt. John C. Fremont in 1844. It was Carson's second trip through the region. He had first been through with Ewing Young's 1830 fur-trapping expedition, which had followed the trail taken by Jedediah Smith (1827) and Fr. Francisco Garces (1776).

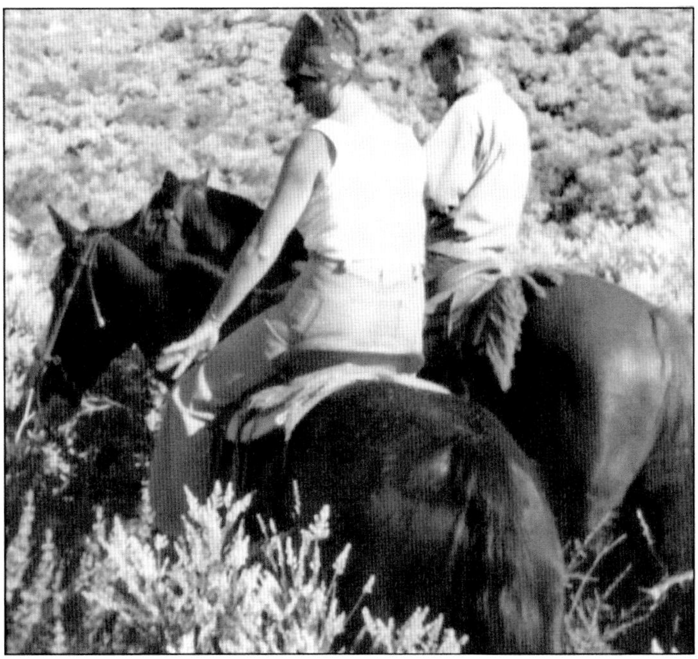

Horseback riders today can still find scenery similar to that which prompted John C. Fremont to write "the land was as rich and fragrant [with wildflowers] as a cultivated garden." A lieutenant with the elite U.S. Army Corps of Topographical Engineers, Fremont kept meticulous journals that included personal observations such as the above quotation describing his journey through the Tehachapi Valley in April 1844. (Author's collection.)

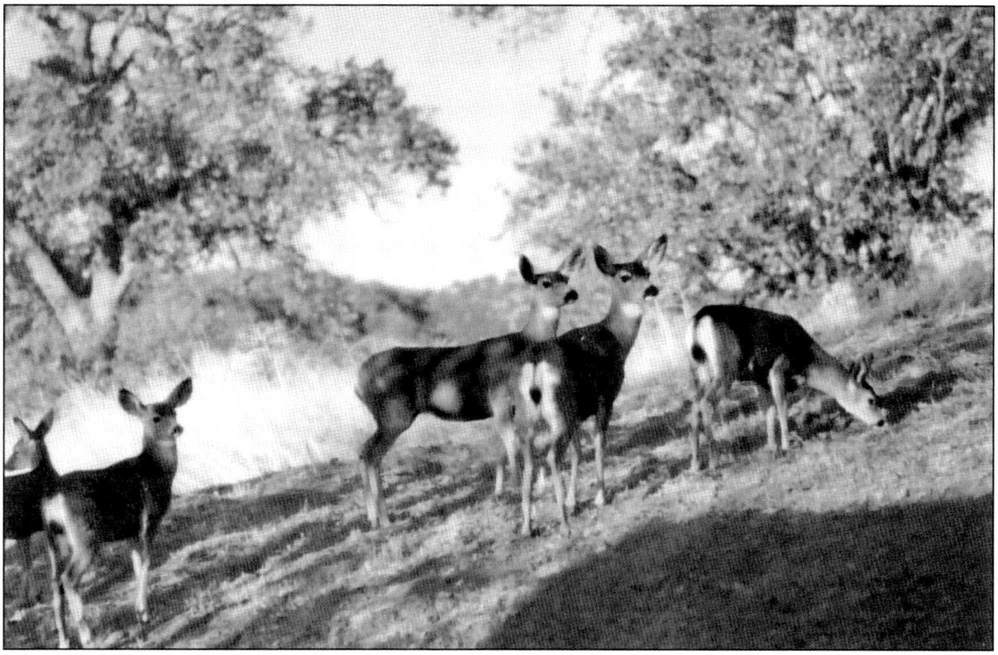

The Tehachapi Valley was a traveler's oasis separating the sands of the Mojave Desert from the marshlands of the Central Valley. There was an abundance of natural food and water; game was plentiful, and mountain springs fed numerous creeks. All this was noted by early travelers, many of whom returned and, like George Cummings, started raising cattle. Moses Hart returned and began farming. (Author's collection.)

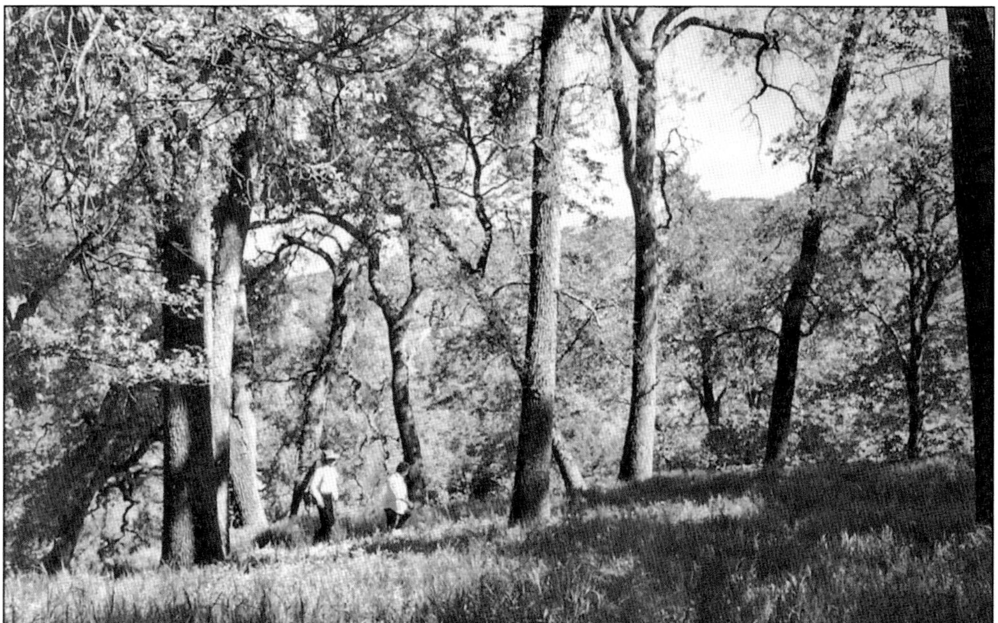

Trees in the bottom of a narrow canyon grew straight and tall in order to reach the sunlight far above. This provided trees taller than usual with few low limbs and attracted the attention of many as an excellent source of timber. (Author's collection.)

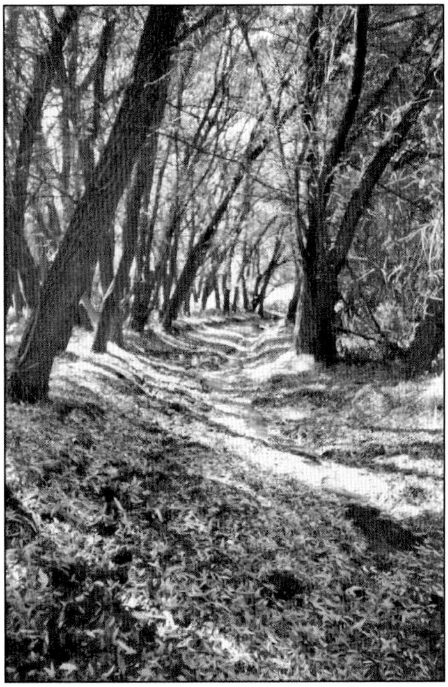

Tree-lined creek beds led through numerous canyons and provided perfect pathways or hideouts for several outlaws traveling through the area. It was not uncommon for a posse from Visalia, Santa Barbara, or Bakersfield to track outlaws and then lose the trail once it entered the Tehachapi Mountains. (Author's collection.)

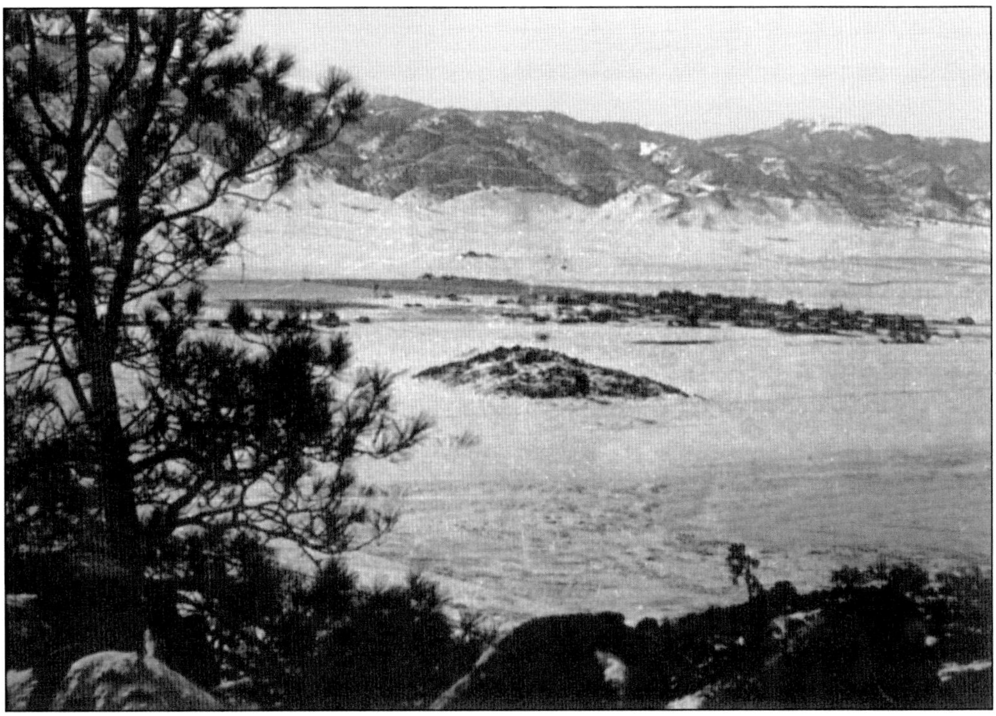

This new land was unique and required one to adjust. "No one ever told us that it snowed in California," was one comment. This gave credibility to the claim that *Tee-hachapi* came from the Paiute word *Ti-ci*, meaning "to freeze." The summers, however, were dry with little rain and little, if any, humidity. The wise farmer quickly determined such weather irregularity could be advantageous and adjusted his techniques. A 320-acre ranch could then raise several different crops.

Two

THE AGRARIAN YEARS

Venerate the plow. Husbandry was the first employment of man, therefore the most ancient, the most honorable, and, above all, of divine appointment.

—*Farmer's Almanac*

Between 1855 and 1875, the Tehachapi Valley was an agrarian society. Everything revolved around the land. In the vernacular of the frontier, this land was not a "one-trick pony." It easily adjusted to new crops such as oats, barley, rye, wheat, alfalfa, and fruit orchards. It provided other benefits as well: gold, salt, lime, cinnabar, timber, and building materials.

Such diversity attracted an equally diverse population. Single men and families came from Vermont, Ohio, New York, Arkansas, Missouri, Tennessee, and Texas. Some left families behind in Canada, Mexico, and Chile or in Wales, Ireland, Scotland, Prussia, France, and Spain. They brought skills and trades as carpenters, coopers, blacksmiths, wheelwrights, farmers, herdsmen, clerks, scholars, and lawyers. In 1866, they helped to petition the state to create a new county (Kern) out of Tulare and Los Angeles Counties, and by 1868, Williamsburg had become the Tehachapi Valley's first town. Peter D. Greene built a new toll road into the Central Valley and, in 1875, created another town, Greenwich, just one and a half miles east of Williamsburg. Both attracted new businesses as farmers increased their planting and cattlemen increased their herds.

Within two decades, the valley was thus leaving behind its earlier image as an isolated and unknown land. "Improvements of all kinds are pushing ahead with vigor," reported the *Kern Weekly Courier* on July 28, 1873. Two years later, on April 3, the same newspaper carried the following: "Settlers are coming in rapidly, the old ones are extending their improvements and land is increasing in value." In the meantime, the Southern Pacific Railroad was steadily pushing south through the Central Valley; its destination, the Tehachapi Pass.

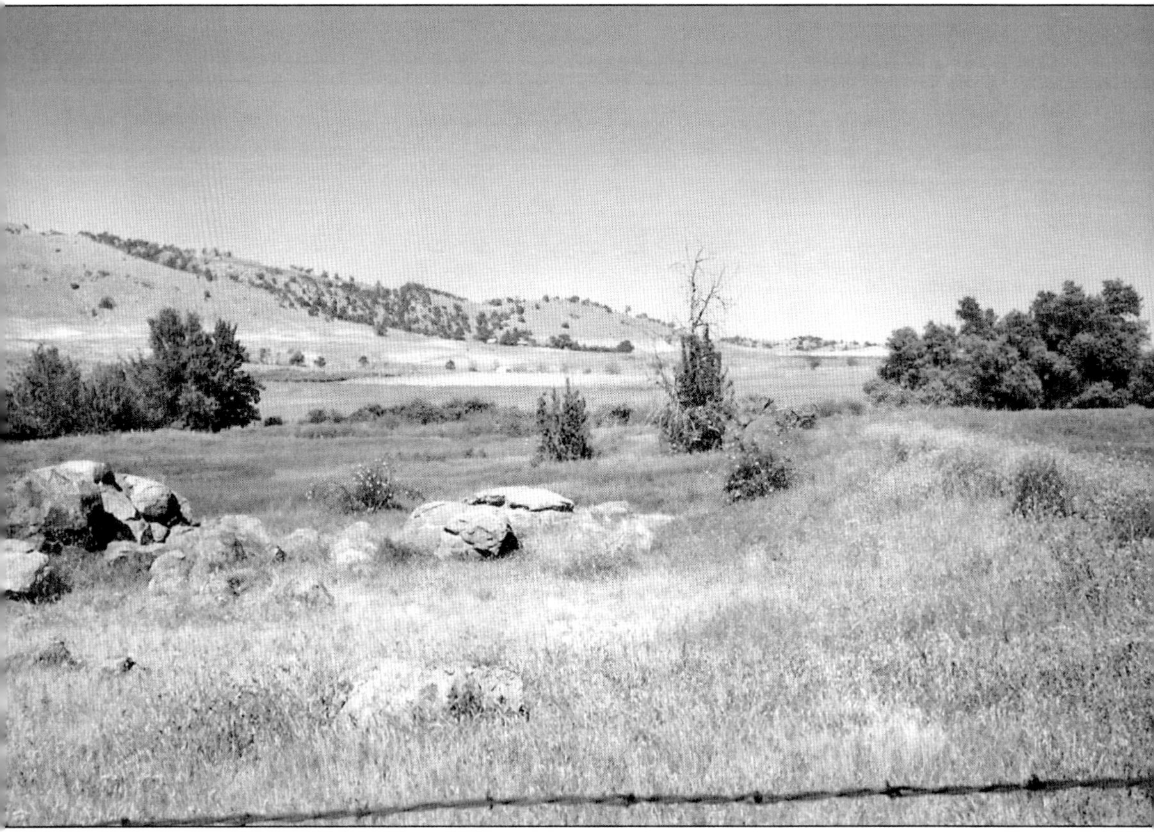

John Brite, his wife, Amanda, and their infant son arrived here in 1854. Their ranch in Brite's Valley, seen here, turned into the center of the growing community. Enterprising and hardy, John was a stockman, farmer, lumberman, businessman, and politician. In 1866, he became the area's first representative on the new Kern County Board of Supervisors. His son Lucas, known as "Gabe," and grandson Perry were also elected supervisors. After dividing the 1,000-acre ranch amongst their children, John and Amanda planned to retire to their new Curry Street home in Tehachapi. Unfortunately, John died before joining Amanda in such comfort. The home was later destroyed in the 1952 earthquake, but the Brite's Valley farmhouse still stands. (Author's collection.)

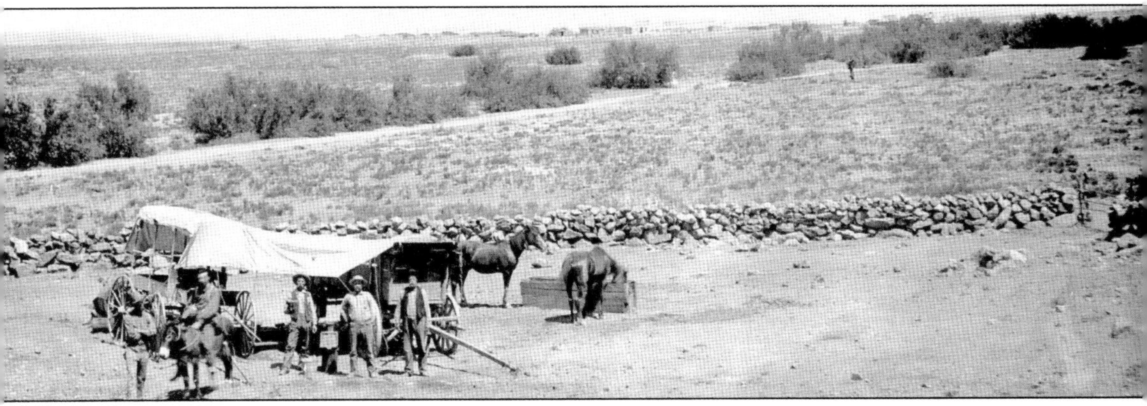

A family would at first live under a canvas shelter until enough trees could be felled to build a crude log cabin. Some families were able to hire local Native Americans to make the mud and straw (adobe) bricks to construct a house that was cool in the summer and warm in the winter.

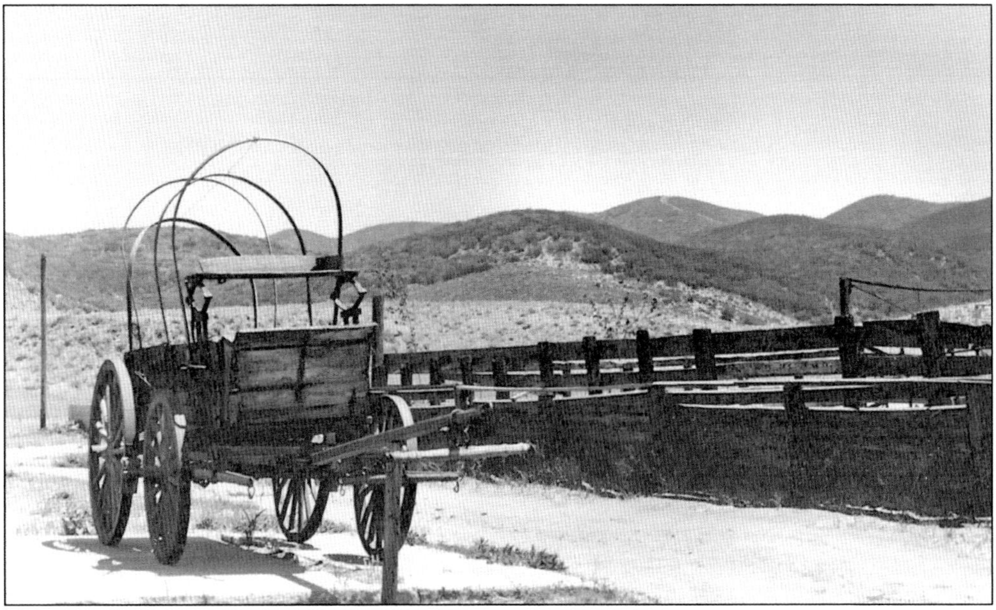

A family's entire life was transported across the country in a wagon. After arrival in the Tehachapi Valley, the wagon was utilized to make semiannual trips to either Visalia or Los Angeles, the nearest commercial centers, for supplies. The round-trip could take up to a week or more. When the town of Williamsburg was established, these long trips were no longer necessary. (Author's collection.)

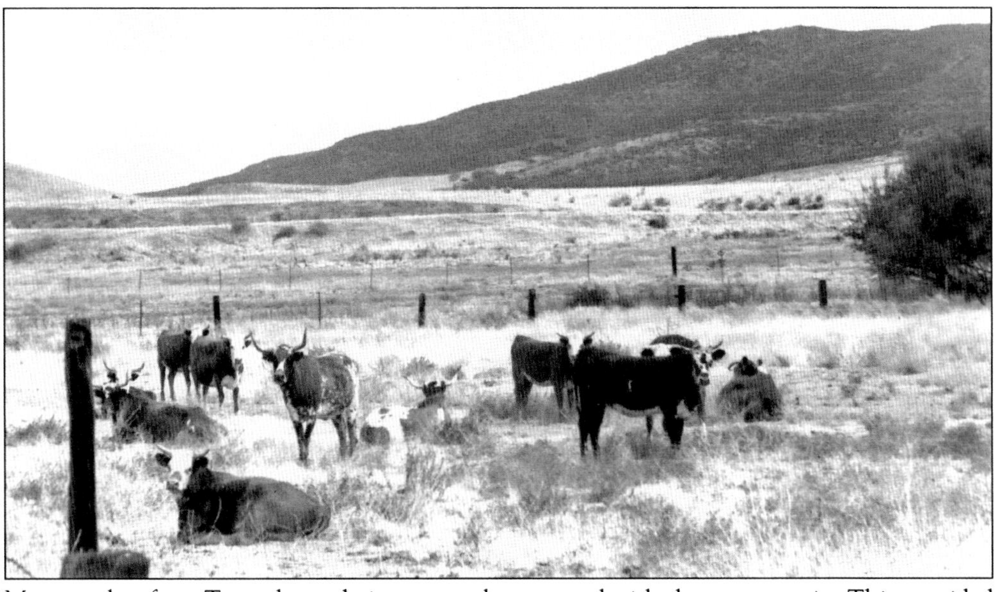

Many settlers from Texas drove their own cattle westward with the wagon train. This provided their first enterprise in the new land. Despite sporadic raids on young calves by the numerous bears and mountain lions, the cattle proved to be a viable investment and added greatly to the area's economy. (Author's collection.)

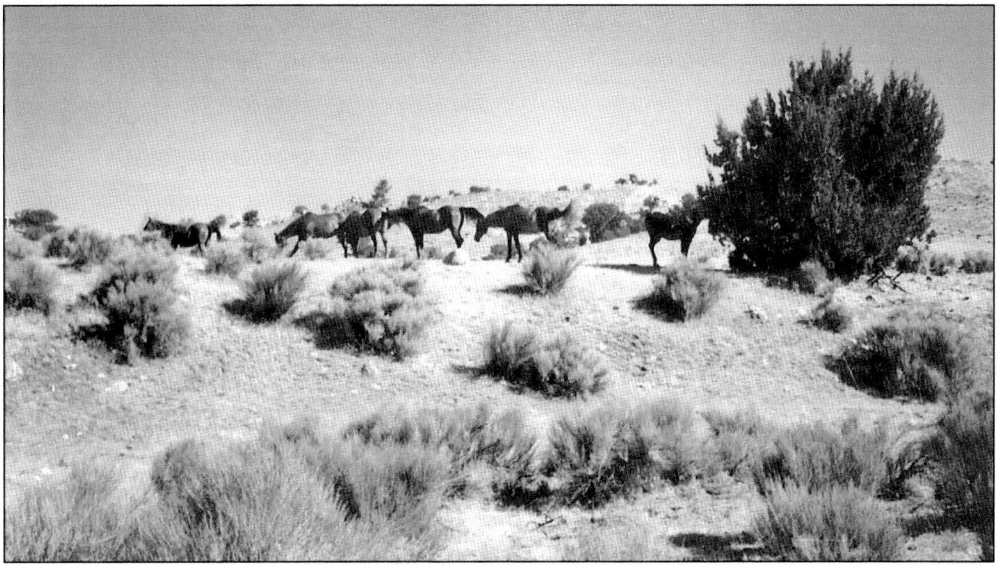

The foothills of Central California were a haven for bands of feral horses, the descendants of those introduced to California by the Spanish in the 1770s. Tehachapi cowboys became quite adept at capturing and breaking these hardy and agile *mestenos* (mustangs) to saddle. (Author's collection.)

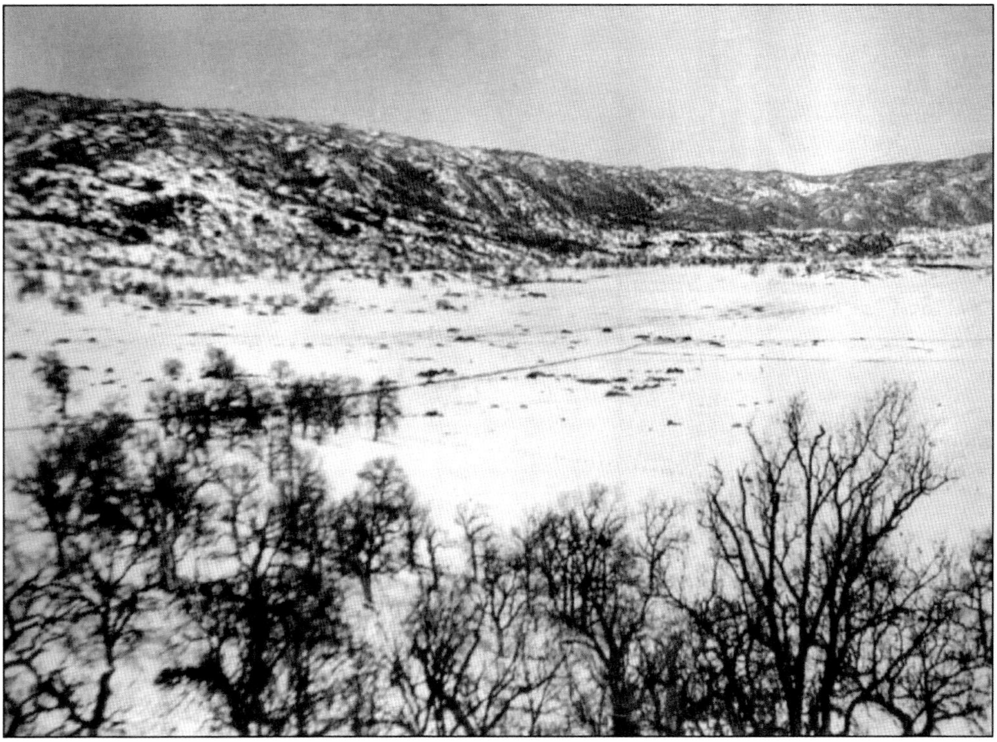

Since several miles separated one family from another, each became self-sufficient by raising its own meat and vegetables. Such isolation was especially hard on the women, who had no social contact with others. The Brites solved this by hosting the area's first Independence Day celebration in 1856. It was a rousing success, lasting all day and into the night.

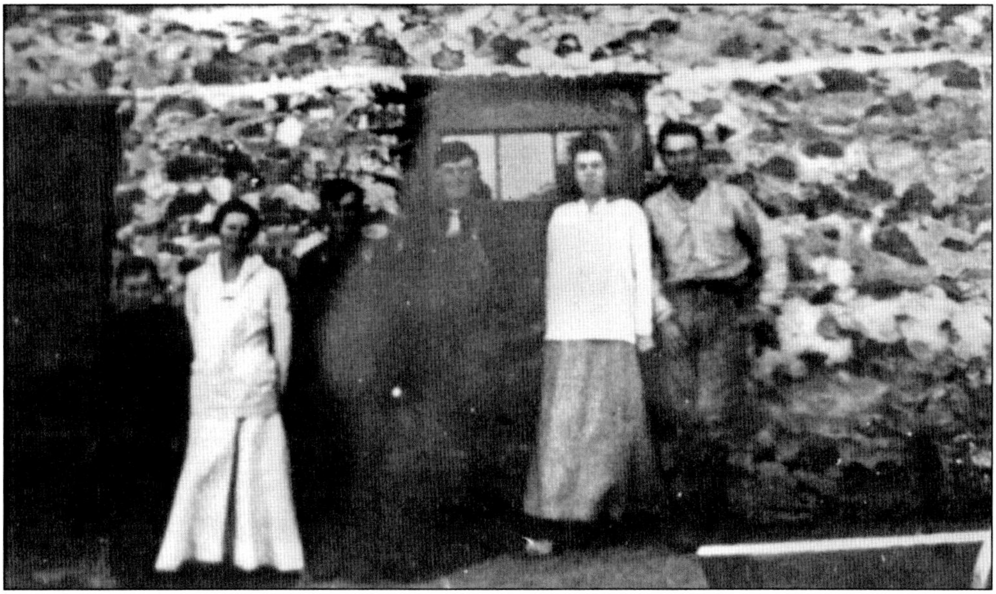

The family was the nucleus of the community. It was customary for a newly married son to bring his bride into his parents' home to live. As the family grew, so did the size of the house. In this way, the parents' workload was gradually assumed by the younger generation.

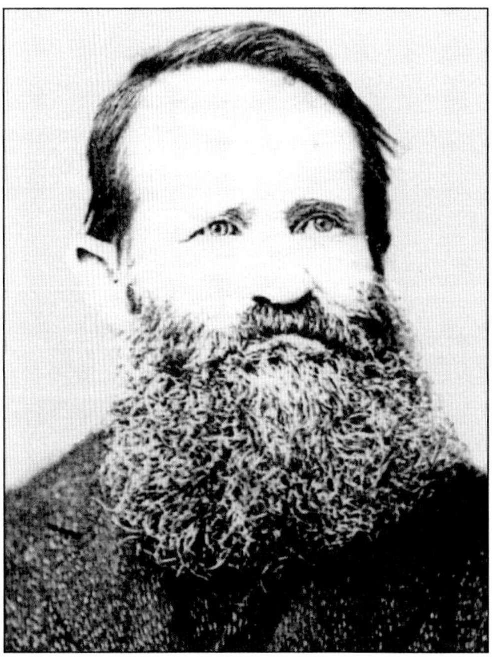

John Narboe; his wife, Johanna Elizabeth; and his brother Paul arrived in 1860 and settled in the northeastern portion of the valley. The brothers came not to farm but to mine. Gold was the primary target, but the 1877 discovery of limestone led to the start of a new industry that lasted well into the mid-1930s.

This seasonal lake, located on the Narboes' property, provided the family's first economic success. During the summer, the water evaporated and left a 3-to-4-inch crust of 93 to 98 percent pure salt. Johanna Narboe sewed the sacks that the brothers filled with salt and sold for $25 each. The lake bed produced between 100 and 300 tons of salt a year.

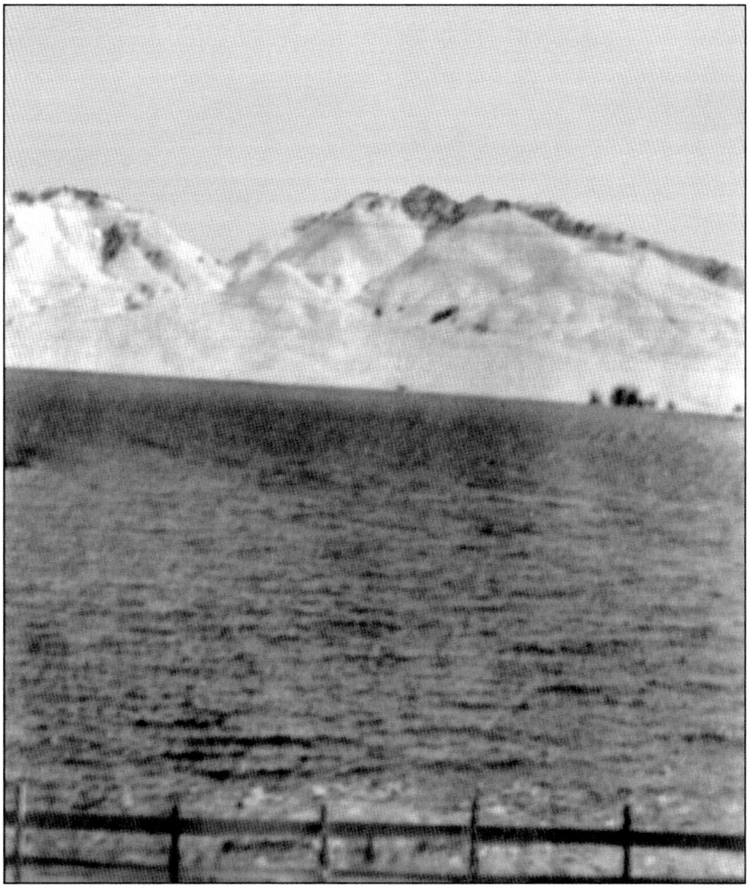

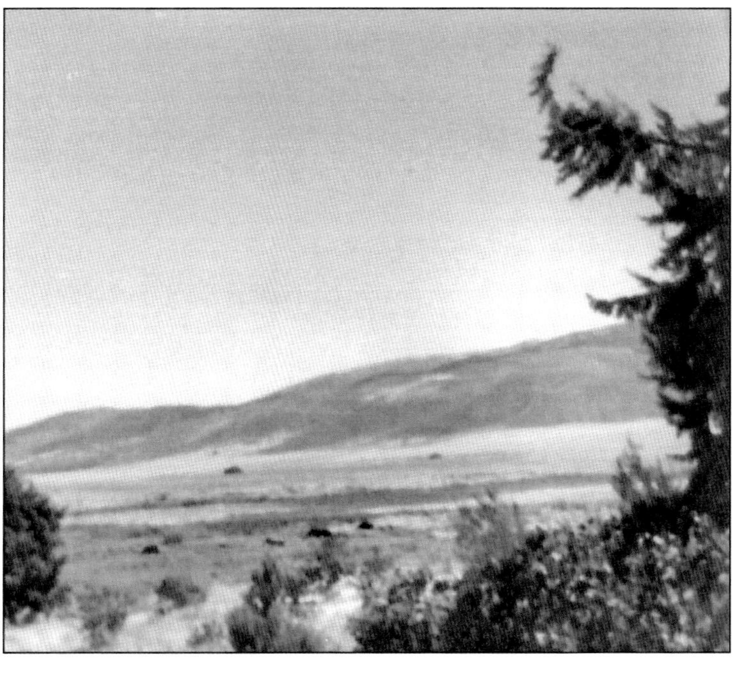

In 1872, a new state law allowed farmers to build fences to prevent roaming cattle from destroying their crops. This allowed more land to be cultivated. For the next two decades, local farmers helped to make California one of the largest wheat producers in the nation. (Author's collection.)

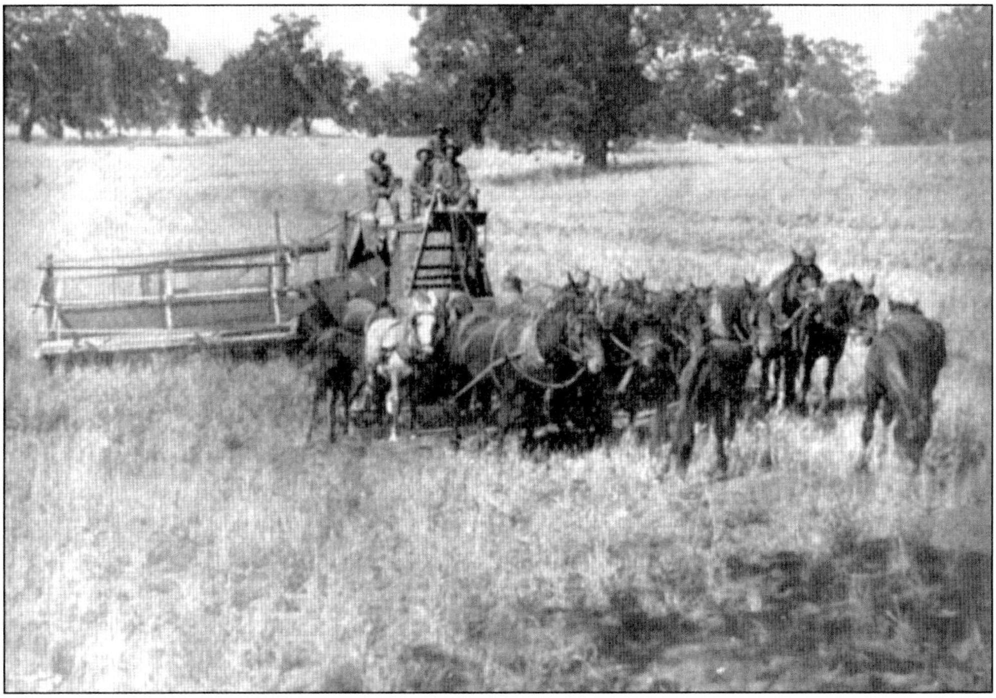

Farmers first raised hay and grain to feed their livestock during the winter. But they soon found their surplus crops in demand to feed the freight teams using the Tehachapi Valley to transport ore from Owens Valley to the railroad at Tipton. By 1875, local farmers were harvesting 300 acres of wild clover and over 1,300 acres of oats and barley.

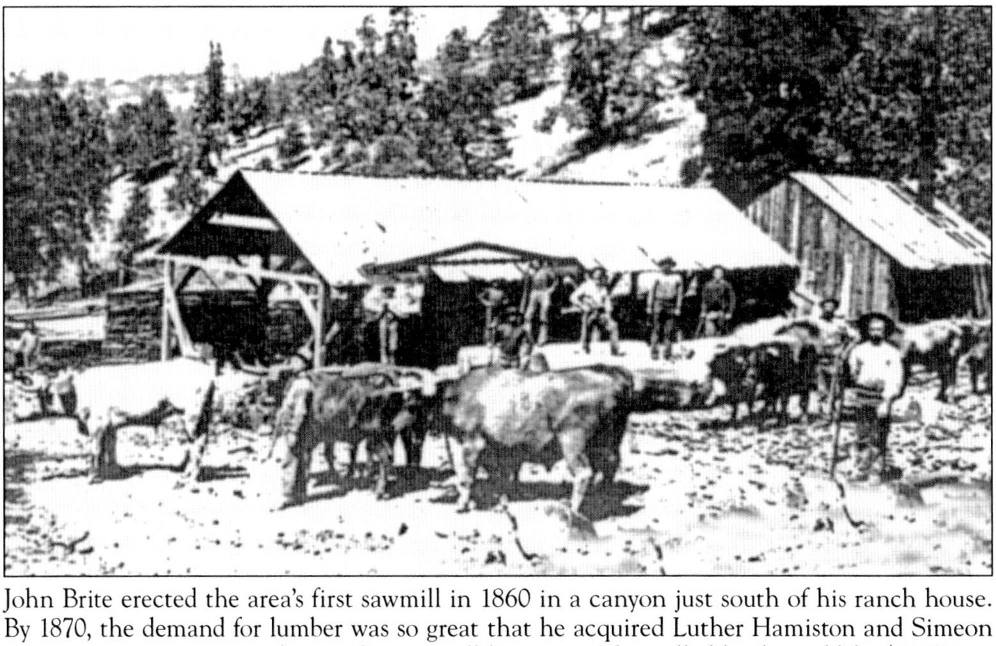

John Brite erected the area's first sawmill in 1860 in a canyon just south of his ranch house. By 1870, the demand for lumber was so great that he acquired Luther Hamiston and Simeon Remington as partners and two other sawmill locations. The milled lumber sold for $22.50 per thousand feet. For 15 years, the partners employed several men at each mill to keep up with the demand for lumber.

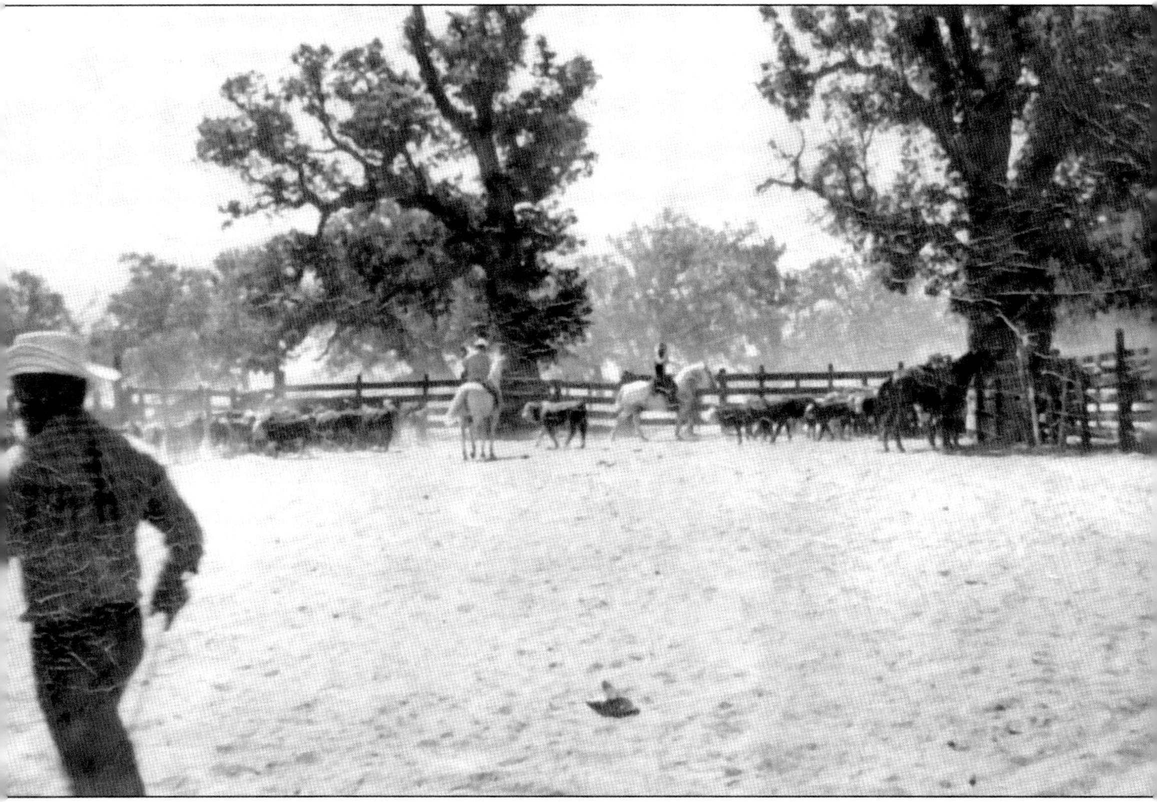

Cattle remained a major factor in the valley's growing economy. Ranches covered several thousand acres and jointly held roundups twice a year. Calves were branded in the spring, and each rancher entered them in his tally book along with losses from severe weather or predators. During the fall roundup, the stock was separated according to those retained for breeding and those destined for the market.

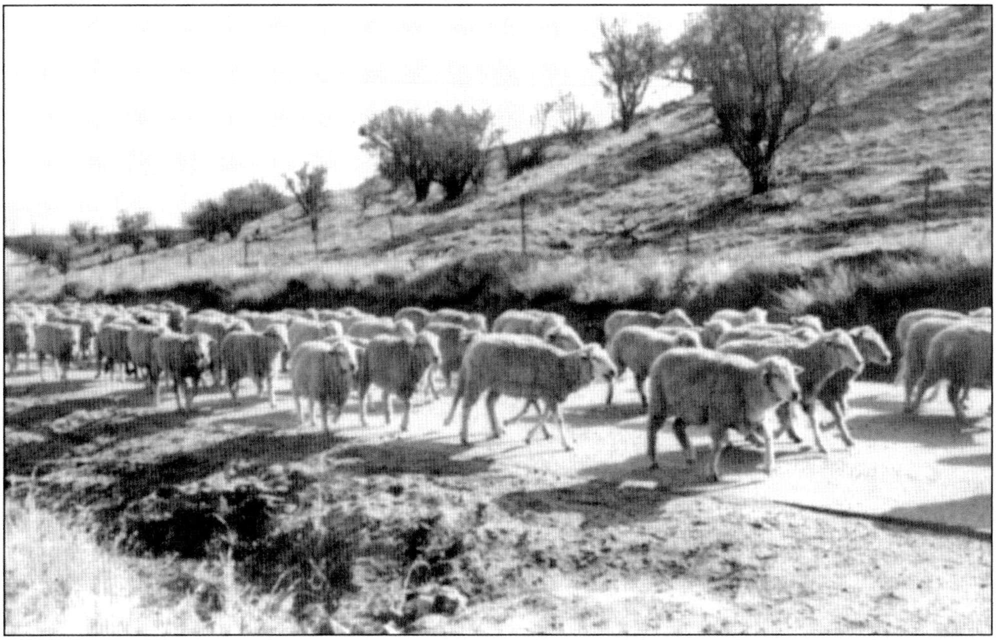

Hostility between sheepmen and cattlemen existed even in the Tehachapi Valley until the arrival of Antone Pauly in 1869. By displaying the wisdom and business sense of his prosperous German father, Pauly acquired 1,750 acres and began raising cattle. The addition of sheep brought him two incomes: one from wool, the other from meat. Others soon followed. Pauly eventually sold parcels of his ranch to Tehachapi businessmen and the town. (Author's collection.)

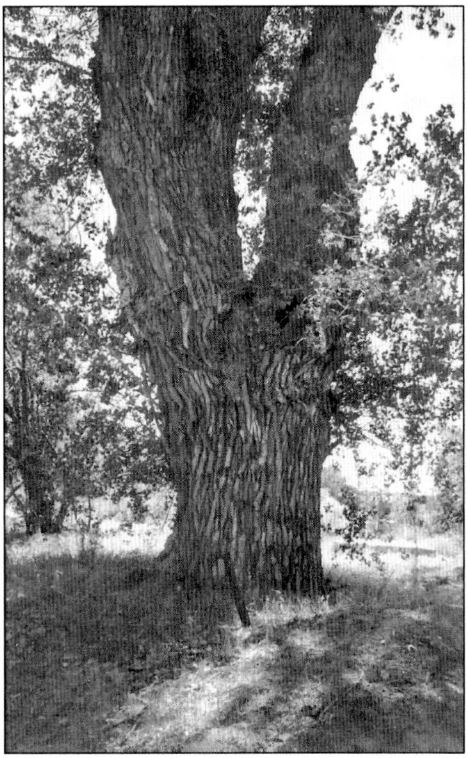

The large oak trees once dominating the foothills were beneficial to both man and beast. The carbohydrate-rich acorns were the staple diet of local Native Americans. They were also relished by the numerous bears that inhabited the region and later by the settler's hogs. Oaks were a source of firewood for the area's homes, wood-burning locomotives, and lime kilns. One tree could produce up to 20 cords of wood. (Author's collection.)

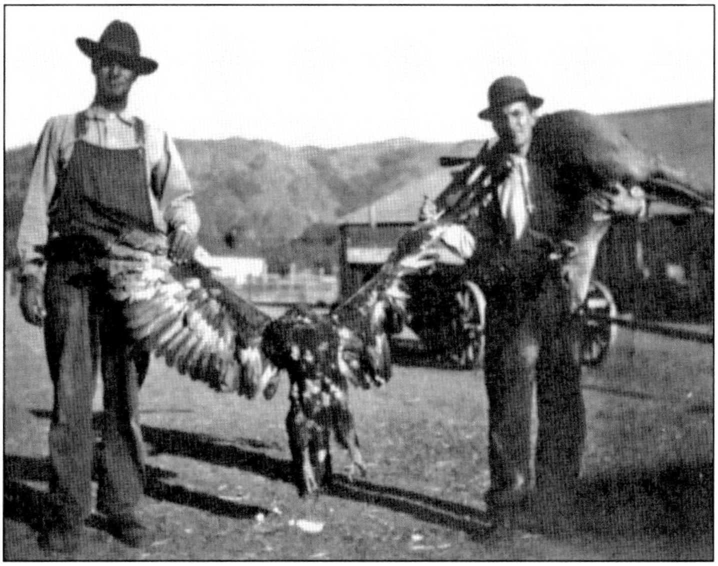

Golden eagles were once so common they provided another erroneous definition of Tehachapa: "eagle's nest." The golden eagle's large wingspan caused some settlers to fear it would carry off small children. Although chickens and small barnyard animals are no match for its keen eyesight and sharp talons, the eagle's primary diet consists of rodents, squirrels, and rabbits.

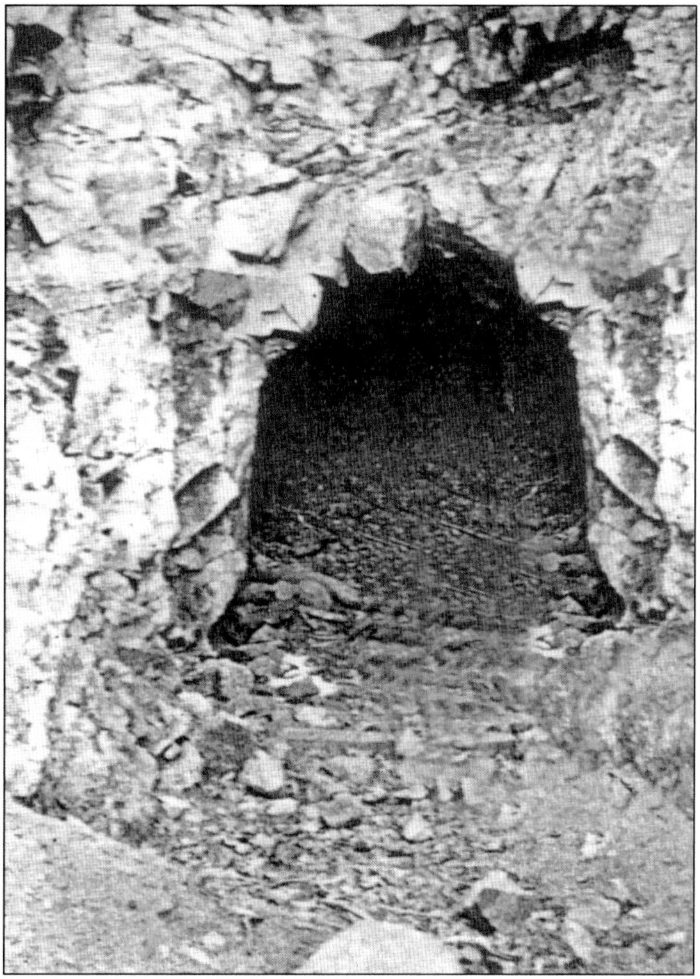

In 1878, a shaft dug into a hillside near Water Canyon became the Pine Tree Mine. It attracted many investors and a succession of owners who added new machinery and expanded operations. The mine never produced any millionaires, but it did add to the economy. By 1897, two dozen men were employed and dividends totaled about $5,000 a month. The mine produced until the price of gold dropped well below operating costs, and the revenue did not justify continued operation.

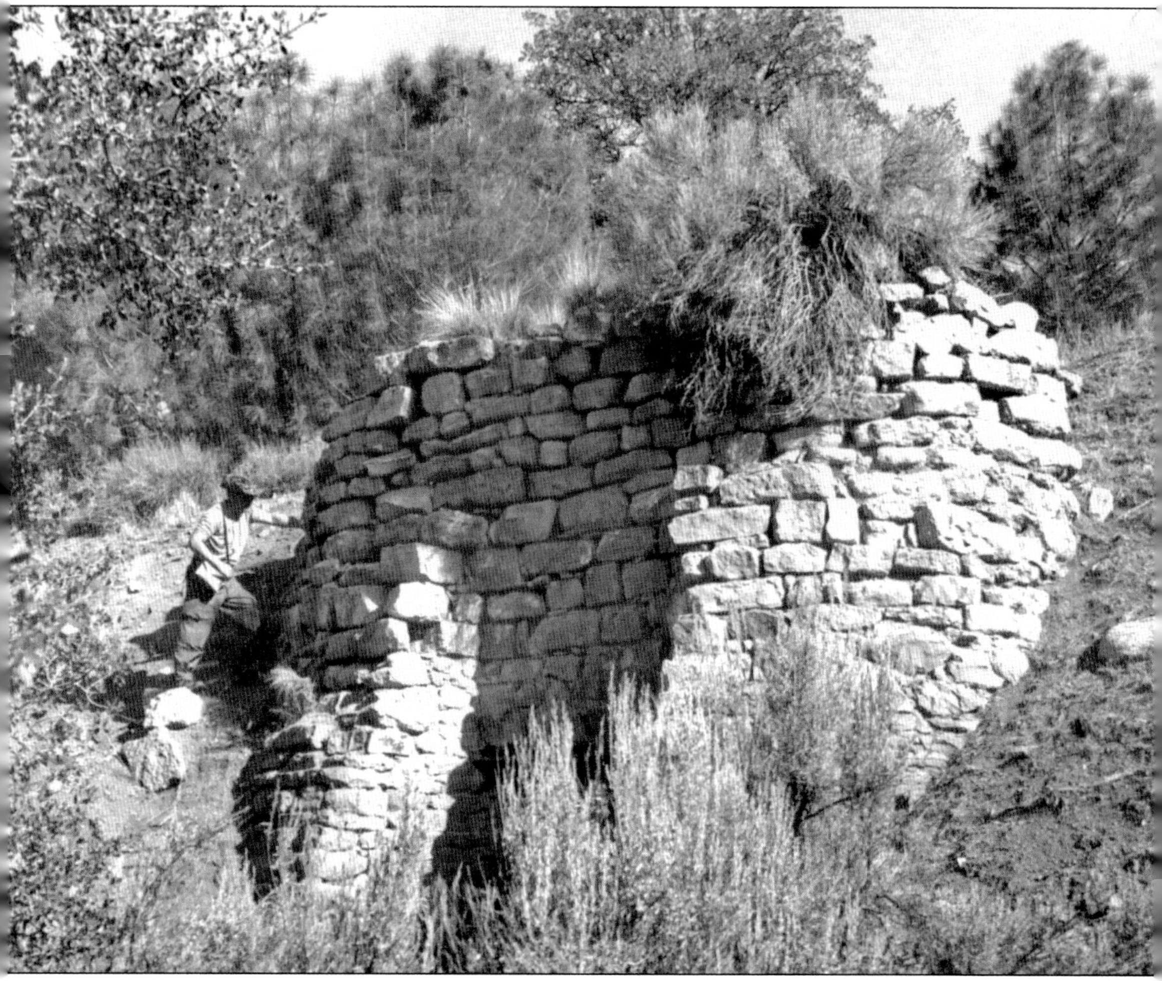

This is all that remains of one of the original lime kilns, called "pot kilns," such as those built by John Narboe and J. B. Malin in 1877. Quarried limestone was dumped inside, covered with cordwood, and ignited. When the temperature reached between 750 and 1,300 degrees Fahrenheit, the stone's carbolic acid burned off, leaving chunks of bluish-white quicklime. In addition to its qualities as a soil additive and stabilizer, quicklime was used in producing whitewash and mortar, making glass, manufacturing paper, tanning leather, and treating raw sewage. Many small lime kilns operated throughout the valley until 1885 when F. O. Wyman made this a major industry. By 1898, Wyman's Summit Lime Company (also known as the Union Lime Company) was a major employer with a $2,500 monthly payroll and shipments of 52,000 barrels a year. In 1900, Wyman introduced oil-burning kilns in Tehachapi near the railroad tracks.

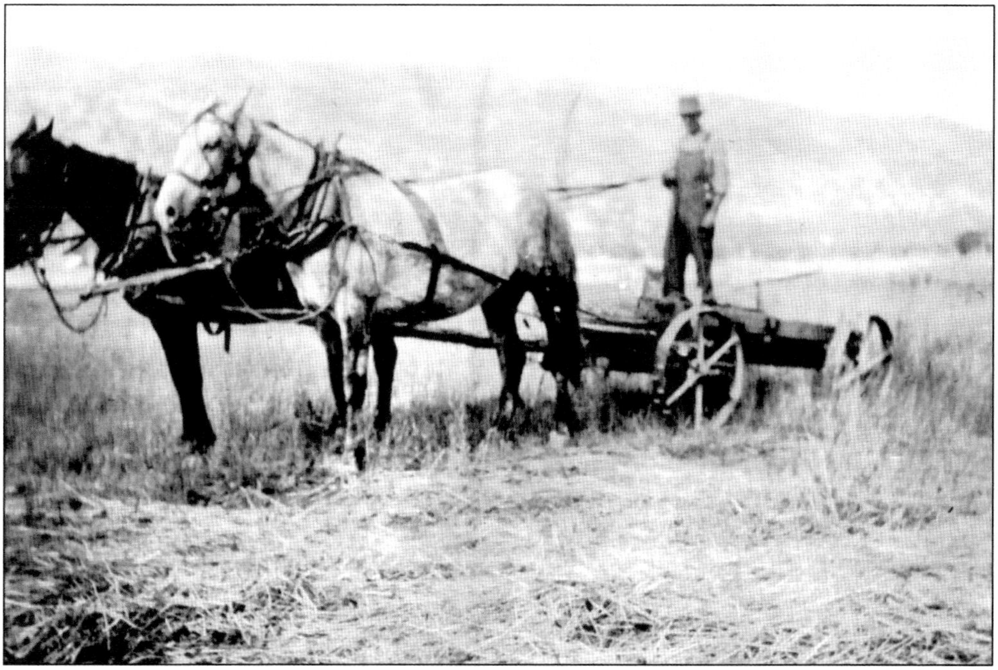

As the year 1860 came to an end, an estimated two dozen families lived in the valley. Most were raising cattle but had also begun to expand their farming operations, like John Brite, who added 80 acres in barley. It was a good move. Hay and grain, followed by wheat, proved beneficial to the economic growth of individuals and the area.

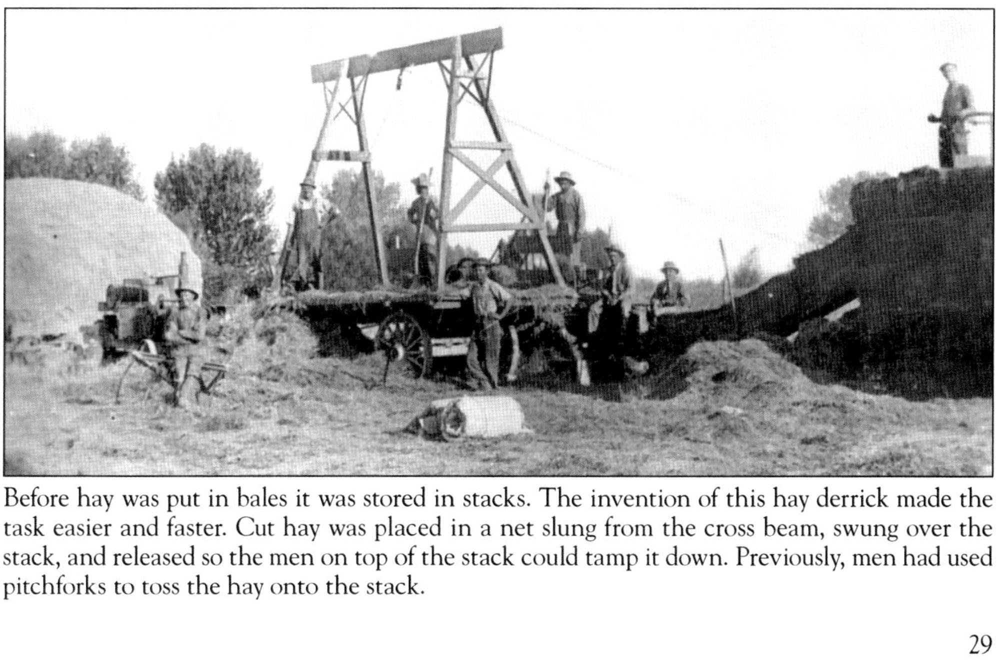

Before hay was put in bales it was stored in stacks. The invention of this hay derrick made the task easier and faster. Cut hay was placed in a net slung from the cross beam, swung over the stack, and released so the men on top of the stack could tamp it down. Previously, men had used pitchforks to toss the hay onto the stack.

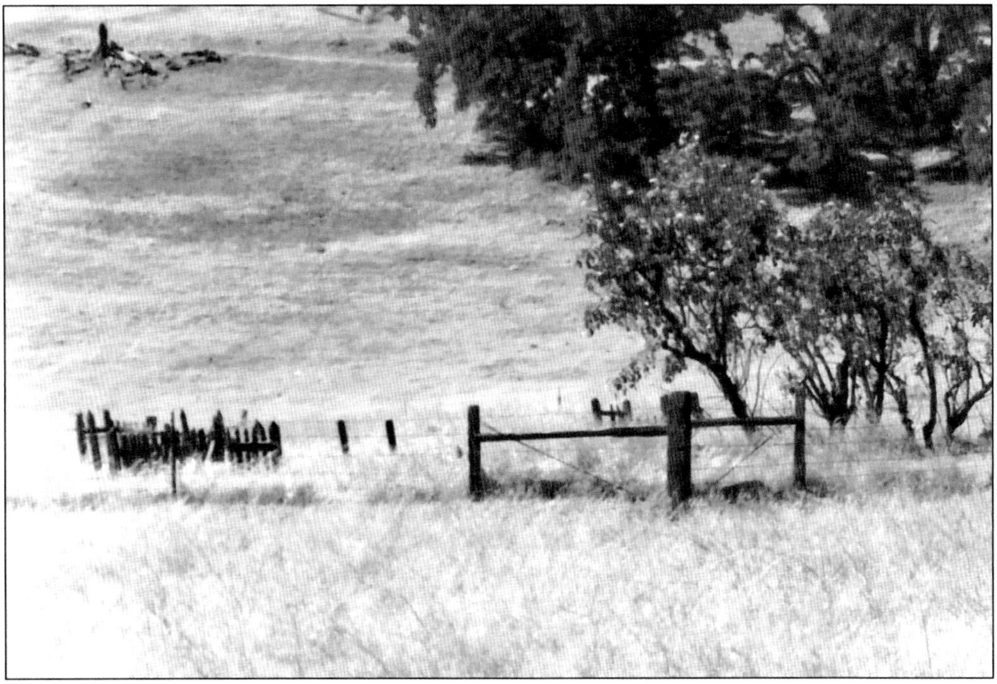

Overgrown with weeds, this graveyard is all that remains of the Sebastian Indian Reservation. It and its neighbor, Fort Tejon, were closed by the government on September 11, 1863. The Native Americans were marched northward to other reservations in the Central Valley, but many Kawaiisus and Tubatulabals managed to slip away to their homelands in the Tehachapi and Kern River Valleys. Here they found employment as vaqueros, farmhands, and laborers. (Author's collection.)

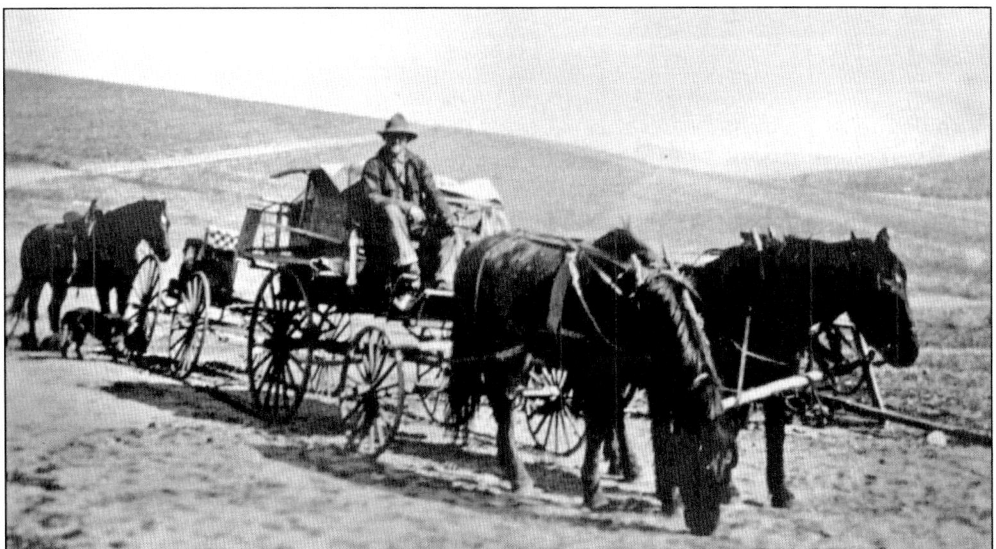

Between 1861 and 1866, journeying in pairs seemed safer because lone travelers were at the mercy of outlaws who once again roamed the area at will. With the start of the Civil War, the troops at Fort Tejon were reassigned. Patrols ended, as did any local law enforcement. Many outlaws also used the war as an excuse to rob and plunder those with strong ties to the Union.

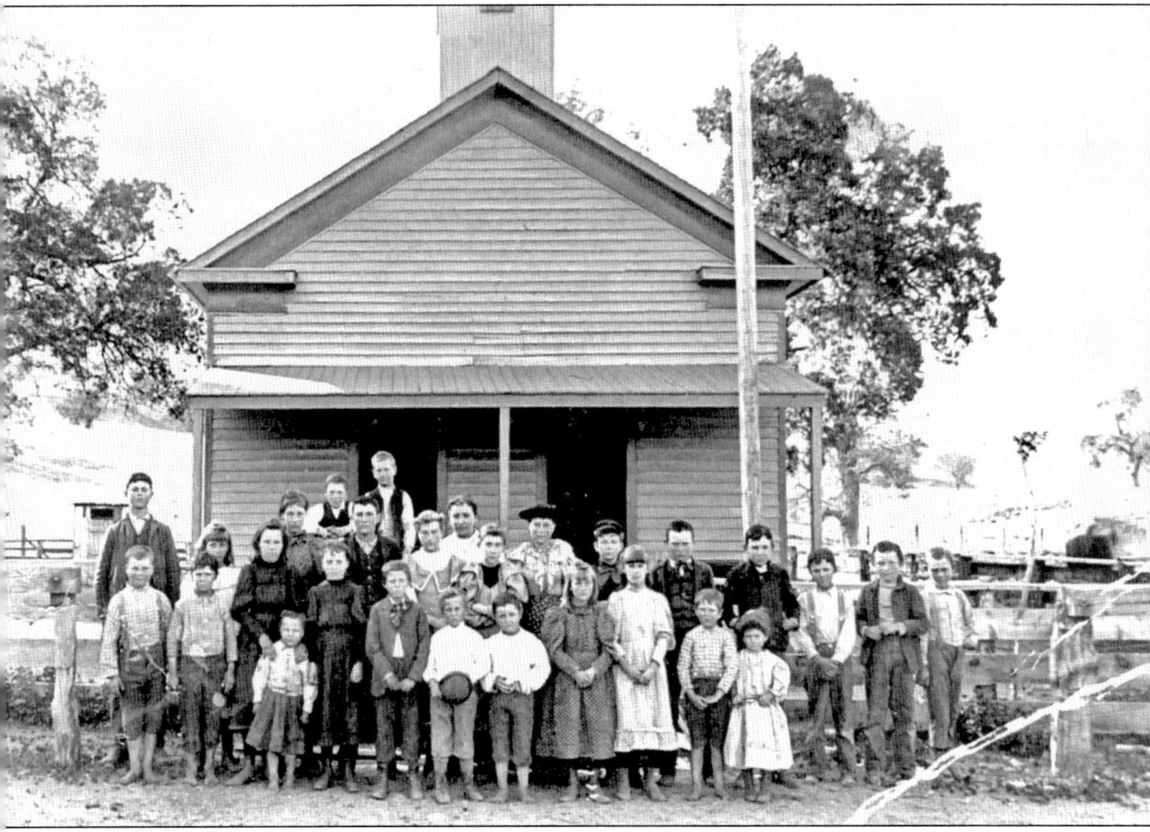

Students and their teacher pose before the new one-room school that represented the Tehachapi School District. The district was created on November 9, 1866, just eight months after state legislators approved the formation of Kern County. The Tehachapi Valley was now part of a judicial district with the ability to make and enforce laws. Nearby Havilah, the county seat, had a sheriff and a jail. Although law enforcement was a top priority, local settlers added education. The Tehachapi School District became the first in the county. (Prior to this, parents had paid William Wiggins to conduct classes at the Brite Ranch.) On June 28, 1868, settlers voted unanimously to finance a new one-room schoolhouse in Williamsburg. Enrollment consisted of 26 students ranging in age from 8 to 18. Their teacher, Miss Louesa Marie Jewett, became the first woman to teach in a publicly funded school in Kern County.

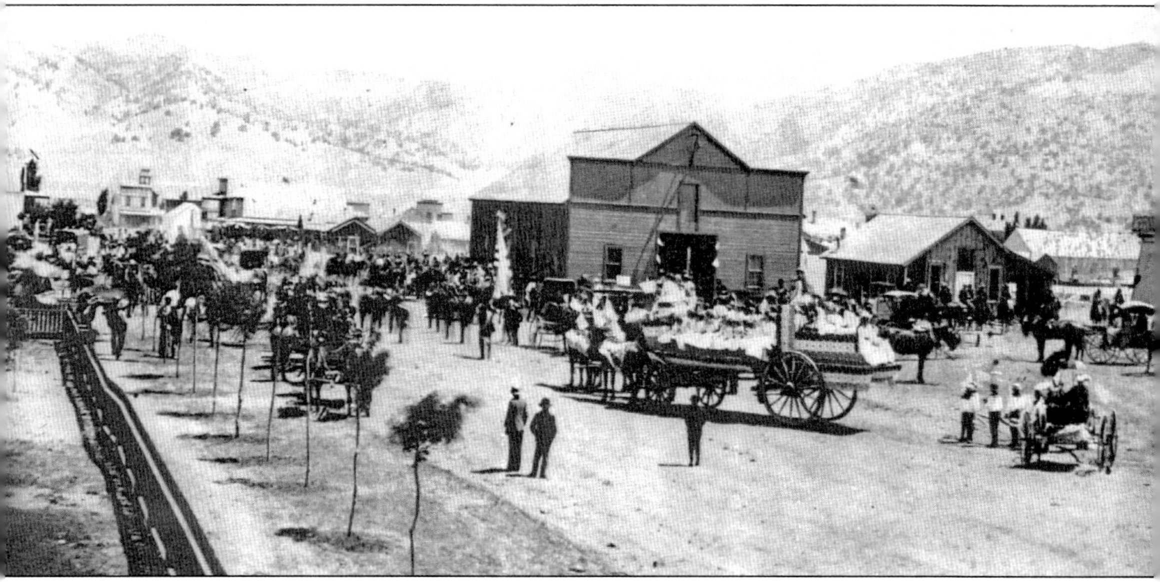

James Williams was a visionary and an entrepreneur. In 1868, when he saw the growing need for a town, he created his own between Black Mountain and the Tehachapi Creek. Williamsburg had just three streets, but the *Havilah Miner* called it "a town already of some importance." The paper described it as follows on December 18, 1872: "There are, at present, two stores, a large school house, one hotel, one blacksmith and wagon-making shop, and several other business establishments are in contemplation. The place occupies a commanding position not only to the Owens River road, but to what will eventually be the greatest grain growing portion of the county. The people of this part of the country are very hopeful and appear to be alive to the prosperous future that cannot possibly escape them." And then came the railroad.

Three

The Railroad

[The] location is the most unsatisfactory . . . on the point of interest, comfort, or possible future growth. It is outside the fertile portion of the valley, is entirely destitute of timber and water, and is on the line of the high winds which sweep from the Mojave through the Tehachapi Canyon.

—*Southern Californian*, May 18, 1876

This editorial reflected the dissatisfaction many felt when the Southern Pacific selected a depot site other than Williamsburg or Greenwich. Unhappy, yes, but not surprised. Ever since the railroad entered Kern County in 1870, word had spread that a town without the railroad was "as good as dead." The bypassing of towns that did not meet the railroad's demands had become all too common. Even Bakersfield, which in 1874 had become the county seat, was avoided by the Iron Horse when its citizens refused to accept the railroad's subsidy terms.

Tehachapi residents had an ace the others lacked: There was only one feasible link between San Francisco and Los Angeles, and that was the Tehachapi Pass. One way or another, Tehachapi would be served by the Southern Pacific.

Many predicted the railroad would never conquer the Tehachapi Pass and that Caliente, nestled at the foot of Bear Mountain and just 16 bird miles west of the Tehachapi Valley, would be the rail terminus. However, local farmers were already getting rich by selling their surplus hay and grain to the stagecoach and freighting teams arriving daily at Caliente. Tehachapi-raised cattle, chickens, fresh eggs, and vegetables helped to feed the 3,000 workers. (Chinese workers alone consumed up to 1,000 hogs in one year.) Local teamsters and their stock were among the 500 horses and mules hired to haul equipment. Hotels, restaurants, and liveries in Williamsburg and Greenwich also benefited from all the activity.

On July 10, 1876, the railroad arrived in the Tehachapi Valley. The bulk of Southern Pacific's workforce was laid off, since from here the task was downhill and therefore much easier. Freight teams and stages arrived daily at the new depot, and business was brisk. Despite its earlier critics, Summit Station proved to be a good location. Another era was about to begin.

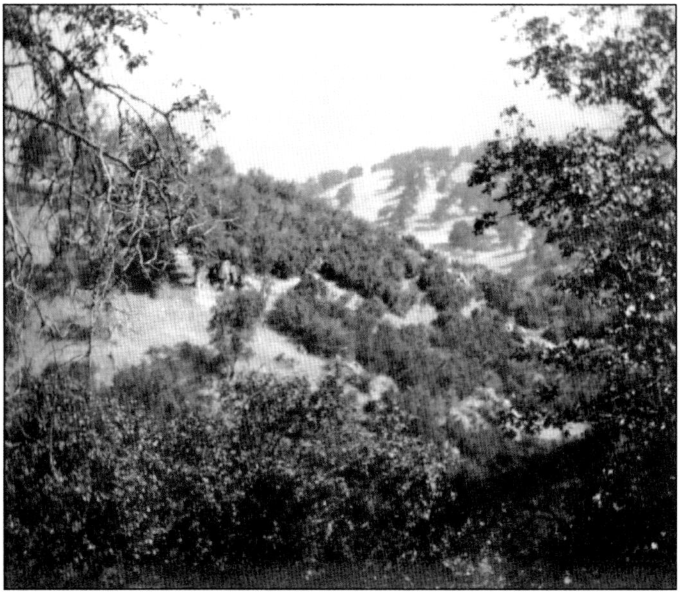

In 1875, the Tehachapi Mountains threatened to stop the steady progress of the Southern Pacific Railroad. At the base of the 4,000-foot-high Tehachapi Pass, the railroad created the town of Caliente. Many believed this would be the terminus, as it would be impossible for the rails to continue. A land boom followed. Within months, Caliente was a wide-open town of over 3,000 residents, including teamsters, investors, gamblers, railroad workers, and camp followers.

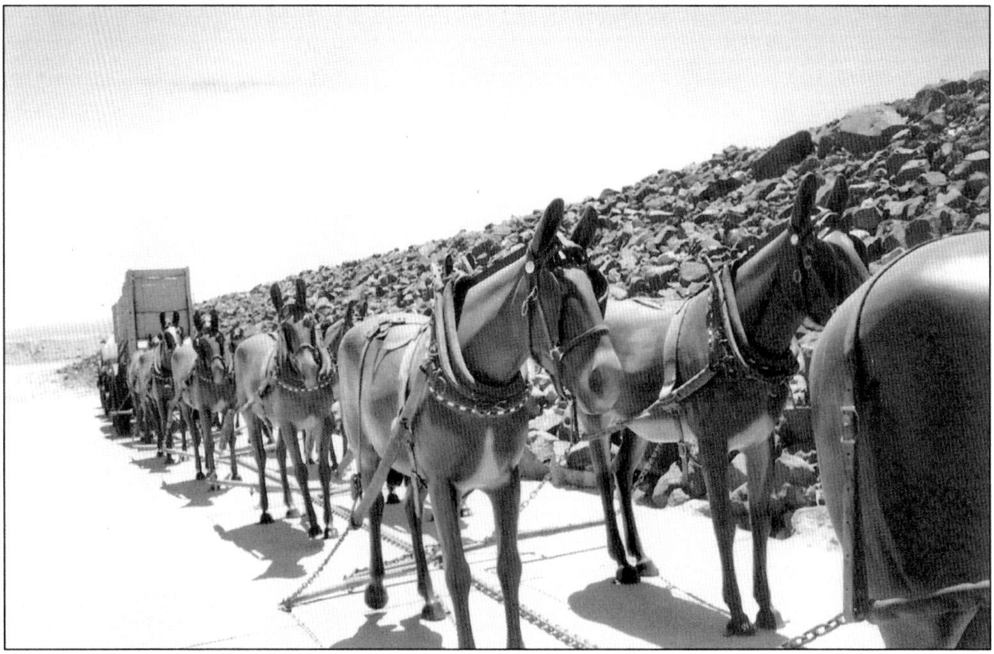

Remi Nadeau's 20-mule teams were so busy hauling ore from the Owens Valley mines to the railroad that he moved his headquarters from Willow Springs to Caliente. The operation, then valued at $500,000, consisted of an office, a blacksmith and wagon repair shop, a harness and equipment shed, a hay lot and steam-powered feed grinder, stables, and corrals. (Author's collection.)

William Hood was a young civil engineer when given the challenge of designing a rail line over the Tehachapi Pass. He accomplished this by creating "the Loop," two large circles that looped over and around themselves within a space of 3,794 feet. When asked how he came up with the idea, he reportedly answered, "It was just common sense."

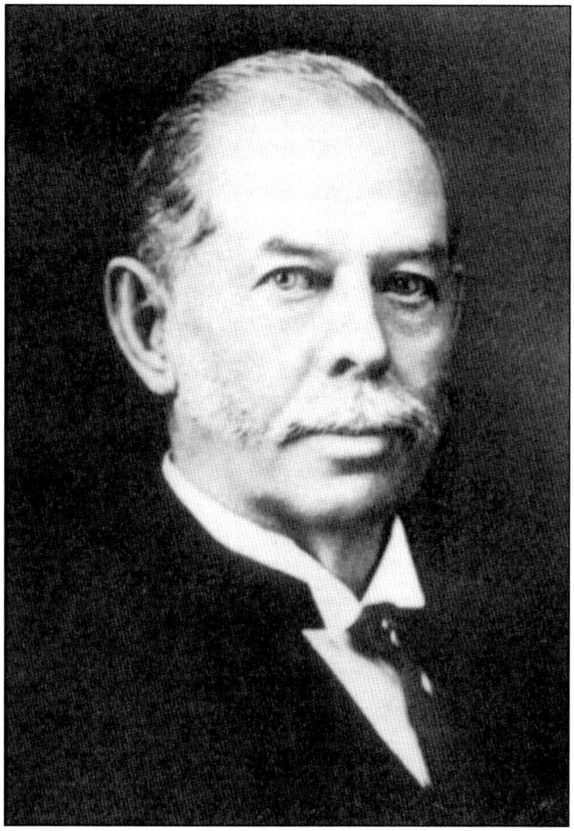

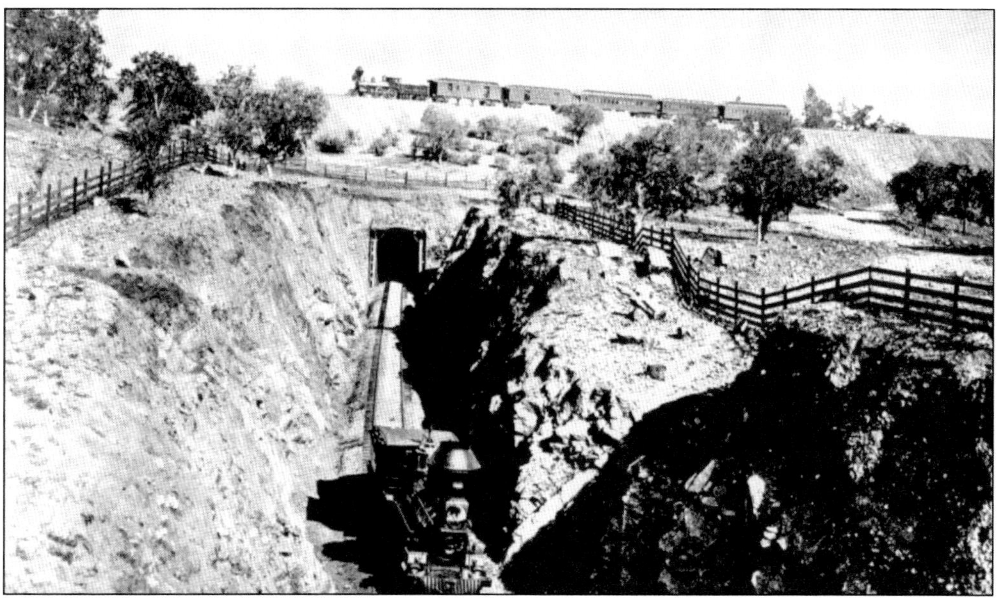

Hood's ingenious design included 18 tunnels on a circular track, allowing trains to travel above and below others. In the *c.* 1879 *Between the Gates*, Benjamin S. Taylor stated, "We seem to be constantly meeting ourselves, pursuing ourselves, contradicting ourselves." According to an unidentified passenger, the Loop was "as crooked and devious as a San Francisco politician."

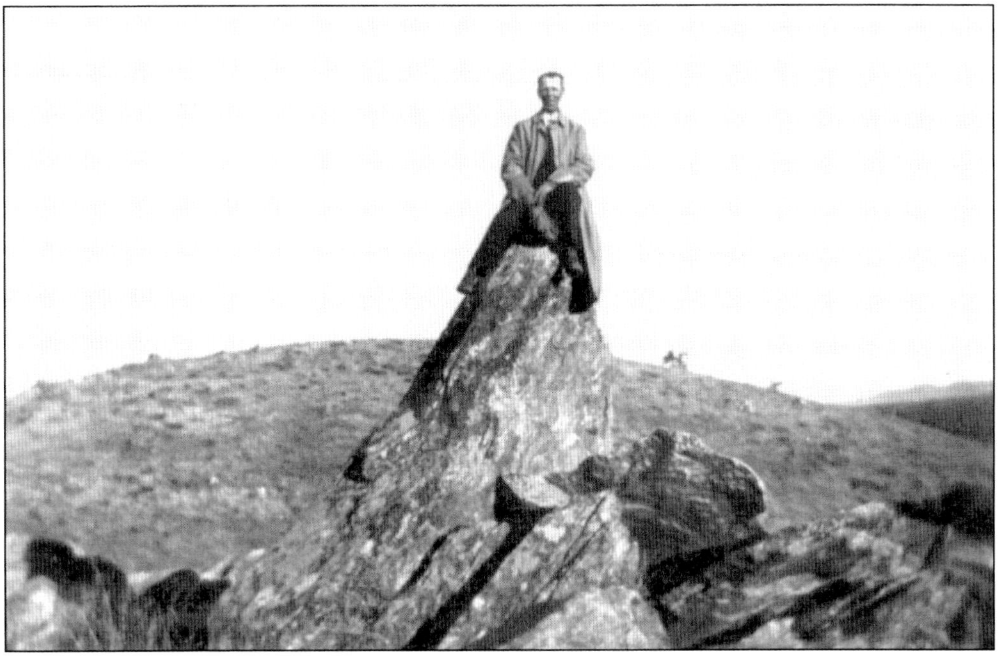

Work on the Tehachapi Pass attracted a number of sightseers. Those from Bakersfield arrived in buggies packed with lunch baskets so they could watch the work progress up the mountainsides. Tehachapi residents got a bird's-eye view by perching on a rocky pinnacle of Bear Mountain and hoping they would not be shaken by the earth-shattering explosions as the rail bed blasted and burrowed up through the mountains.

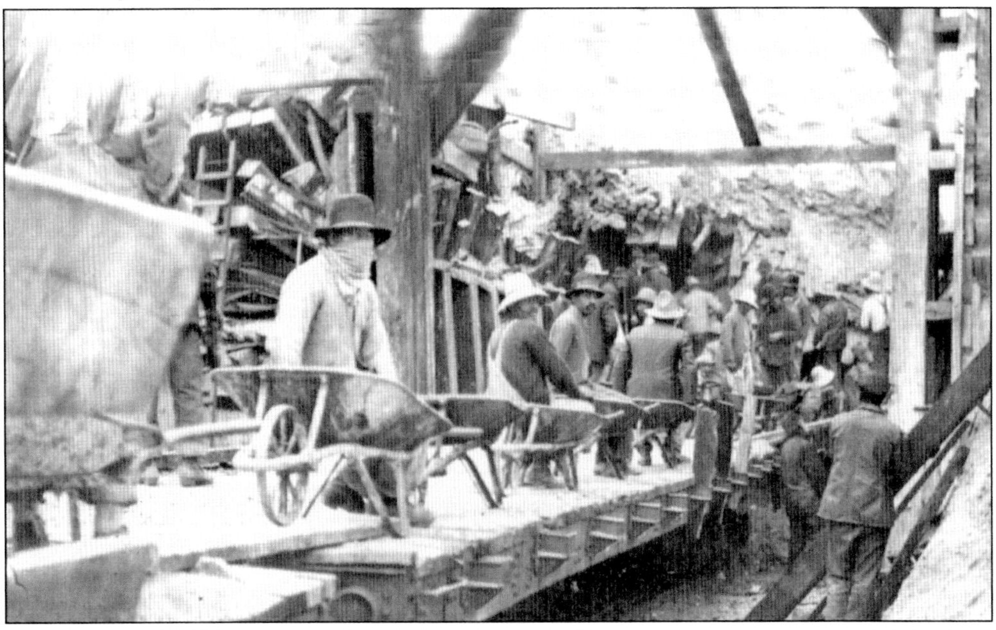

A workforce of 3,000 men dug, shoveled, and tunneled its way through the rugged Tehachapi Pass. Some 1,000 Chinese were hired to handle the 600 kegs of blasting powder used per week. Mule-drawn scrapers followed and cleared a pathway. The final work was accomplished by men using picks, shovels, crowbars, handcarts, and wheelbarrows.

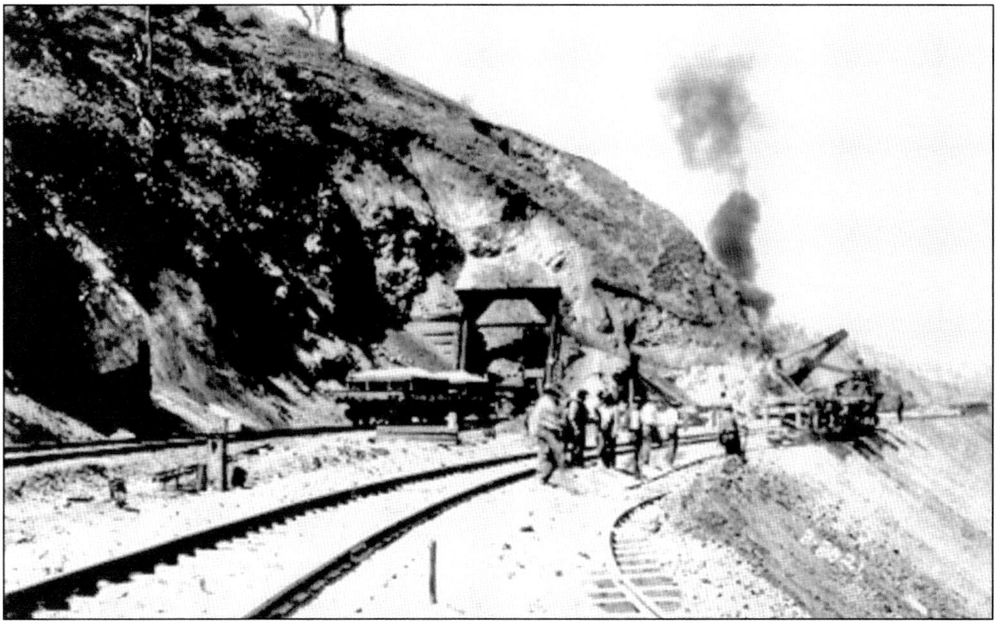

"I had no idea of the magnitude of the work," wrote an early traveler through the pass. He described the rail trip as "clinging to the face of a precipice" and being "surrounded by rock walls rising on both sides."

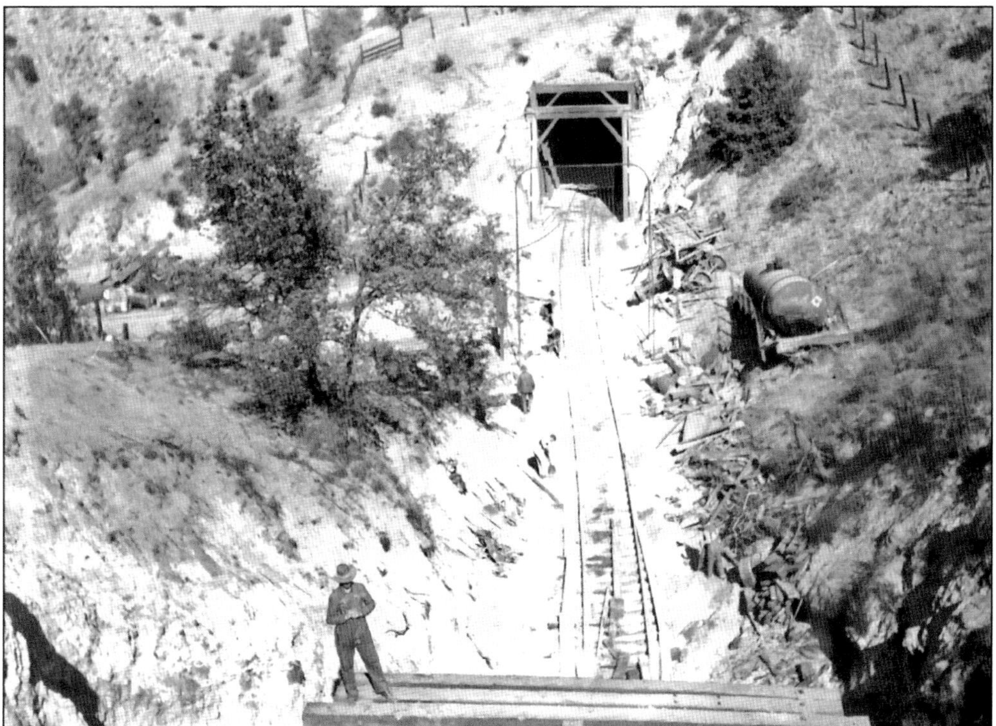

Originally, 18 tunnels were created. Some of these were later day-lighted (opened to the sky). Others had a shoo-fly (detour) built around the side of the mountain, and the tunnel was abandoned. Ultimately, only 11 tunnels remained in service.

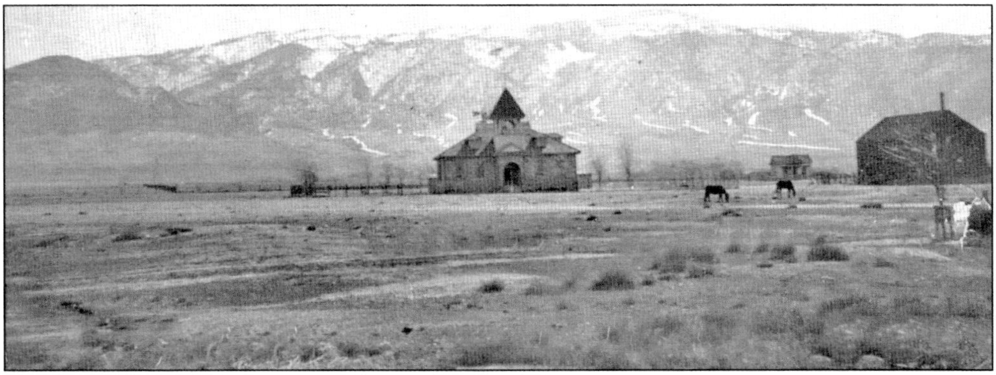

The railroad bypassed both Williamsburg and Greenwich to establish its own town. Summit Station was located on a barren section of the Tehachapi Valley, but it was exactly what the Southern Pacific needed. There was enough nearby timber and water to supply the needs of both humans and the steam-powered locomotives. Above all, the railroad held the deed to acres of open land that it could divide and sell.

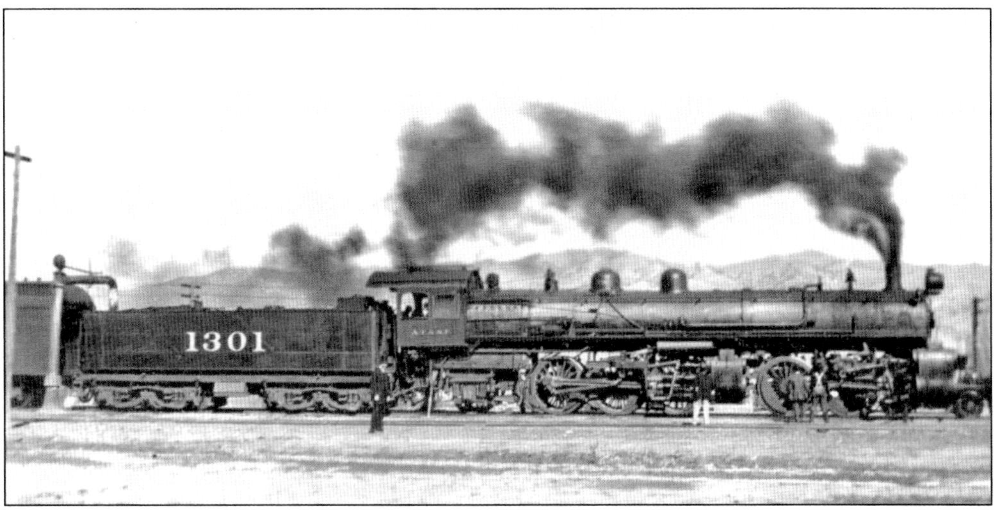

Amidst a plume of thick black smoke, the first train pulled into Summit Station on July 10, 1876. From there, it was an easy task to continue on to Mojave and south through the Antelope Valley. Another construction crew was laying track north from Los Angeles. The two crews would meet just east of Newhall for the completion of the north-to-south rail line.

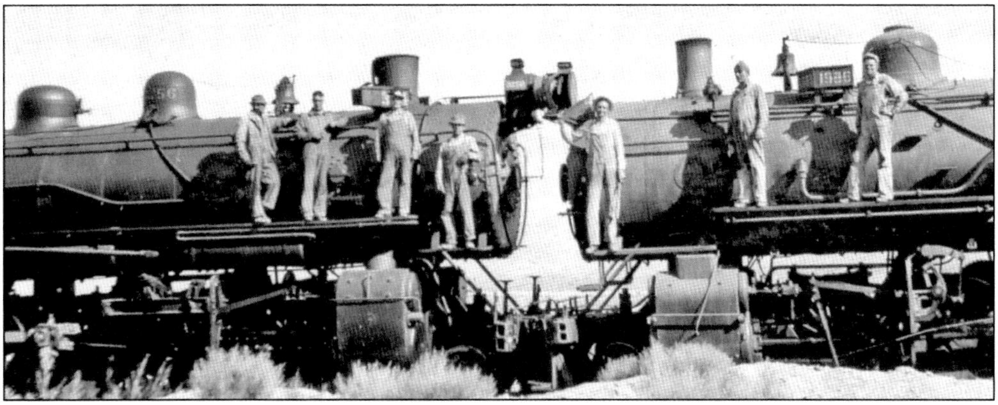

On September 5, 1876, the rail line connecting San Francisco with Los Angeles was completed. The ceremonial spike was driven at Lang, a station just north of present-day Newhall. Witnessing the event were dignitaries and reporters who had arrived on special trains—one out of San Francisco, the other from Los Angeles. A reporter for the *Sacramento Daily-Record-Union* wrote, "What a contrast to our swift flying trip to Los Angeles is the slow, lumbering speed of the stage coach."

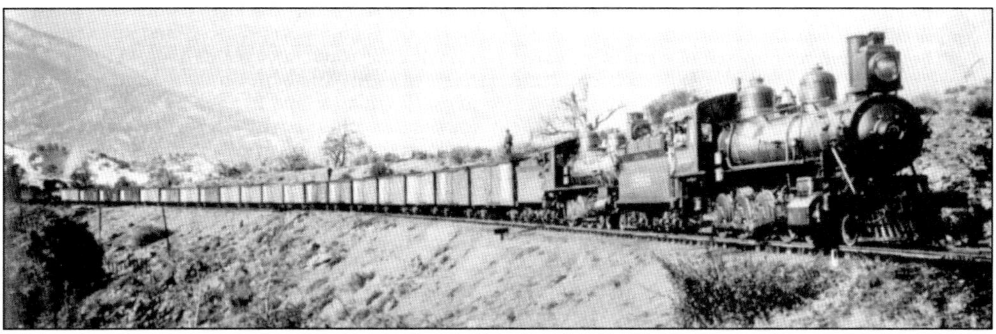

The first regular passenger service between San Francisco and Los Angeles was inaugurated on September 6, 1876. The 484-mile trip took 24 hours and 40 minutes. A brochure published by the Southern Pacific encouraged travelers to use the train, describing the Tehachapi Pass as "quite picturesque and often grand."

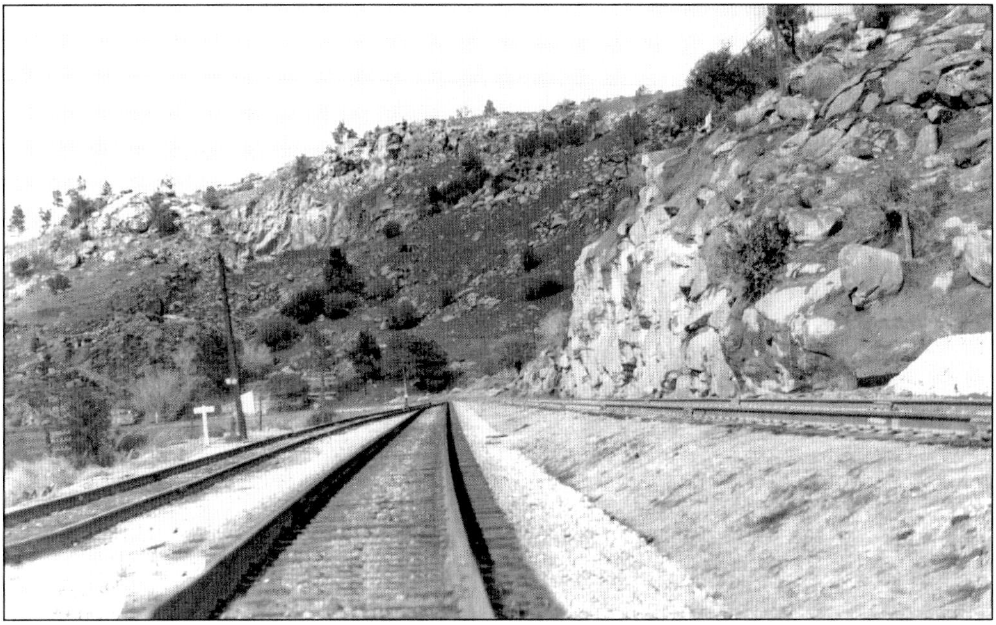

In *Between the Gates*, Benjamin S. Taylor described his 1879 rail trip through the Tehachapi Pass. "The heights were impractical," he wrote. "The rocks were immovable, and so the train climbed as high as it could, and crept into a burrow [tunnel] like a fox." The ascent took its toll on the engines until *El Gobernador*, or "the Governor," (below) was introduced. It was a 217,000-pound engine made in Sacramento especially for the Tehachapi Pass. It was put into service in 1884, and for 10 years, it did the work of two "cook hogs" (the 12-wheelers introduced in 1880). Despite the engine's power, its size was still a problem. The behemoth was too large to be turned around for the return trip to Caliente, so it had to be backed down the twisting grade. This limited its use to daylight hours. At the end of 1894, it was considered too impractical for further use. Deemed obsolete, it was broken up for scrap. *El Gobernador* was the only engine of its kind.

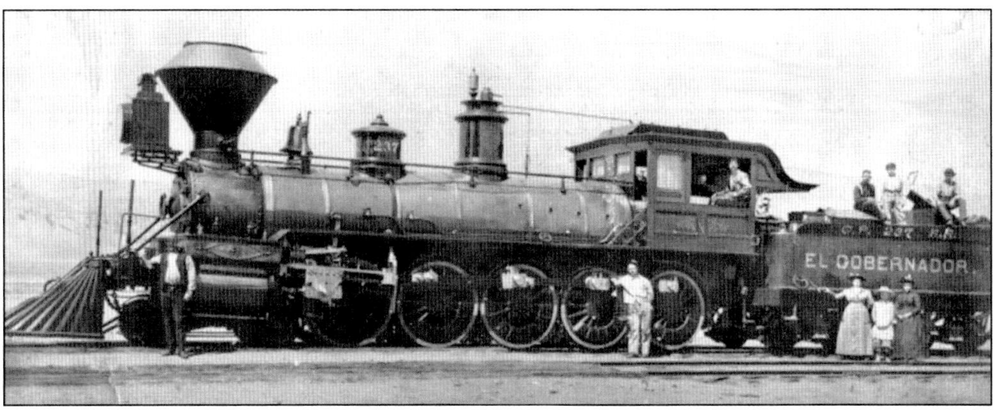

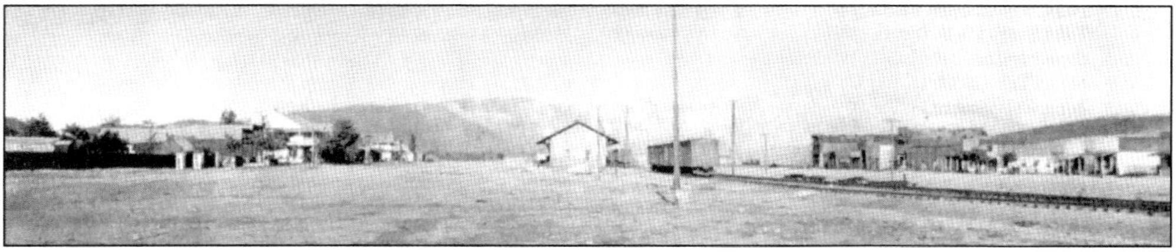

Tehachapi Summit is pictured here in the early 1880s. To the left is Railroad Avenue (the main street), which runs parallel to and south of the tracks. To the right (north) was housing for the rail workers and other fixtures of a typical western town like cheap saloons and "bawdy houses."

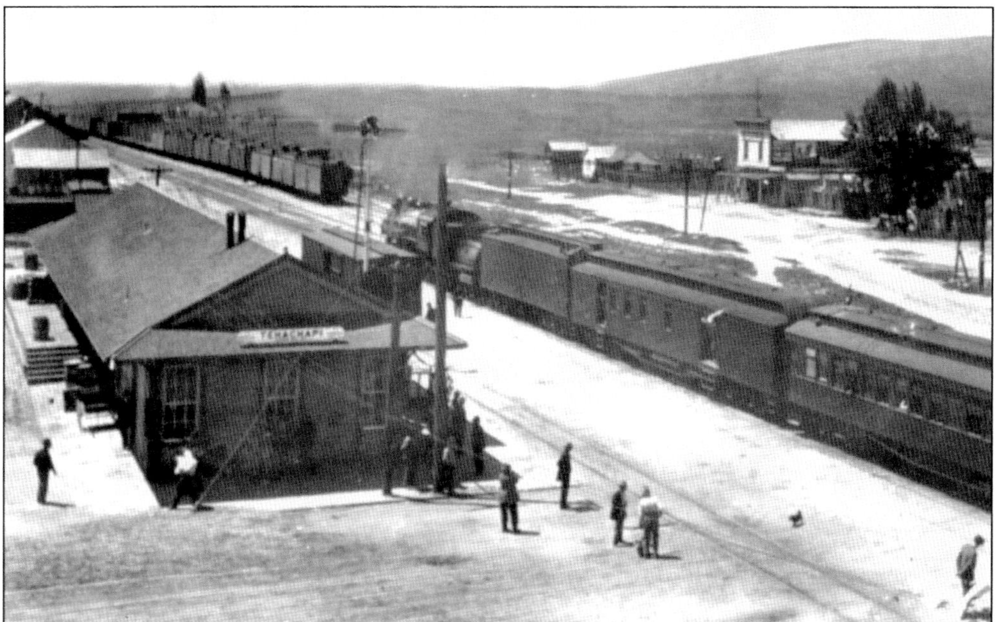

Business was brisk at the depot. During the week, four trains arrived daily—two of them passenger trains, the others freight only. Exports exceeded imports. Freight cars left the depot with shipments of grain, produce, lime, lumber, and livestock. A stationmaster's report for 1890 listing exports included 1,490 full and part carloads. A year later, this had increased to 1,500 full carloads. Such activity was in direct contrast to the doom and gloom predicted years earlier by the *Southern Californian* that claimed Summit Station was "lacking in any point of interest, comfort, or possible growth."

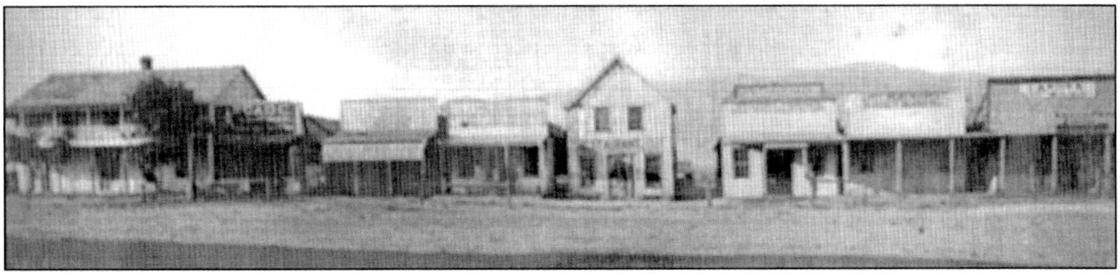

Growth was slow but steady. Willard's Saloon and Billiard Parlor (with furnishings imported from San Francisco) was the first to attract steady customers. Mary Ann Haigh's restaurant also thrived. Next to come were a boardinghouse, hotel, general merchandise store, two livery stables, blacksmith shop, hay and feed lot, lumberyard, and several new saloons. Businessmen built warehouses next to the railroad tracks, enabling storage for the goods awaiting shipment. Livestock pens held cattle, sheep, hogs, and crates of turkeys.

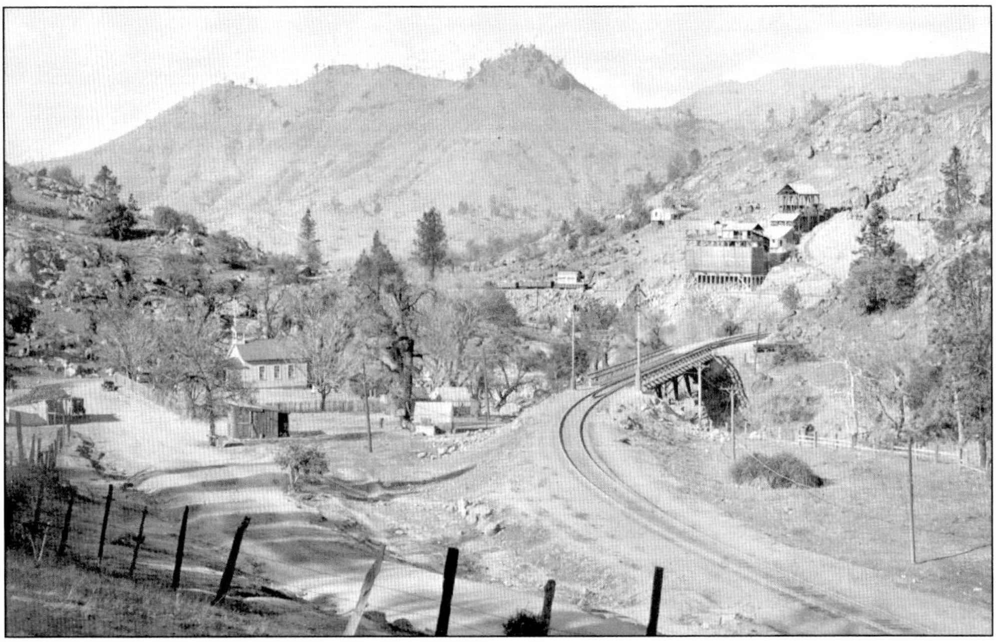

When the railroad continued to the Tehachapi Valley, Caliente lost over half of its population, economy, and dubious reputation as another hellhole of the West. But it was not a ghost town. The mines along Caliente Creek and Walker's Basin were still sending ore to Caliente depot for shipment to San Francisco. Ranchers continued to drive steers to the railroad's stock pens. Trains stopped at Caliente and picked up fuel, water, and a "helper" engine or two to negotiate the pass.

Four

Tehachapi

A recent excursion to Tehachapa [sic] convinced us that the Summit, the name by which it is chiefly known, is soon to be the principal town and center of trade of that section of the country.

—*Kern County Californian*, November 14, 1885

Summit Station did not begin as a boom town. Its first and only building was a 7-by-9-foot wooden telegrapher's office. William S. Knapp, the telegrapher, was therefore the town's first permanent resident. Ironically, he was also the son-in-law of James Williams, the founder of Williamsburg. The railroad's tent city, which once housed workers and assorted camp followers, was now a mere shadow of itself. Once the bulk of workers were no longer needed, the tents disappeared as rapidly as mushrooms in a drought.

Unlike Caliente, Summit Station was already divided into lots, and streets were laid out. Railroad Avenue, the main street, ran south of and parallel to the tracks. A saloon and billiard parlor (its furnishings imported from San Francisco) was the first to open for business. It was followed by a restaurant run by Mary Ann Haigh, Tehachapi's first businesswoman. Others soon followed: two hotels, liveries and feed lots, and a mercantile store. All were wooden structures with false fronts facing a board sidewalk with an assortment of hitching racks. Growth was slow but steady. Residents believed in the old farmer's proverb, "The fastest grown pumpkin usually turns out to be the 'pore' one."

Nevertheless, Summit Station's growth was consistent enough for Greenwich to vanish within a year. Founder Peter D. Greene transported his post office franchise to the new town and later became its justice of the peace. James Williams died in December 1876, so he was not around in 1885 to see his town completely disappear.

With completion of the rails into Los Angeles, four trains (two of them passenger trains) arrived in Tehachapi on a daily basis. Summit Station became Tehachapi Summit and eventually just Tehachapi. A new century was on the horizon, and with it, more changes were in store.

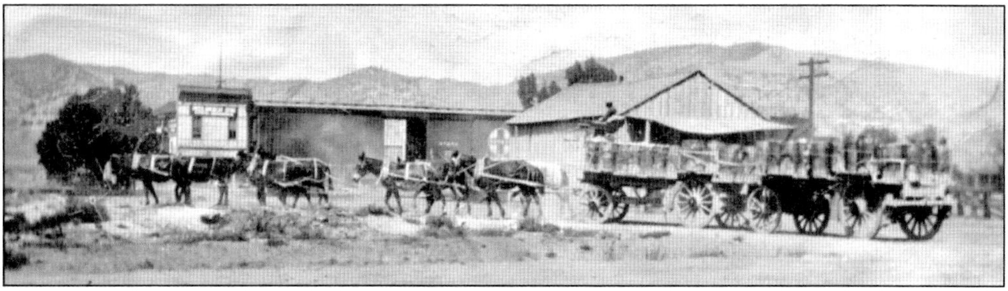

Freight teams were a common sight along Railroad Avenue, transporting gold from the Owens Valley mines, along with local farmers' hay and grain, lumber and cordwood, and sacks of salt. New businesses opened, and Summit Station grew. A hotel, saloon, and store were operated by Ben Kessing; Mary Ann Haigh's cooking kept her restaurant and boardinghouse busy; and the saloons of J. W. Wheeler and Frank Cooper thrived. The livery stables and feed lots of L. Dillon and L. F. Gates also did brisk business. On October 7, 1876, the *Gazette* proclaimed, "The little town of Summit Station is going ahead in population and improvements, and is competing for the Tehachapi [Williamsburg and Greenwich] trade." Meanwhile, cattle remained a major source of income for many. Experienced *vaqueros* (cowboys), such as those seen below, could find work at any of the many ranches scattered throughout the valley. Between 1854 and 1940, there were some 35 brands registered to Tehachapi ranchers.

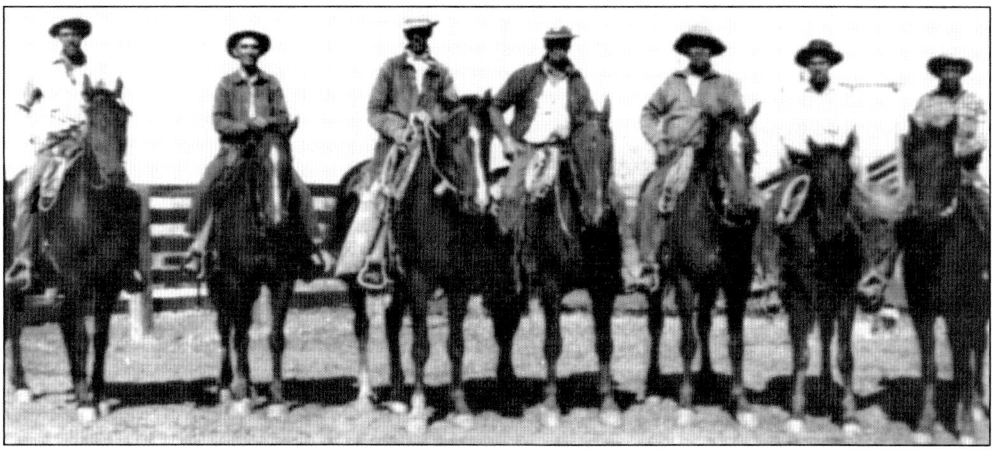

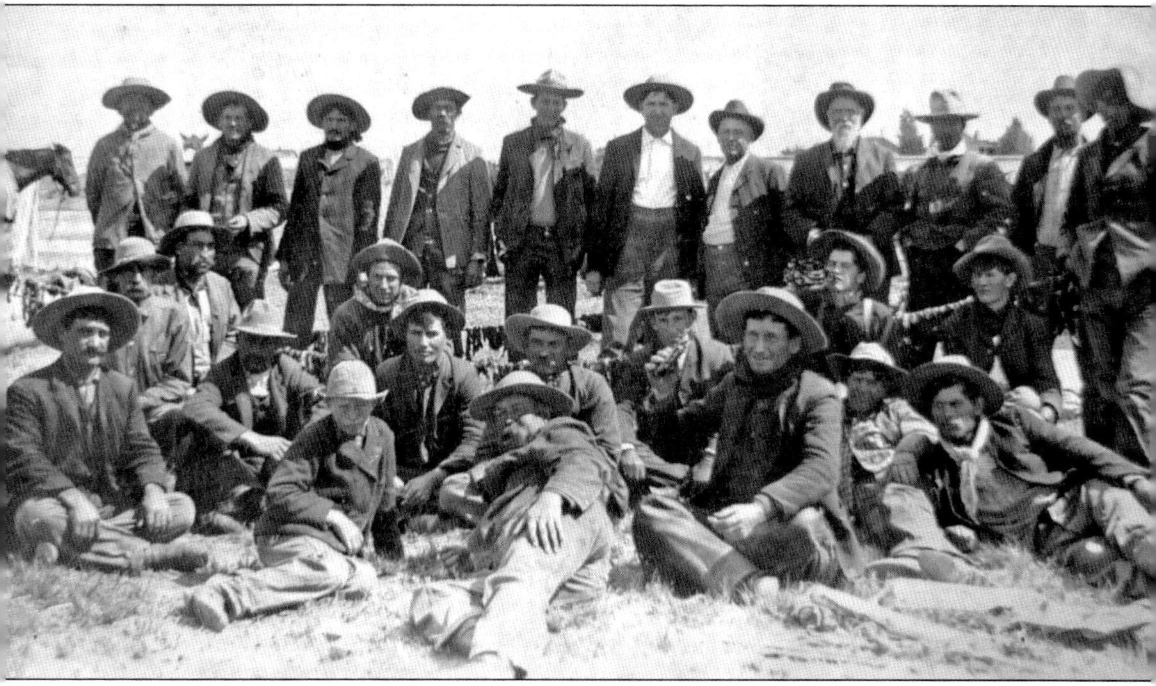

Excluding the lime kilns, most work was seasonal and consisted of long hours and hard labor. The harvest season was the shortest. Men worked from before sunup to dark to accomplish the task before wet weather ruined the crops. The mines and quarries could not operate during rain or snow, nor could the timber crews and lumbermen. Many spent the winters as carpenters, blacksmiths, or anything that would provide an income.

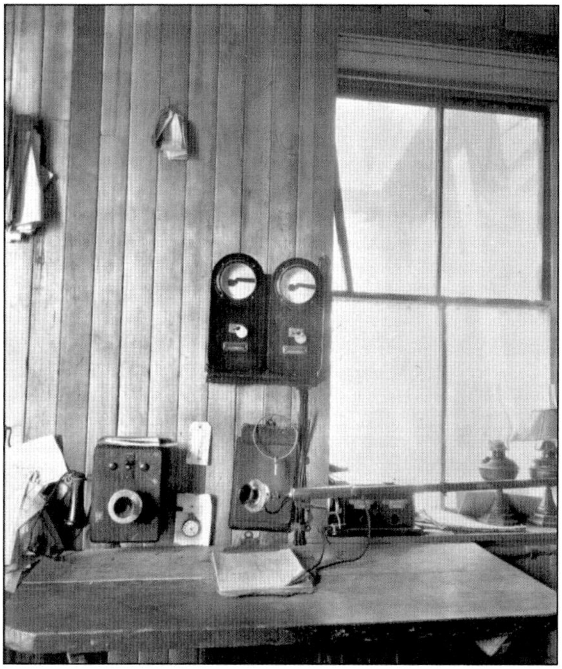

This 1940s railroad office is similar to the one in service during the late 1870s. San Francisco has been credited with having the first telephone service in 1878, but according to the May 9, 1878, issue of the *Courier Californian*, a primitive telephone exchange was in operation between Summit Station and Williamsburg. W. H. Knapp served as the Summit Station operator, and young Paul Narboe operated the system in Williamsburg.

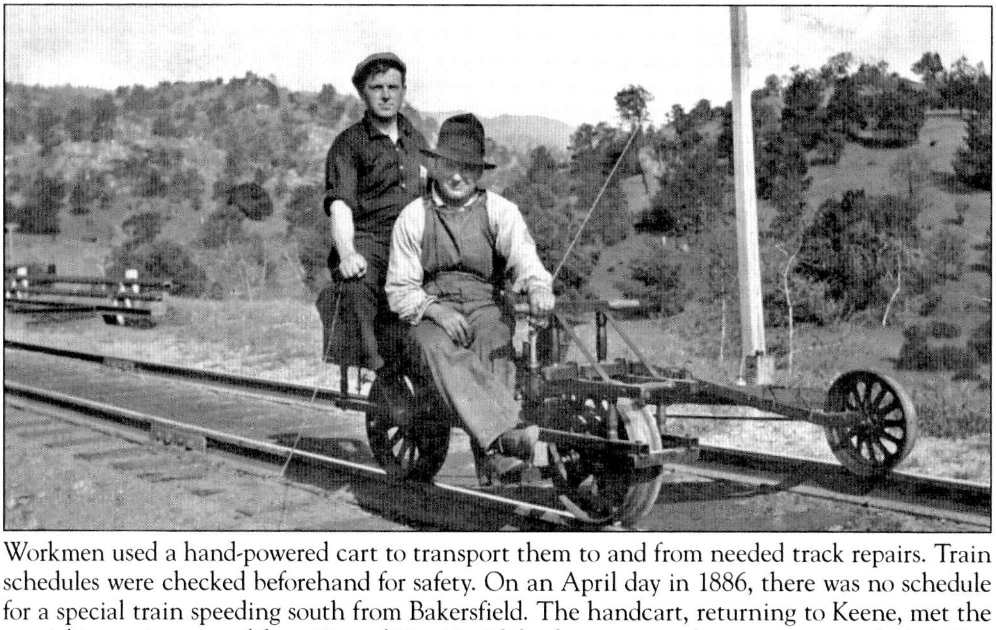

Workmen used a hand-powered cart to transport them to and from needed track repairs. Train schedules were checked beforehand for safety. On an April day in 1886, there was no schedule for a special train speeding south from Bakersfield. The handcart, returning to Keene, met the special just as it emerged from Tunnel No. 10. Of the four men on the cart, two were killed. The remaining two jumped and were severely injured.

The original Summit School was located north of the depot by a grove of oak trees. Its surrounding meadow became ablaze with wildflowers each spring and was favored by picnickers, especially on the First of May. That day's celebration consisted of a picnic, a grand ball, and a late supper. Summit Station received its own school district in 1877, and in April 1878, a two-story schoolhouse was constructed for a daily attendance of 15 students.

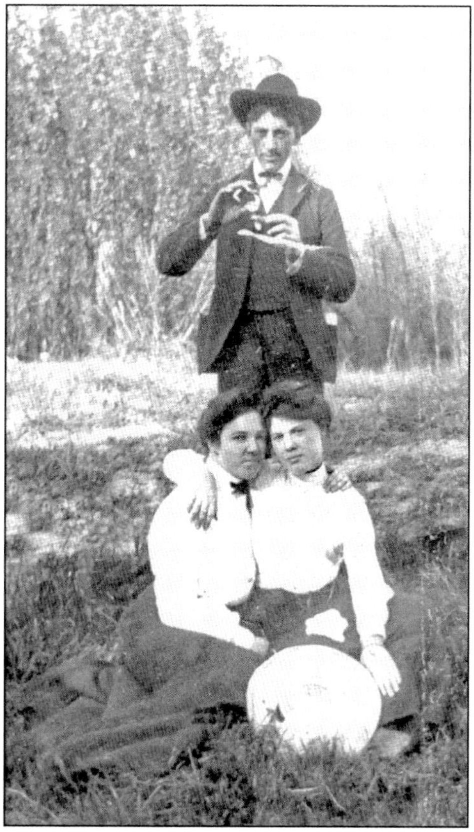

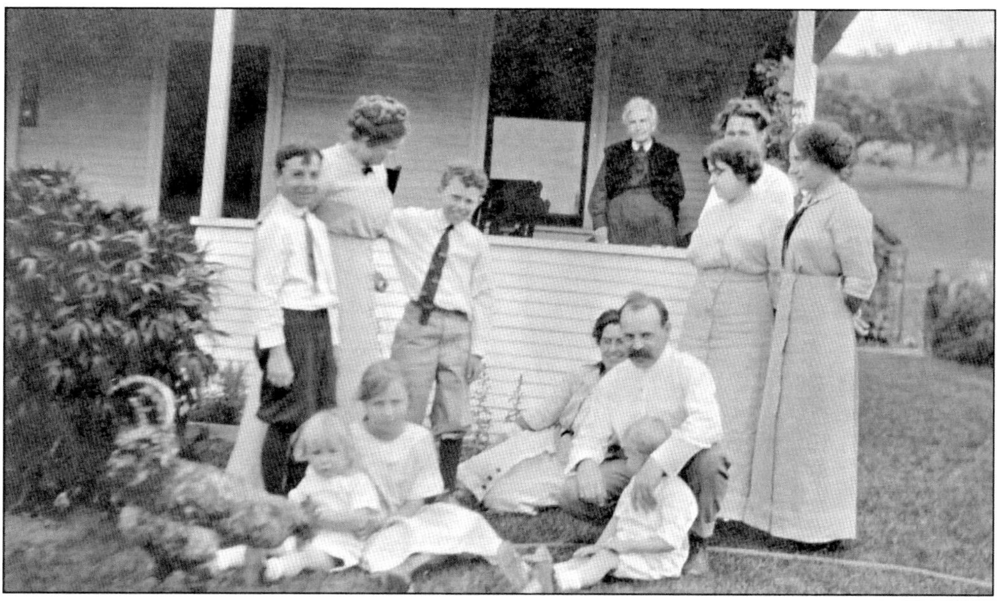

The family was considered the cornerstone of society, and great pride was taken in preserving the family's name. It was not uncommon for a family to consist of both parents, 8 to 10 children, and the grandparents. Many family members lived under one roof or, if in town, within close proximity of each other.

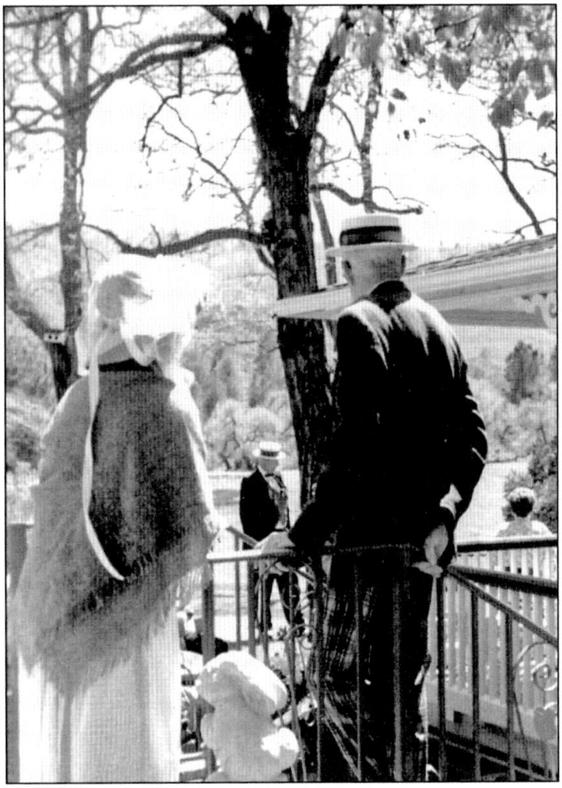

By 1892, Tehachapi was, according to a Bakersfield newspaper, shaking its image of "a hard town and attracting a more refined class of people." Social clubs, which included both men and women, were becoming popular. The Wednesday Club met weekly to advance the literary and educational interests of its members. It replaced the Debating Society, which had been formed in Williamsburg in 1878. (Author's collection.)

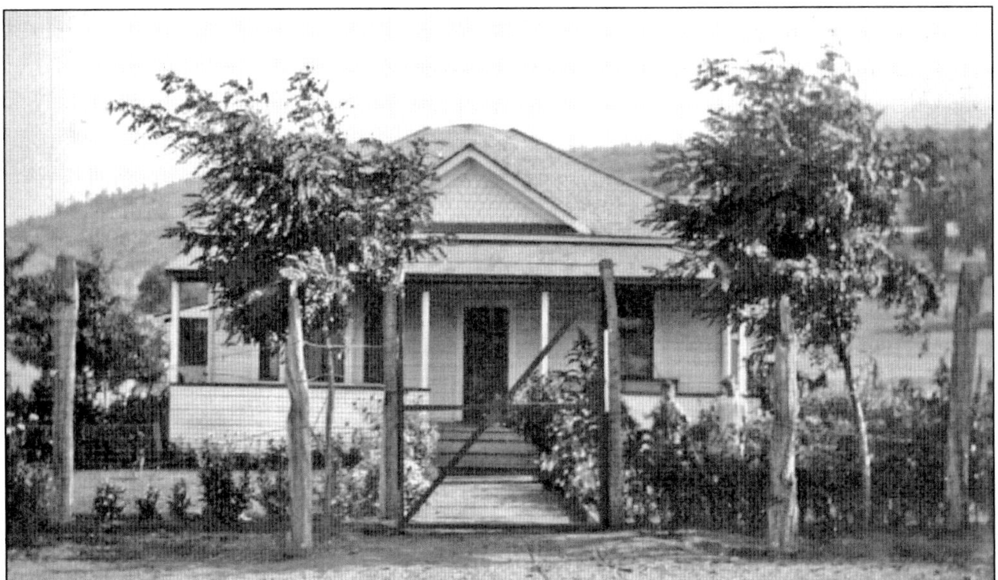

As the number of businesses grew, so did the residences. More and more homes were constructed in the town, which was now called Tehachapi Summit. Some had been moved from Williamsburg. Owners made their homes attractive by planting trees and flowers, cultivating lawns and lilac bushes, and adding picket fences.

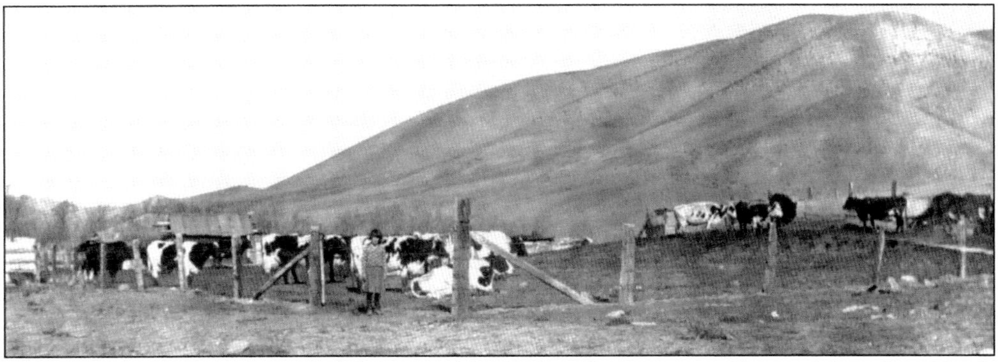

With population increasing, so did the need for fresh milk, cream, and butter. Mary Ann Haigh first started serving milk and cream to her restaurant and boardinghouse customers. It proved so popular that she began selling milk and cream to others, who would bring their own containers. A full-fledged dairy soon opened outside of town, and a regular milk route was established. The Meadowbrook Dairy eventually had its own customized milk bottles.

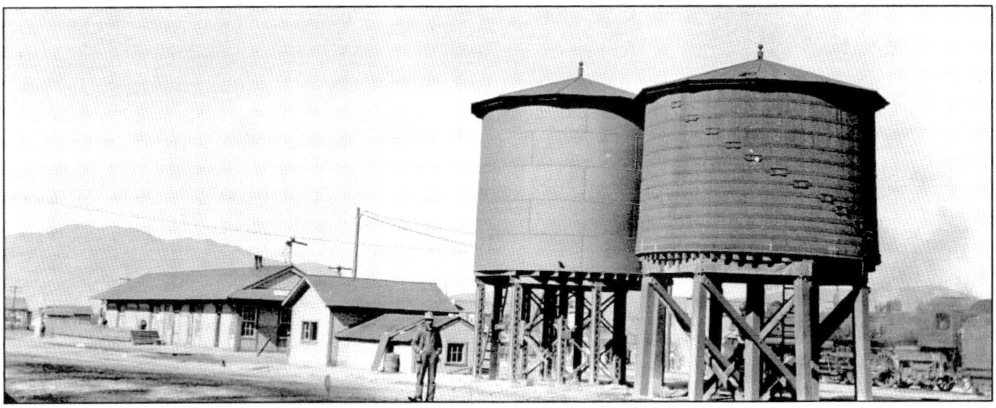

Steam locomotives required an ample supply of water, and these twin water towers at the Tehachapi depot became a landmark. In 1878, the Southern Pacific considered bringing additional water to Tehachapi by means of a pipeline from the mountains. It never transpired, as wells dug to a depth of 40 to 60 feet seemed adequate and inexhaustible. It would take several years to prove such theories wrong.

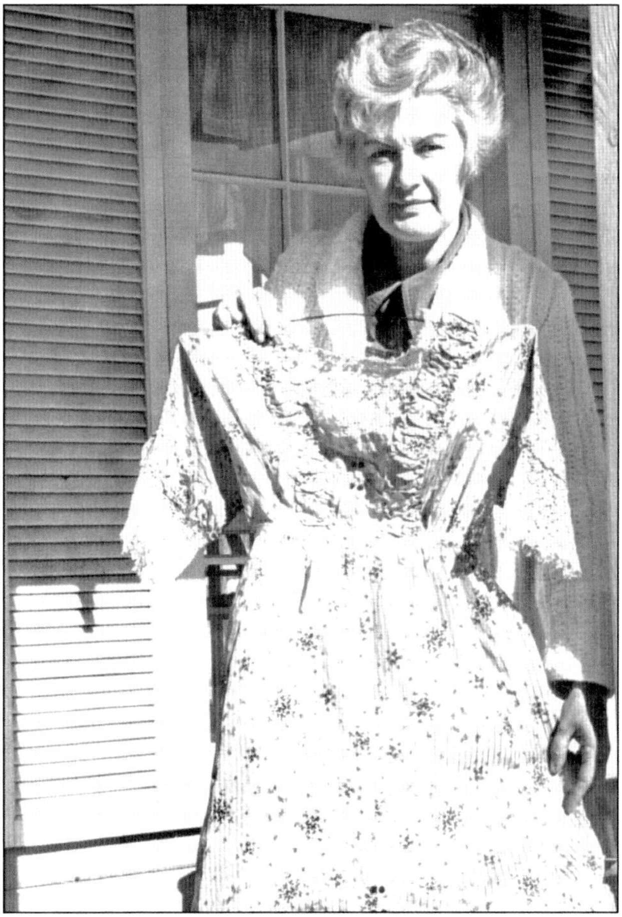

A museum docent (left) displays a dress once worn by the wife of John C. Downey, governor of California from 1860 to 1862. Mrs. Downey was the victim of a major railroad disaster on January 15, 1883. During a routine stop at Tehachapi to disconnect a helper engine, seven cars, three of them sleepers, accidentally broke lose and began sliding back down the grade at an estimated speed of 90 miles per hour. Where the track curved and crossed over a ravine, two cars passed in safety but the other five left the track and crashed—two into a hillside, three into the ravine. Stoves and lamps fell over and set the cars ablaze. Nearby residents heard the crash and rushed to rescue what passengers they could, including a dozen with severe injuries. The wreck (below) claimed 21 people, including Mrs. Downey.

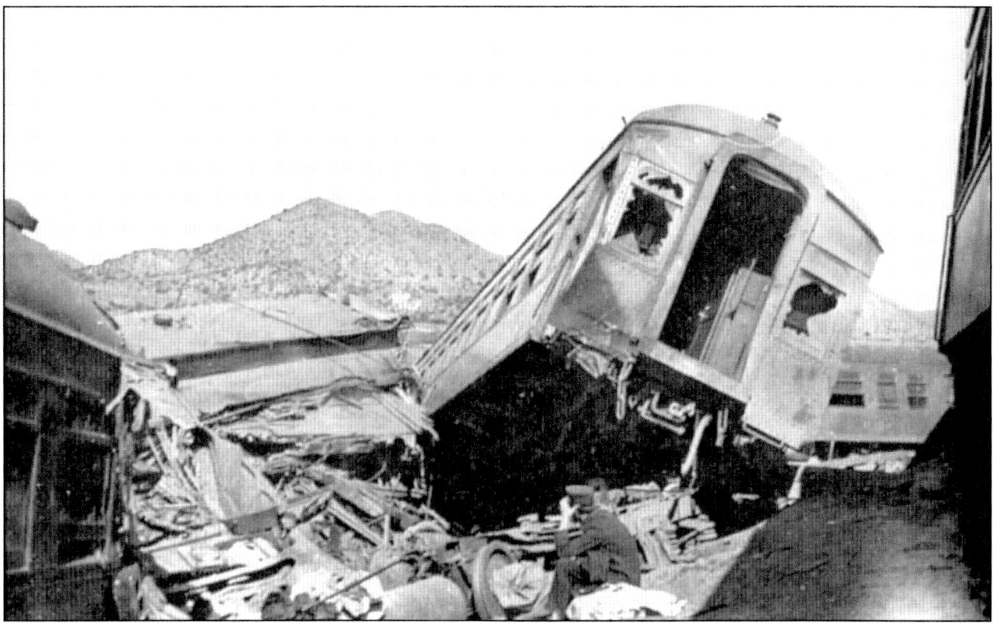

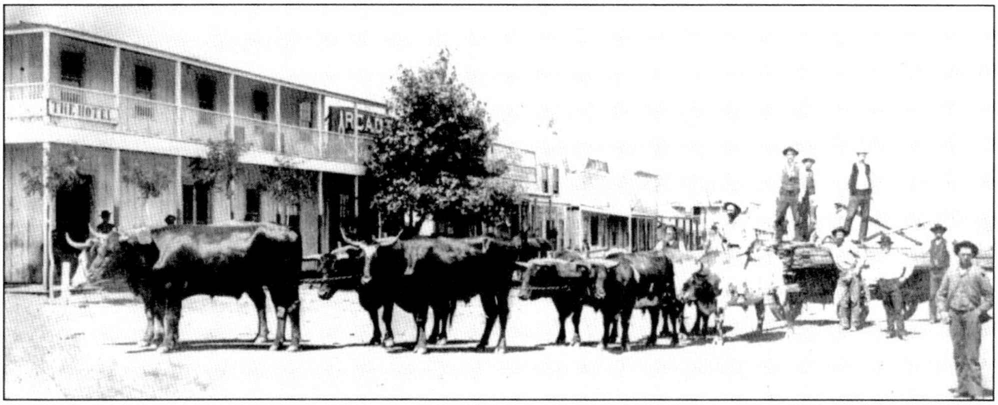

This photograph, taken in the late 1890s, shows Tehachapi's frontier appearance as its growth became a blend of the old and the new. Even as the railroad was converting to coal instead of wood, teams of oxen (the beast of burden since biblical times) were bringing freight into the depot as late as 1910.

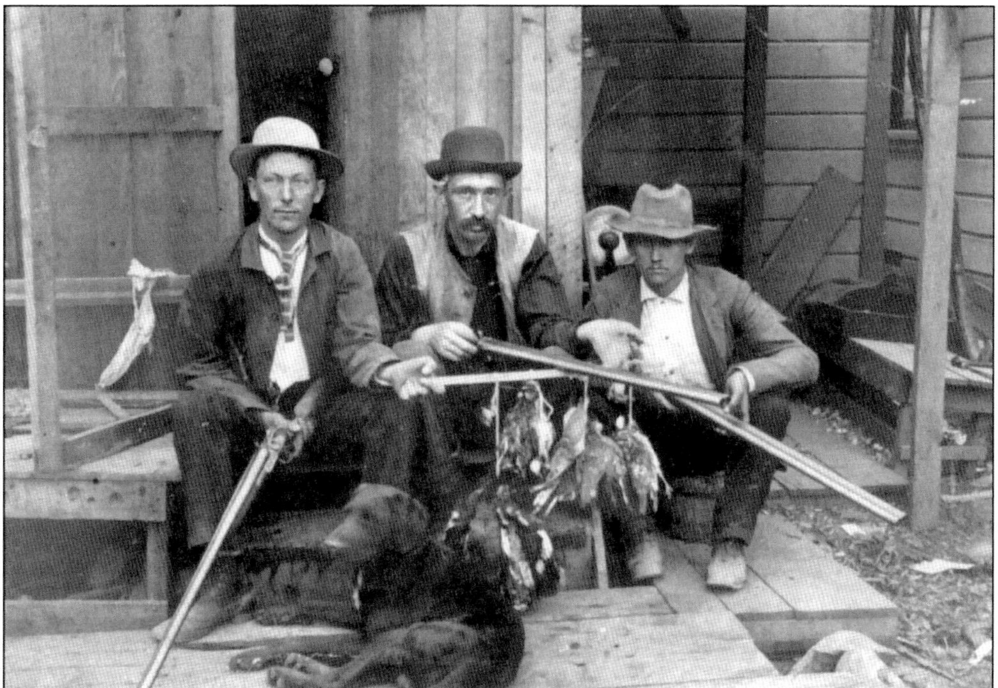

The February 15, 1879, issue of the *Gazette* carried this report from Tehachapi: "For a good time just come up and take a good hunt after ducks and geese. Our little lake is fairly swarming with them." Paul Narboe had mineral rights to the lake bearing his name, but this did not affect one's right to hunt the waterfowl that landed on the lake during their annual migration.

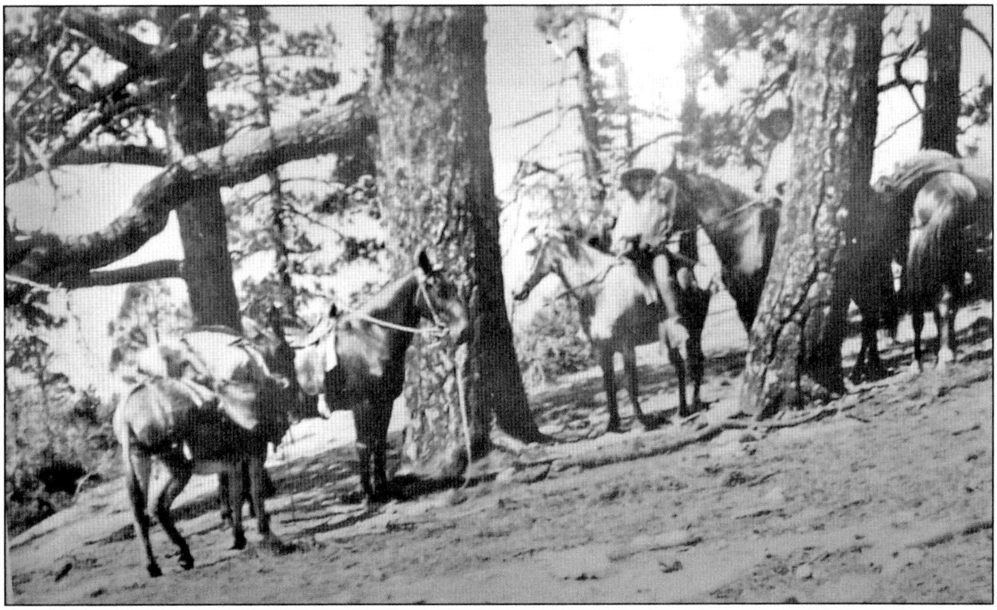

The Southern Pacific Company published a brochure promoting Tehachapi for hunting and camping holidays. It described the scenic timber country with its numerous deer and bear populations and the migrating ducks and geese. However, the company failed to create an influx of visitors since the same attractions then existed in areas closer to Los Angeles.

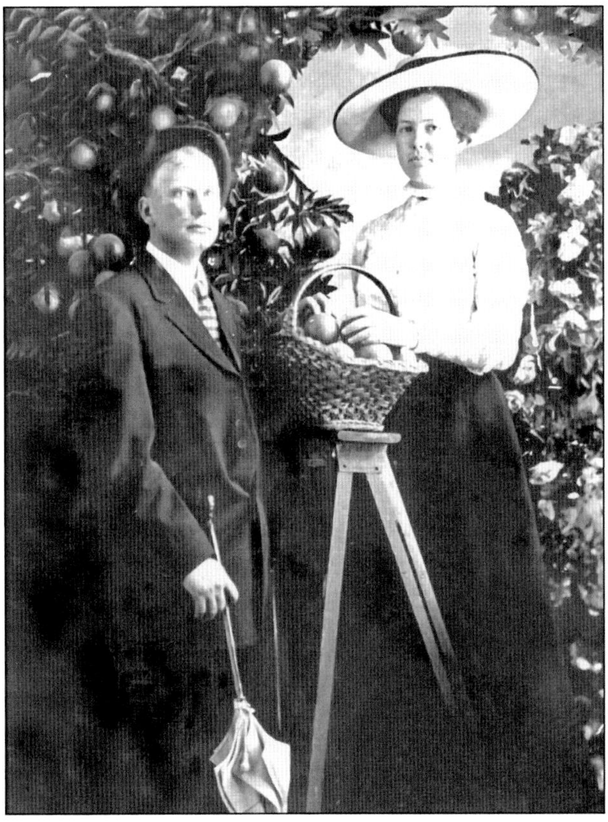

Itinerant photographers would occasionally visit Tehachapi and set up a temporary studio inside one of the hotels. Their business was advertised well in advance and was generally good since there were no commercial photographers in town. The nearest studios were in Bakersfield, which allowed a photography session to be combined with an afternoon of shopping or dining.

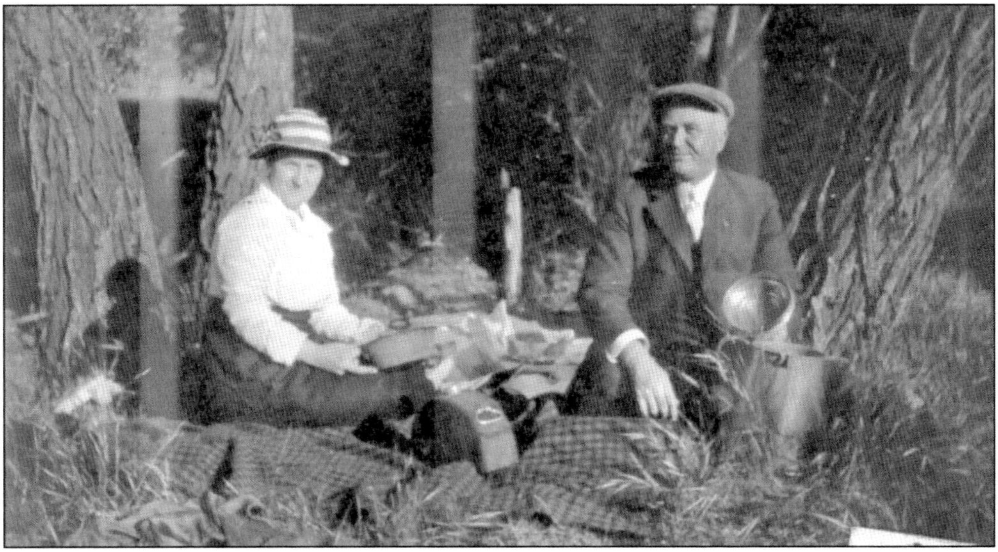

The nearby mountains afforded a pleasant day's outing. Amidst a grove of softly scented pine trees, a basket of food was set out next to the clear waters of a rippling creek. A picnic could consist of an interlude for two or up to a dozen hungry revelers.

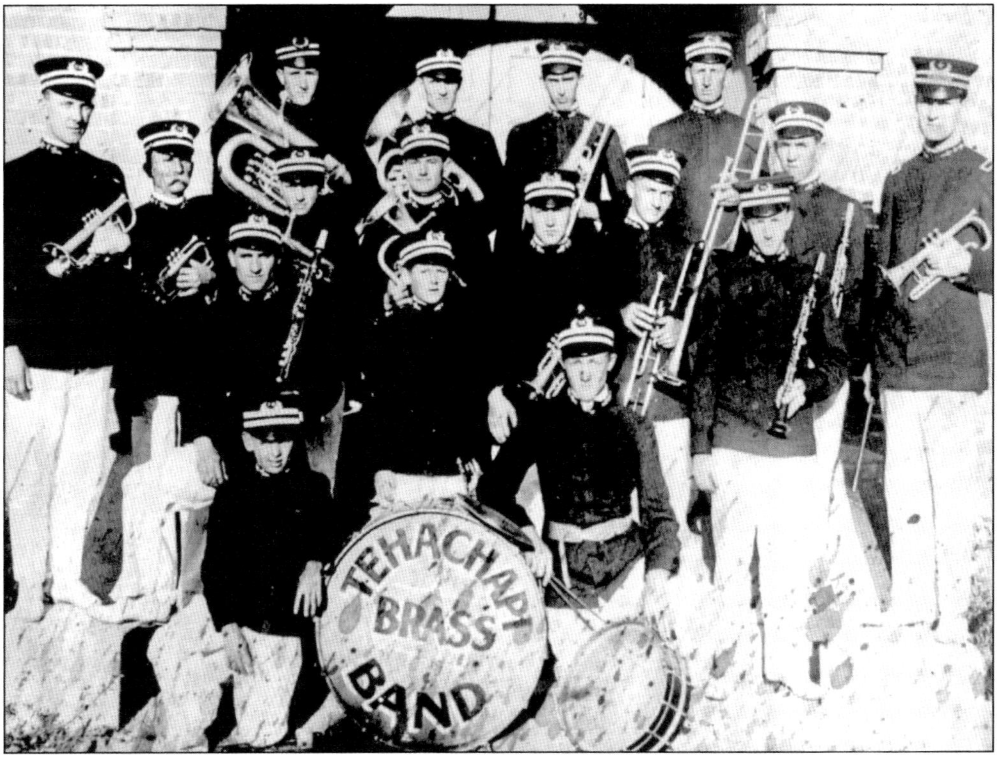

"The Tehachapi Brass Band is no longer a thing of conjecture," reported the *Kern County Californian* on August 15, 1891. "All the new instruments arrived yesterday, ten in number, . . . Professor Roth as leader." The instruments consisted of three coronets, one clarinet, two alto saxophones, one tuba, one trombone, and a drum. The band underwent several reorganizations until 1916 when it was replaced by the Tehachapi Jazz Orchestra.

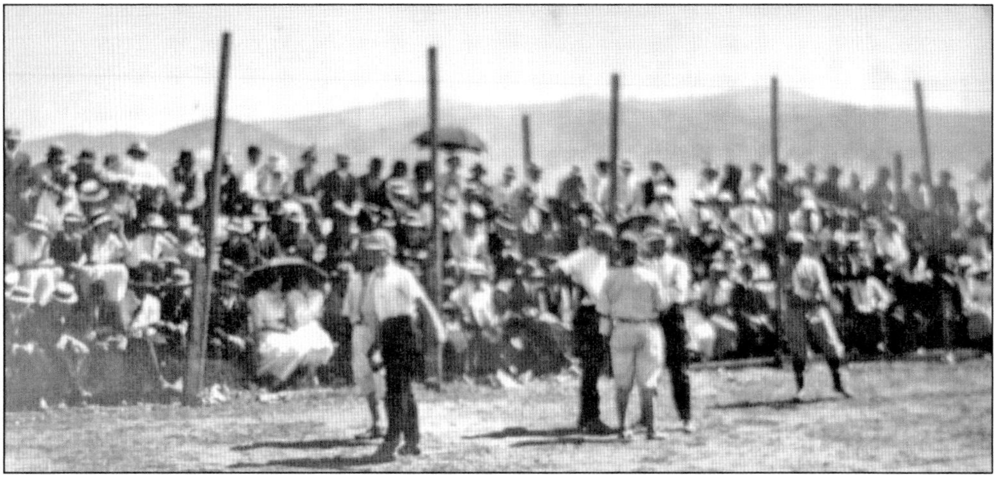

Baseball fervor spread to Tehachapi as early as 1899 when games were played on Sunday afternoons on the racetrack north of town. Several businessmen then sponsored the Tehachapi Baseball Club. Games were staged between teams from Bakersfield, Mojave, and Lancaster. The Mojave-Tehachapi rivalry was so intense that matches often ended with a brawl. Many players sported black eyes and assorted bruises as souvenirs of "a great game."

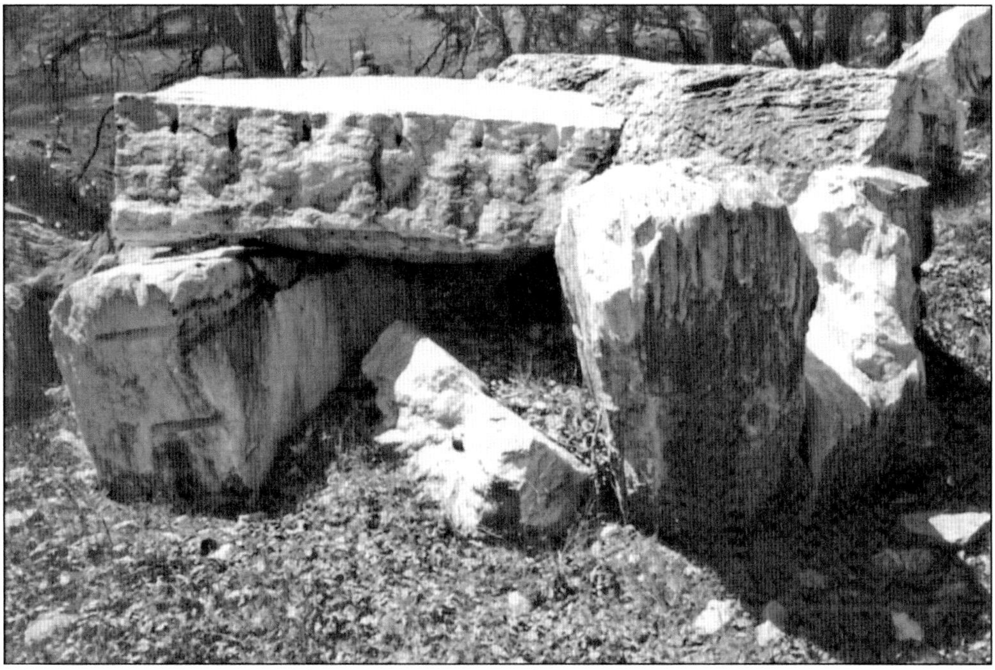

These scattered slabs of marble are the remnants of a quarry discovered in Brite Valley in 1874. The claim was purchased in 1876 by the Merrill Marble Works of San Francisco, which shipped some 6,000 tons to the City by the Bay, where it was used in the construction and beautification of several civic buildings and private mansions. One ledge alone measured 200 feet wide and 26 feet deep. (Author's collection.)

In 1887, the discovery of a ledge of colored sandstone led to the incorporation of the Tehachapi Building Stone Company. Its quarries produced blocks of sandstone ranging in color from green to tan, blue, red, and beige. The product was shipped by rail to the Los Angeles area where it was used in various construction projects, including the Pasadena City Library.

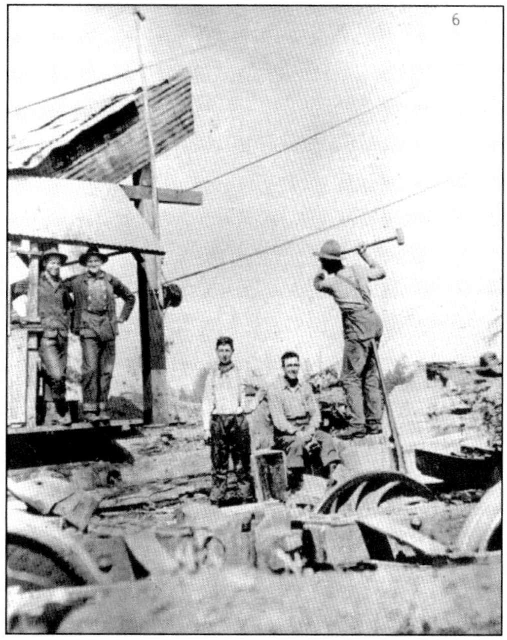

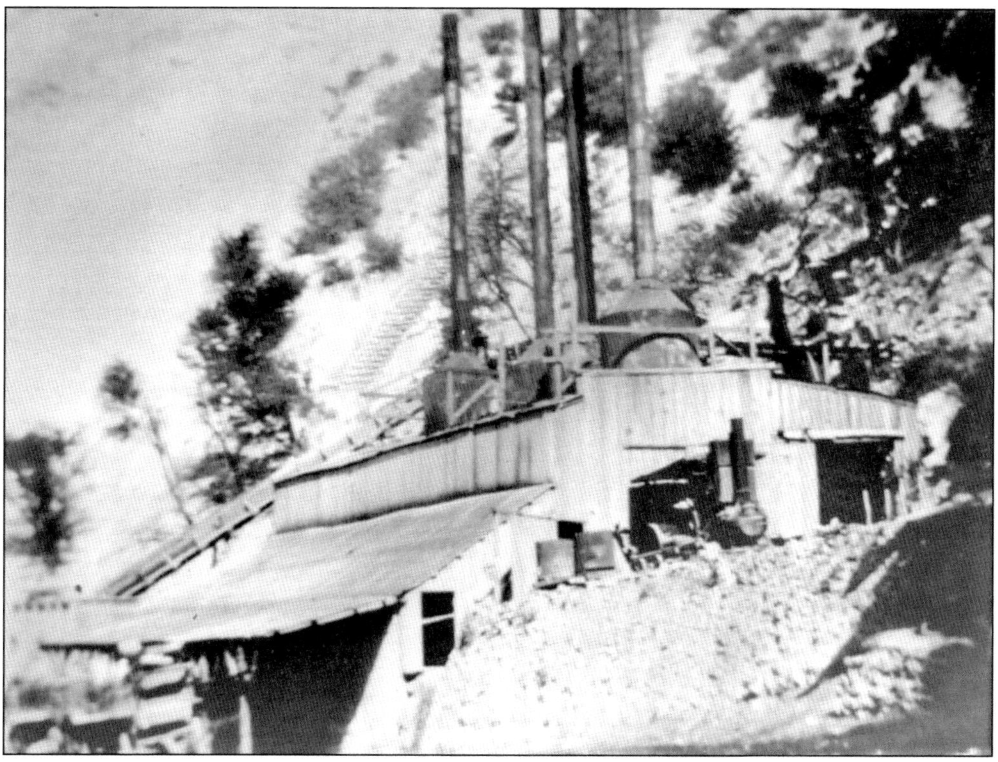

With the arrival of F. O. Wyman in 1885, the Union Lime Company became a major business in Tehachapi. Wyman's previous experience with the dolomite lime fields in Ohio kept him abreast of the latest improvements in the industry. Only the best stonemasons were employed in building the large kilns. The company operated until the 1930s and, during that time, produced over a million tons of quicklime.

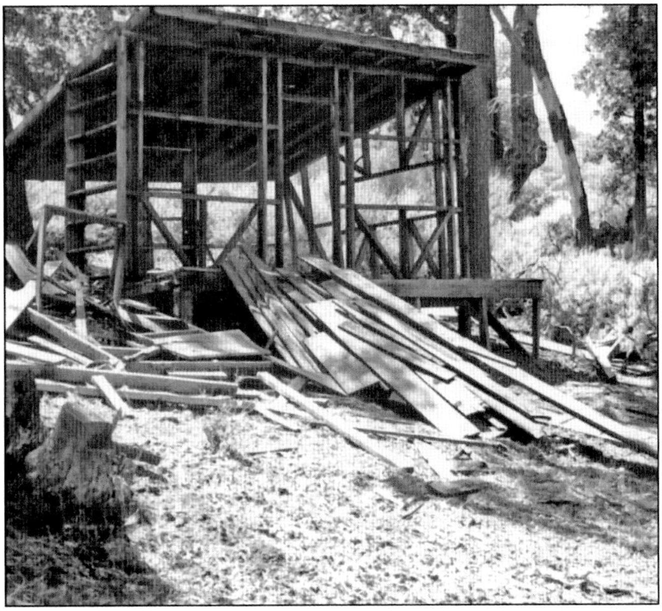

The California Pine Box Company was a branch of the Oak Creek Lumber Company. Owners Burt Denison and Jack and Dan McFarland milled lumber and made fruit crates. The crates were shipped to Los Angeles to supply the growing citrus industry. They were also used to transport Denison's pears to outside markets. The company operated for a full decade, from 1880 to 1890, before closing down.

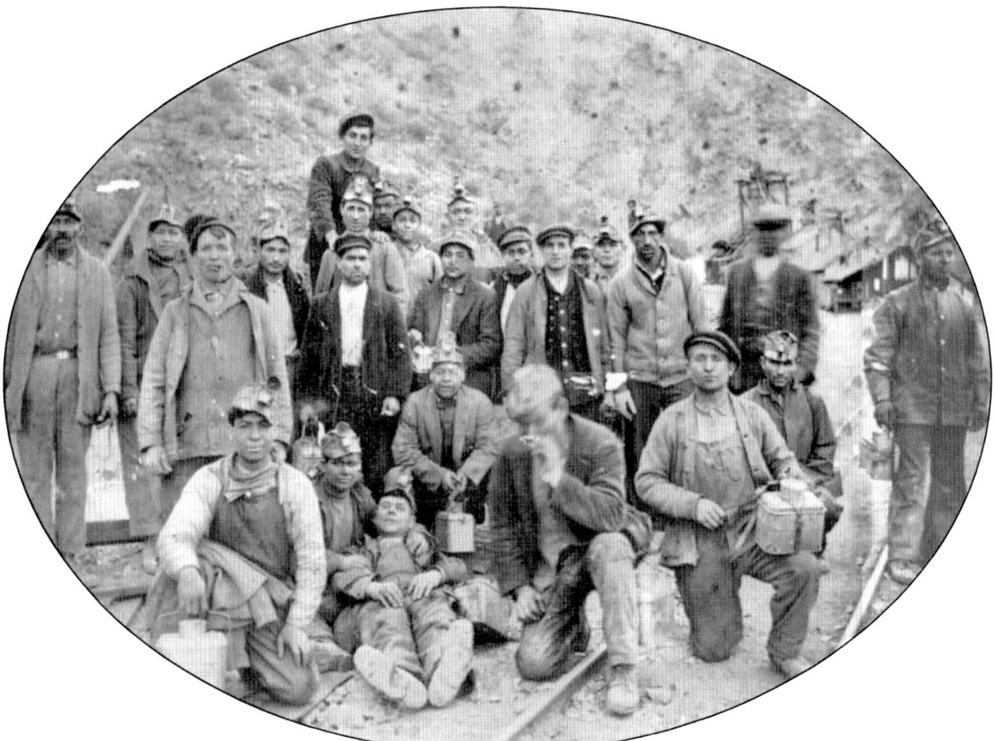

It did not take long for Tehachapi settlers to establish a diversified economy. On January 26, 1878, the *Kern County Gazette* provided the following description of what men did for a living: "Some of us work placer mines, some gather salt, some raise stock, some burn limestone, some manufacture lumber, and some raise grain and vegetables."

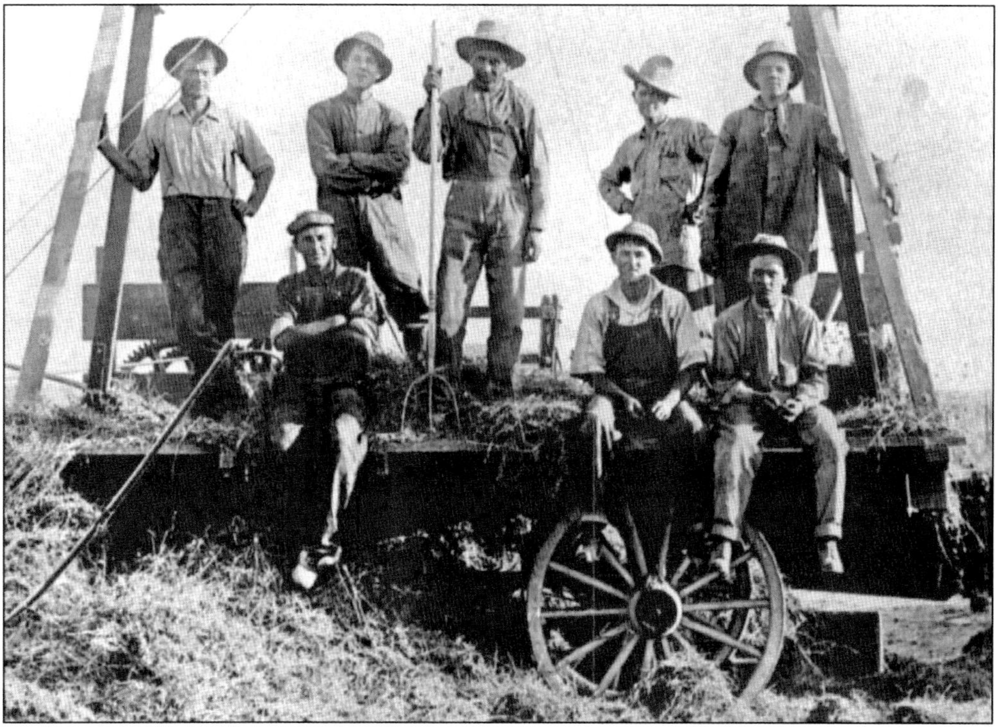

By 1890, Tehachapi also had a diverse population in which men still outnumbered women. The *Daily Californian* of April 17, 1894, printed the following results of the 1893 census: "Males-401, Females-228, Children-13. Residents totaled 642 of which 571 were born in the United States, 10 in Germany, 12-China, 3-the British Isles, 1 from Italy, 7-Ireland, 4-Mexico, 3-Spain, 1-Portugal and 16 from France."

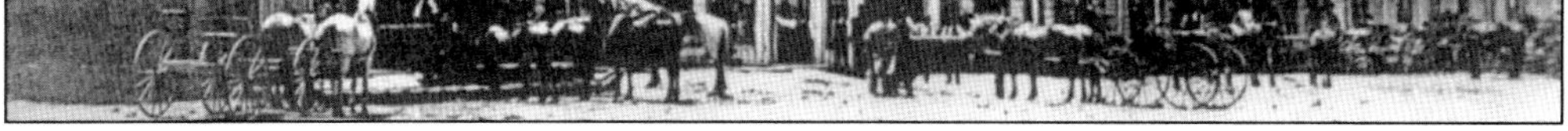

The Tehachapi Summit of 1885 was outgrowing its earlier critics. One previously critical editor changed his opinion to predicting a bright future. Many editors made trips to Summit to provide firsthand reports. In the November 14, 1885, issue of the *Kern County Californian*, one writer observed, while partaking of the hospitality of Summit's numerous saloons: "As an indicator of its growth and prosperity we mention the fact that it has eight saloons which barely suffice to supply the demands for bilious refreshments stimulated by the pure, bracing, mountain air." He added, "Other branches of business are equally well represented."

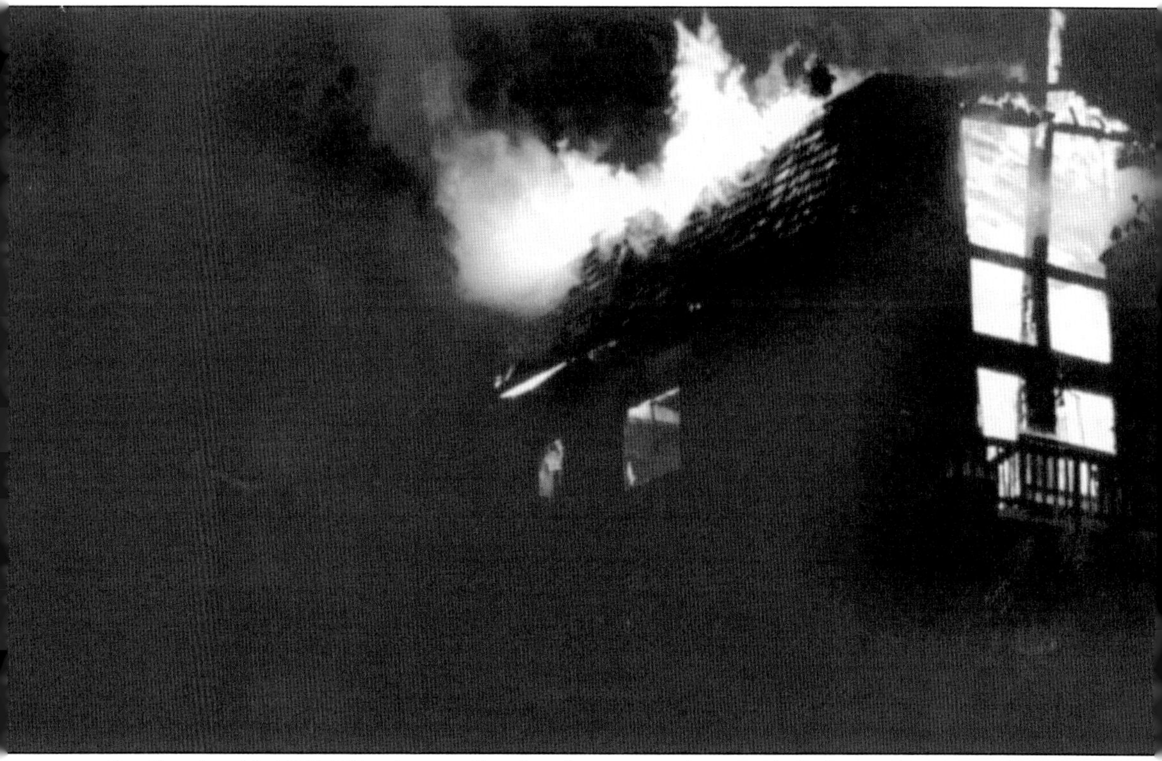

On October 15, 1895, Tehachapi suffered its first major disaster. A faulty coal stove inside Harry Coleman's Shoe Repair shop ignited the conflagration at 8:00 p.m. The flames quickly spread through wooden buildings along Railroad Avenue. Lined with cloth and wallpaper, they quickly ignited. A swiftly formed bucket brigade proved useless, so volunteers helped business owners rescue what they could. In the end, 18 businesses were reduced to ashes, including Coleman's Shoe Repair, the Piute Hotel, Mary Ann Haigh's restaurant, and the post office. Also burned out were businesses owned by the Cuddeback brothers, Charles Hart, John Irribarne, Charles Heath, H. M. Jacobs, C. A. Lee, H. Wilkison, E. L. Spencer, D. S. Clark, A. F. Burke, C. Walsh, and S. Thompin. Within two days reconstruction had begun as re-builders turned to the newly opened brickyard for material. Tehachapi went through several more fires and years before a volunteer fire department was organized. (Author's collection.)

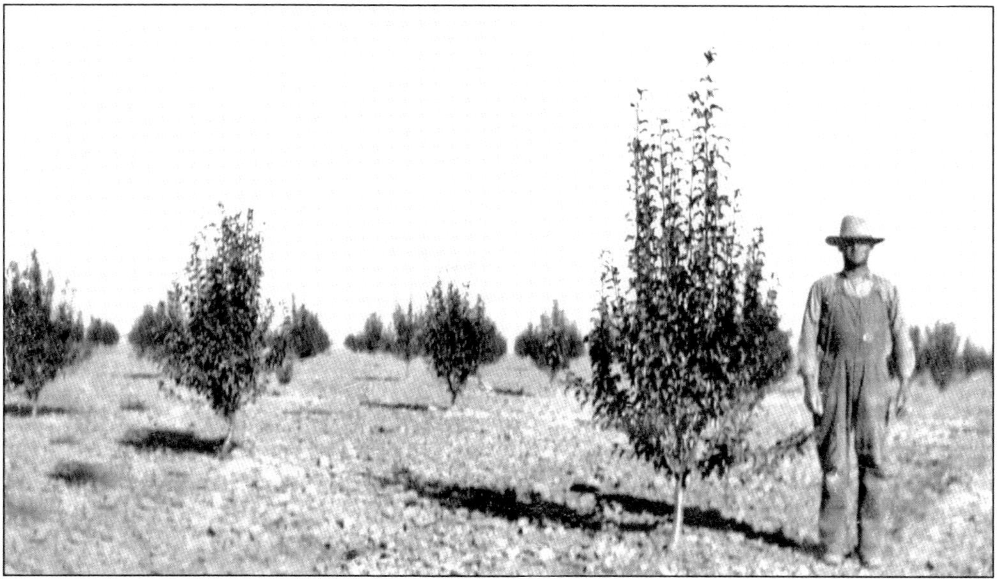

The arrival of the railroad helped to convert family orchards into a cash crop. Joseph Kiser sold his apples to the Southern Pacific for their chain of Harvey House restaurants. In 1891, two fruit stands opened next to the depot and did a brisk business. Locals and travelers alike enjoyed the cherries, pears, peaches, apricots, and the "finest apples in the state," which sold for 3¢ a pound.

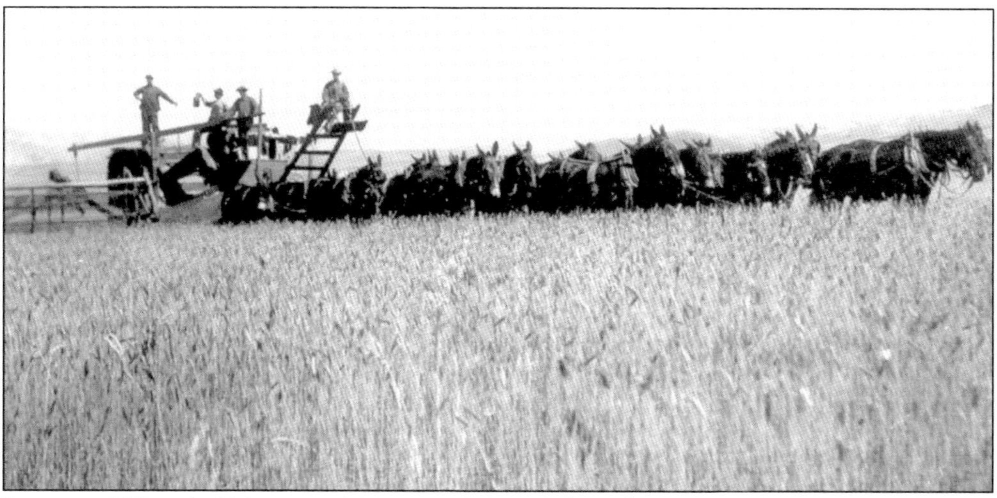

Between 1870 and 1900, some 100,000 acres were under cultivation in the valley, requiring up to 600 horses to pull the machinery used during the harvest season. Tehachapi farmers helped make California one of the nation's top producers and exporters of wheat. England, France, and Italy were particularly fond of Tehachapi's hard-grain, white wheat, which made excellent breads and pasta.

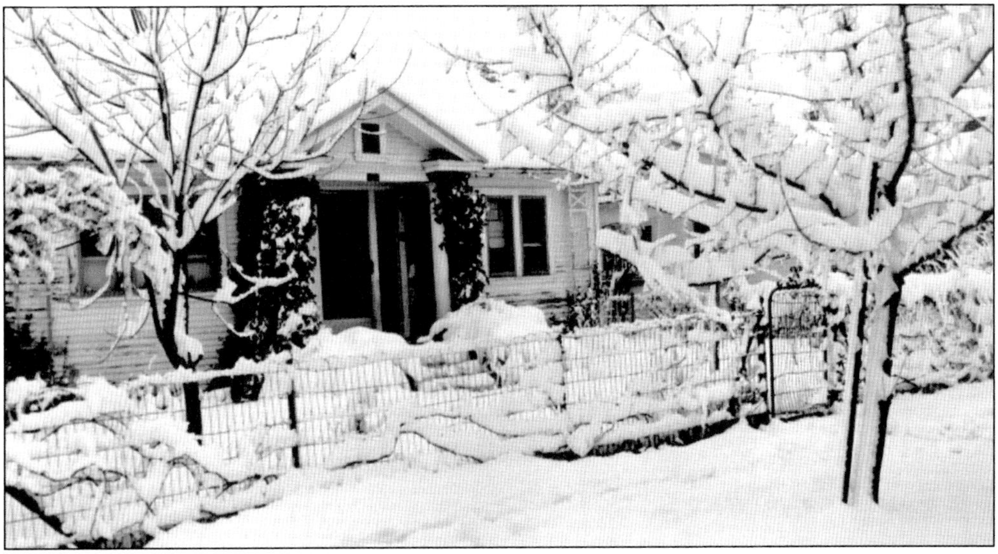

A winter storm proved Native Americans' predictions correct. Wise residents kept ample wood for kitchen and parlor stoves. Nellie Bly, a reporter for the *New York World*, was coming by train through Tehachapi, and snow or not, locals planned to welcome her. But Bly's train did not stop. "Her failure to appear induced the crowd to snowball the train and her car left here with a coat of snow," stated the *Kern County Californian* on January 8, 1890.

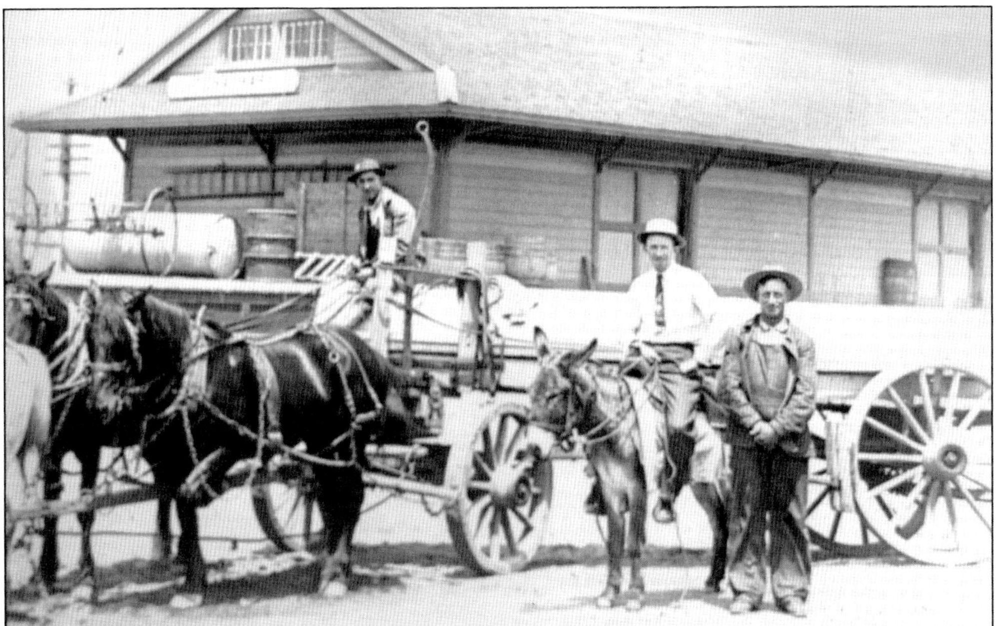

The depot was a window to the outside world. Some came just to watch people arrive or boxcars being loaded. In 1891, the stationmaster forewarned residents of a forthcoming train bearing Pres. Benjamin Harrison. Residents flocked to the depot to hang banners and display flags but to no avail. On April 24, 1891, the *Kern County Californian* reported, "The President's Special passed through here Tuesday too early to see the display in his honor. Mr. Harrison was probably not aware that Tehachapi is the largest town between Girard and Cameron but it is!" Both Girard and Cameron were relay stations between Caliente and Mojave.

Five

THE CHANGING SCENE

In 1900 America presented to the eye the picture of a country that was still mostly frontier of one sort or another.

—Mark Sullivan, *Our Times, Volume 1: The Turn of the Century*

The Tehachapi of 1900 was a typical small western town that one visitor described as "not too pretty." The streets were dirt, and the buildings were made of board and mostly unpainted with false fronts. The population, wavering between 500 and 600, was outnumbered by cattle, horses, and sheep.

Some 45,000 acres were sown with oats, barley, and wheat. Orchards were making an initial appearance, and by 1910, apple and pear trees covered 5,000 acres. The land was still producing lime, salt, and gold along with marble and colored sandstone. By 1905, there were 22 businesses in town, including the weekly *Tehachapi Tomahawk*, which was advocating incorporation. Four years later, on a 36-23 vote, Tehachapi became an incorporated town. Its five-man board of trustees had the legal authority to pass and enforce ordinances.

But it really took the automobile to hasten progress. In 1906, autos were such an oddity that a huge crowd turned out to witness a six-passenger touring car come through town. Some 10 years later, the Ramina Livery Stable added a full-service garage. Electricity came in 1915 when trustees approved a contract with Pacific Light and Power. Natural gas followed in 1927. Next were the phonograph, the radio, and the cinema. From products to services to new styles in hair and clothing, it was an era of change. The widow Mary Kessing, who had run the Summit Hotel since 1876, later gave this description: "The town has gone through many changes. Now Tehachapi is such a quiet little town with its electric lights and automobiles, so different from the old stage depot and cowboy town of the past."

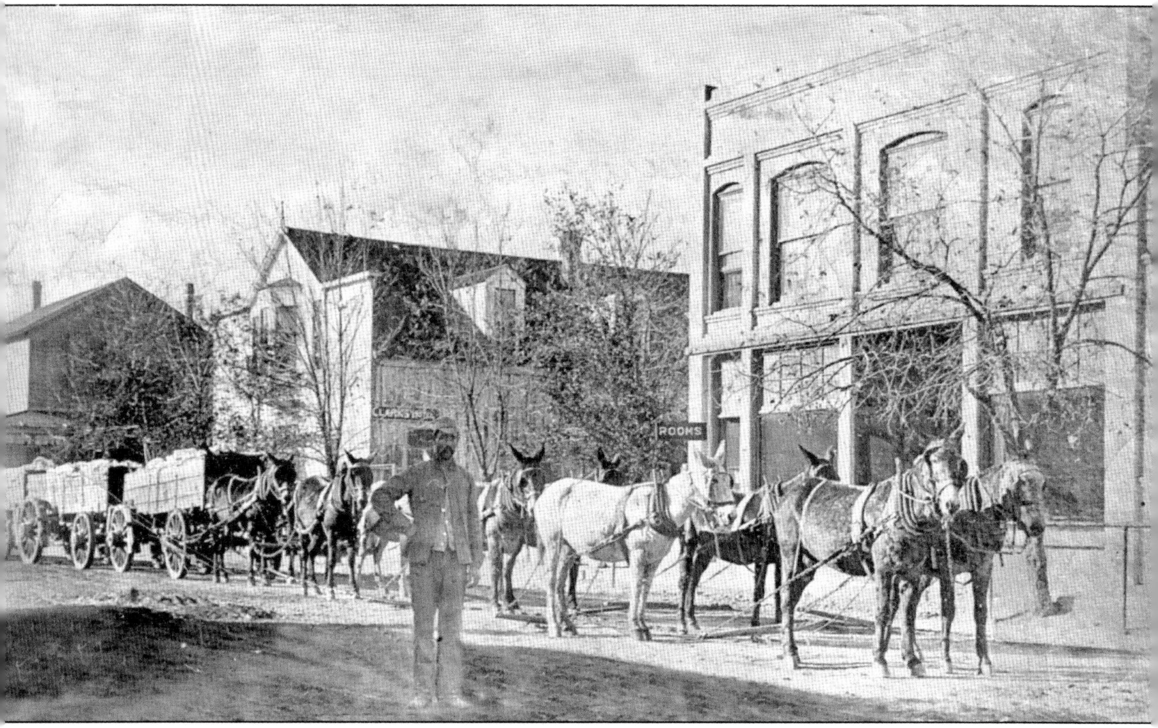

"Few Clothes Slim" was an excellent teamster. For years he was employed by the Union Lime Company to bring the wagonloads of lime from the company's kilns in Antelope Canyon to the rail depot in Tehachapi. Even as the automobile began making an appearance, he and his mule team were a familiar sight to young and old alike.

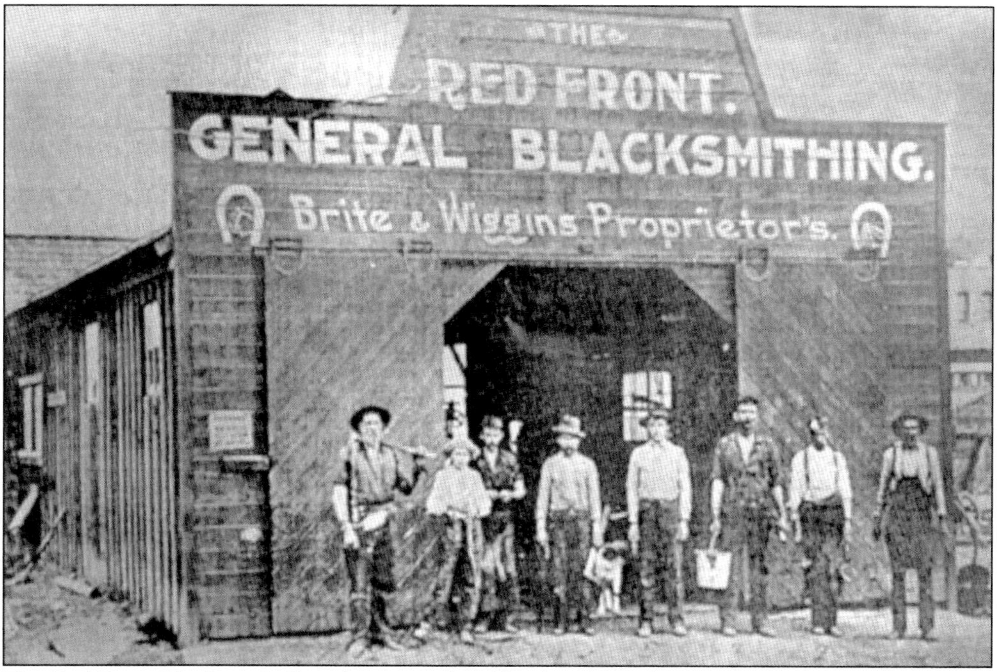

The Red Front Blacksmith Shop became a local landmark on the corner of Green and F Streets. Directions were based on turning right or left or going one block beyond the "Red Front." This partnership of John Brite and William Wiggins was only natural since both families lived near each other. The children grew up, attended school, and rode horses together.

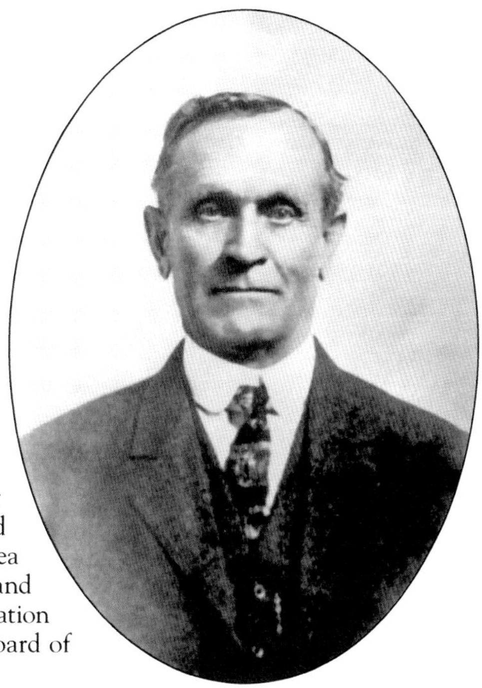
John Hickey was one of the leading proponents for the incorporation of Tehachapi. Born in Ireland and educated in the United States, he came to this area in 1875 and worked as a farmer, schoolteacher, and itinerant preacher. Following the town's incorporation in 1909, Hickey was elected to serve on the board of trustees, a position he held for several terms.

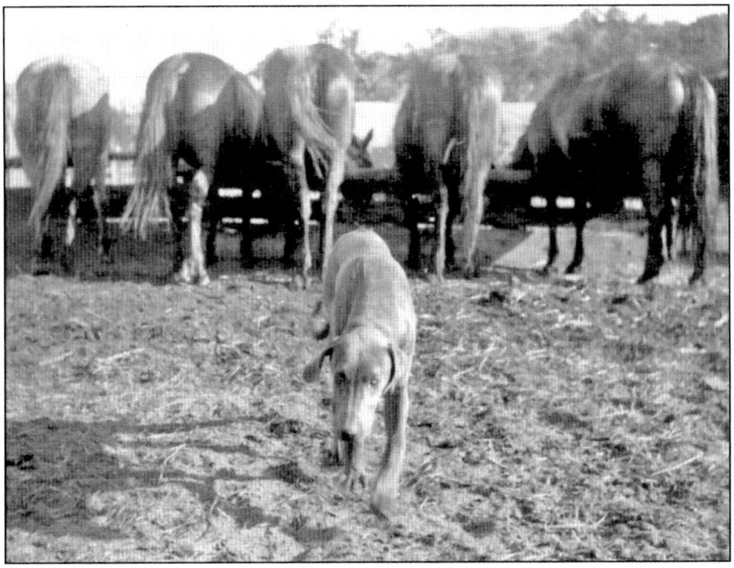

One of the first actions taken by the board of trustees was to pass an ordinance regulating stray domestic animals and approving a tax on all dogs ($1 males, $3 females). Stray dogs had obviously become such a nuisance that, in 1897, the *Tehachapi Times* reported, "It would not be out of place for the [county] poundmaster to get a move on to protect our trees and yards."

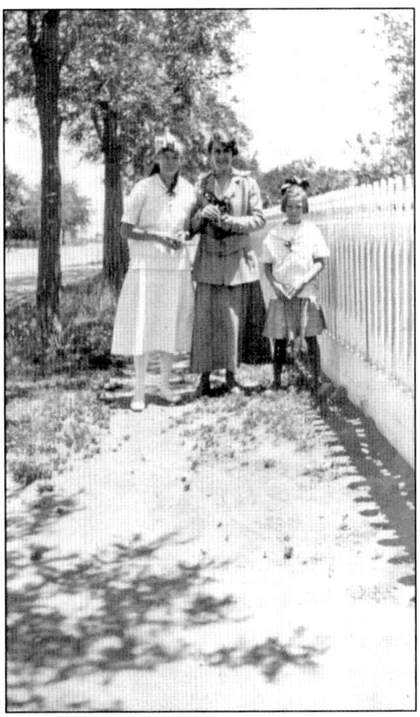

Sidewalks also posed a problem for the town trustees. Wooden walkways, once touted as vast improvements, had become so dilapidated as to become hazardous. But property owners objected to paying for new sidewalks, curbs, and gutters that would cost $2.50 per foot. It would be several years before improvements were made.

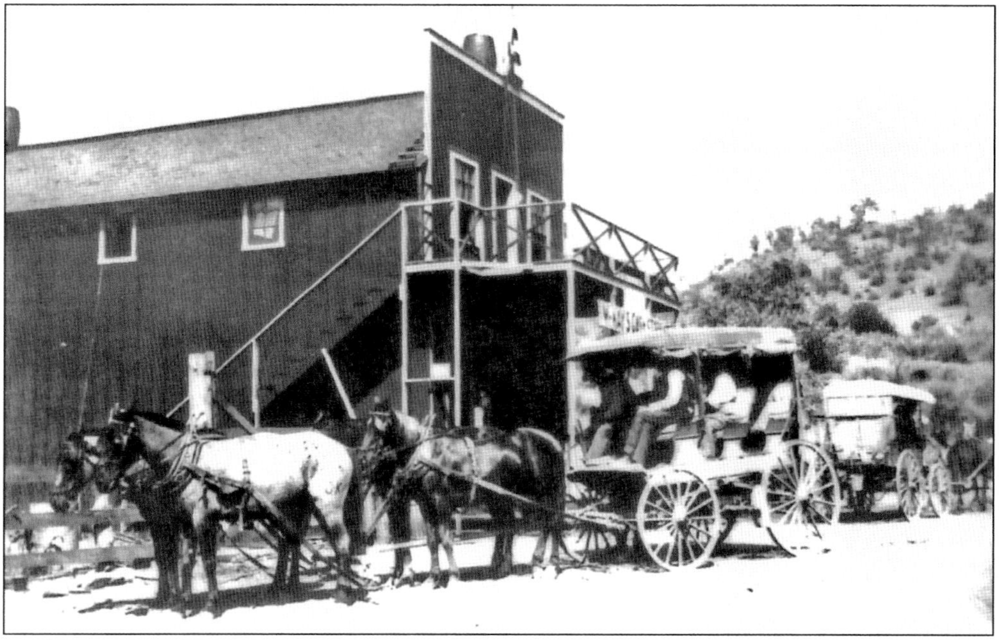

As the nation embraced a new era of industrialization and the changing appearances of the 1900s, Tehachapi remained a typical western town with dirt streets and hitching racks. The buildings were made of unpainted wood, some with false fronts and others with porches.

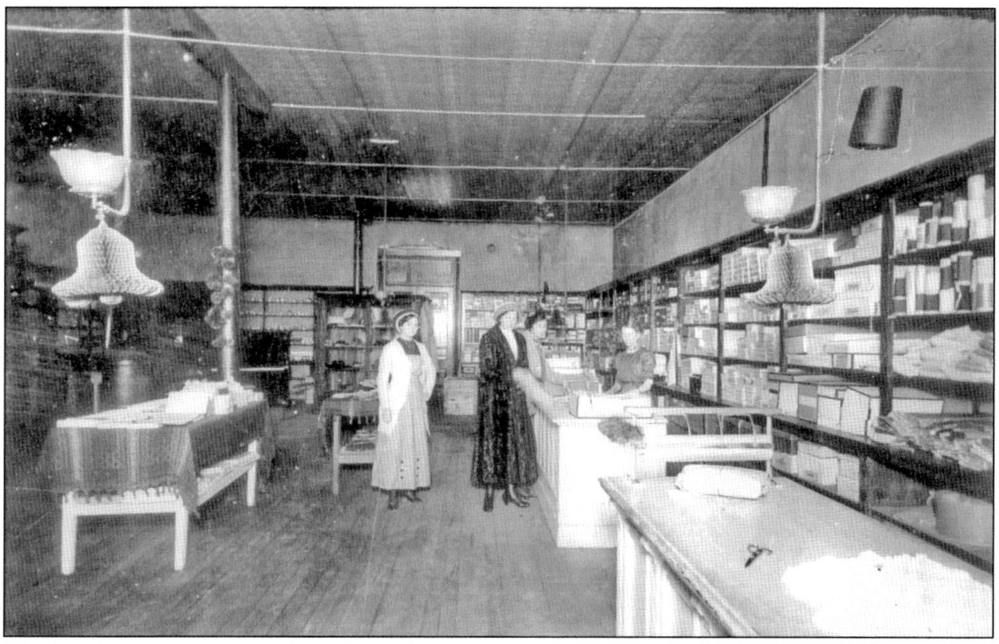

The 1900s saw an increased number of women entrepreneurs. Laura Wiggins Weferling owned this millinery shop in Tehachapi and employed women salesclerks. The shop, located inside the Vernon Hotel on Green Street, sold readymade or individually designed hats from its stock of forms, colored ribbons, lace, artificial flowers, and real feathers.

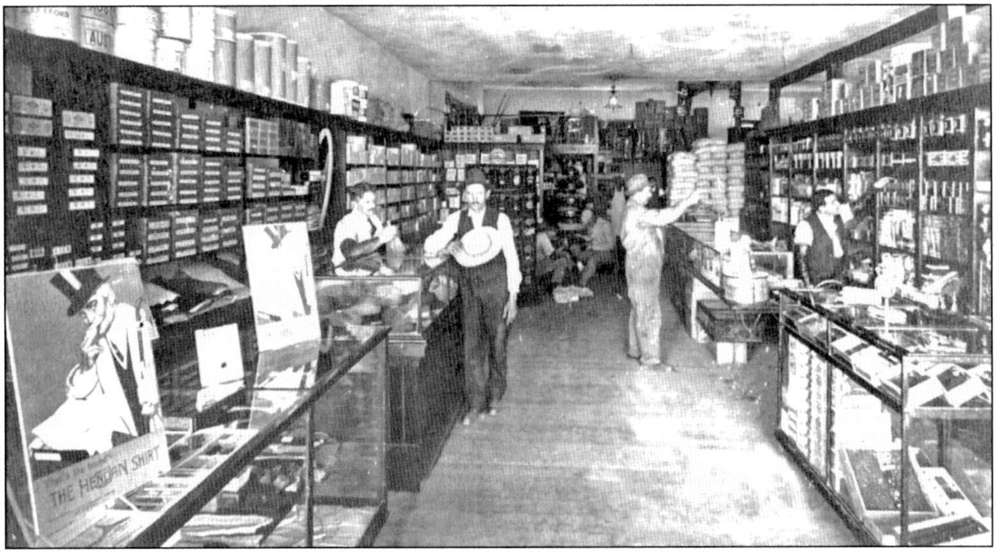

Isador Asher's mercantile was one of Tehachapi's finest stores. Built in 1892, the 50-by-100-foot, all-brick shop included a basement for storage. Asher first clerked at Hirschfield and Green's store in Williamsburg until 1885 when he opened his own store in Tehachapi. The second floor became known as Asher's Opera House, which was the scene of lectures, plays, and gala balls.

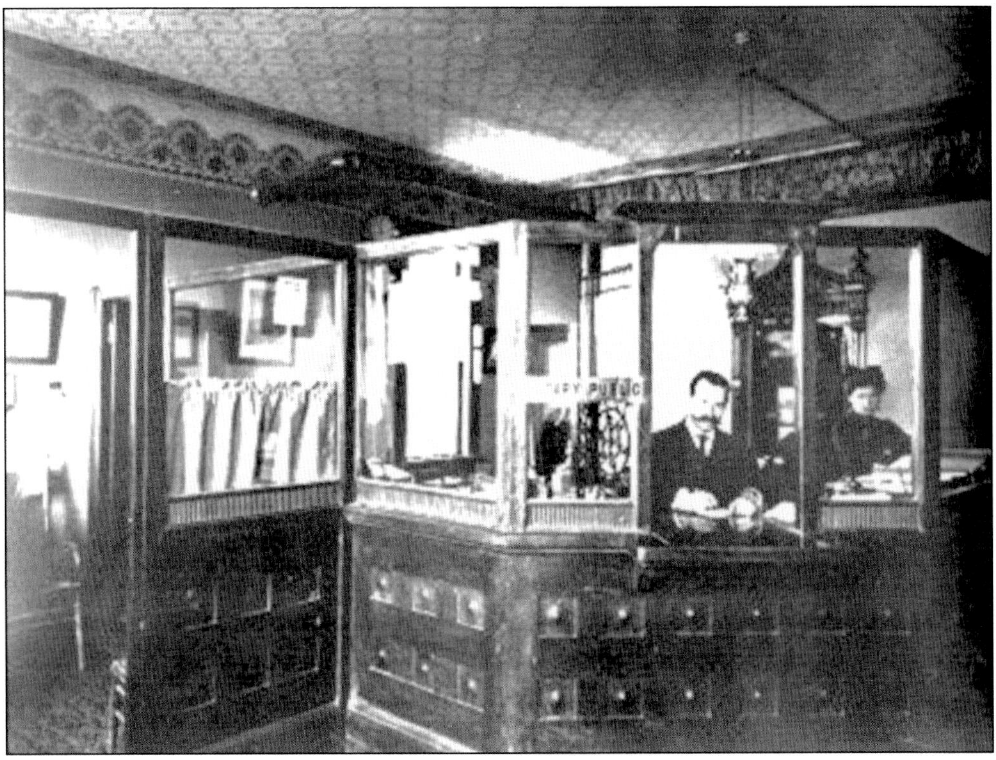

In 1892, the Bank of Tehachapi became a duly authorized and incorporated bank. The board of trustees consisted of president Isador Asher and members L. Harris, H. A. Blodgett, and H. Hirschfield. By 1906, it had outgrown its original location inside Asher's store and moved into its own building. A hometown bank, it remained solvent even during the Great Depression.

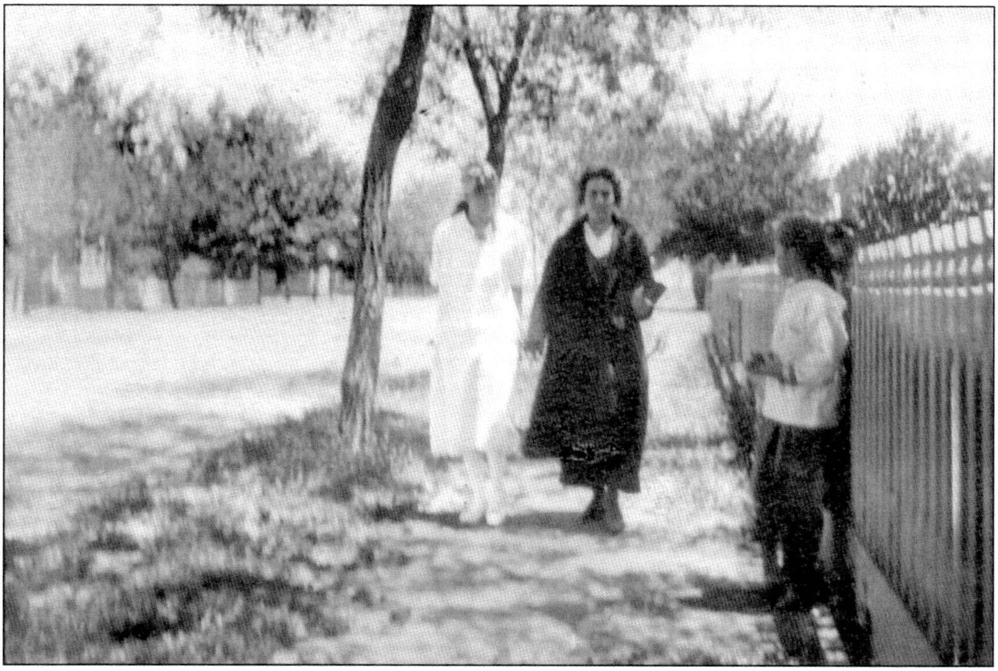

Tree-lined streets provided welcome shade for pedestrians—and horses. A large tree on G Street presented an unusual problem: it became such a favored spot at which to tie one's saddle horse that there was no room for pedestrians to walk! In order to keep the tree intact, town trustees posted this warning sign, "NO hitching. Do not disturb the tree."

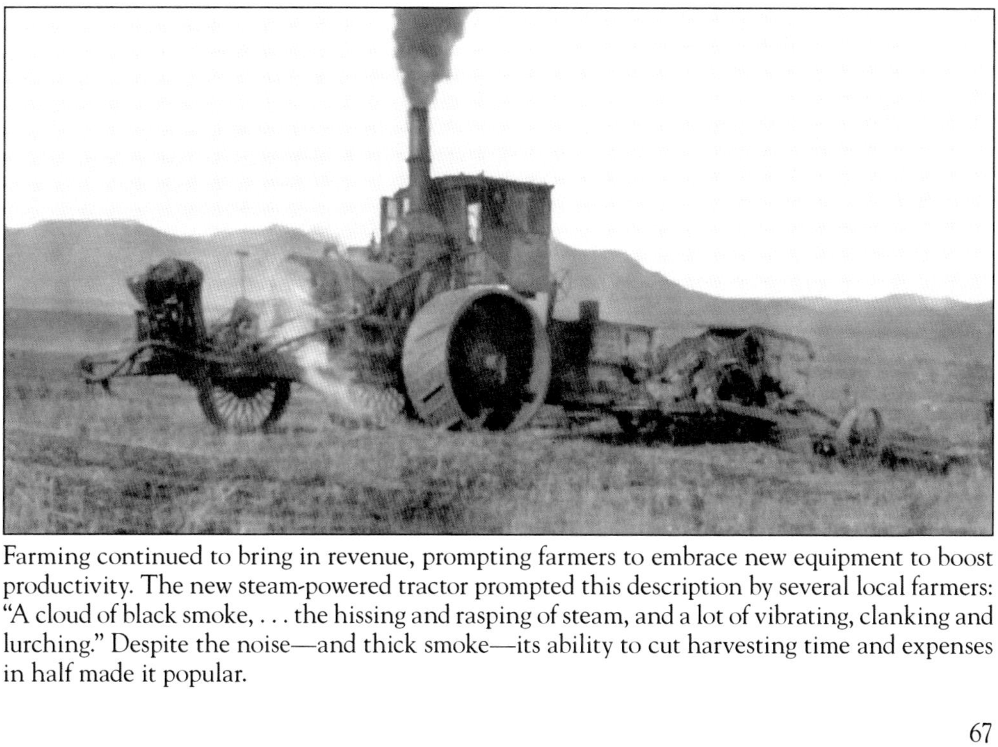

Farming continued to bring in revenue, prompting farmers to embrace new equipment to boost productivity. The new steam-powered tractor prompted this description by several local farmers: "A cloud of black smoke, . . . the hissing and rasping of steam, and a lot of vibrating, clanking and lurching." Despite the noise—and thick smoke—its ability to cut harvesting time and expenses in half made it popular.

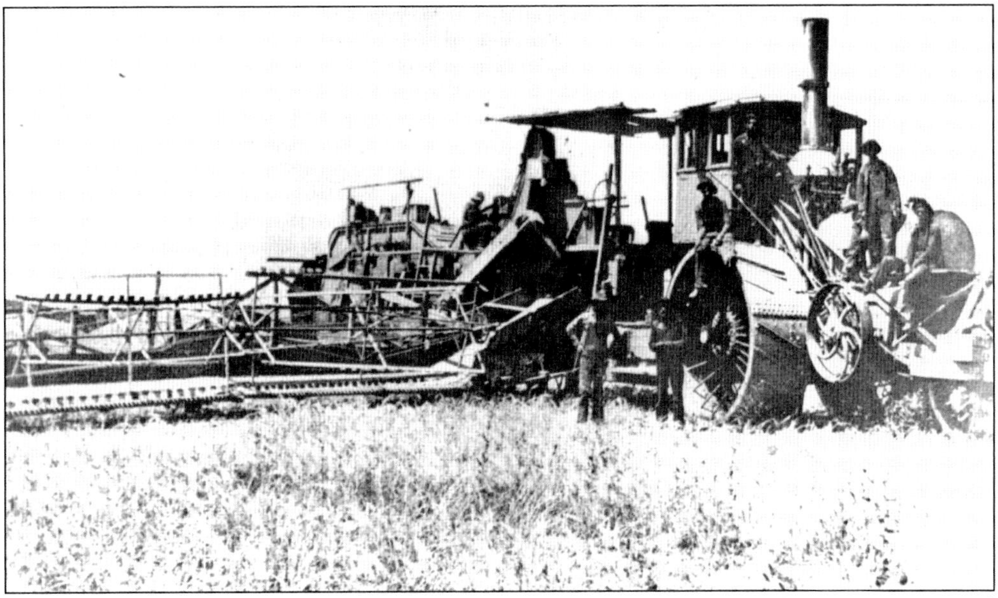

The California Steam Tractor Company began farming operations in 1900. The firm was so named because when the giant, two-wheeled tractor started up, it reportedly reminded the owner of an old steam locomotive. Owned by former Nevada senator John Percival Jones, the company had over 3,000 acres running east, south, and north of Tehachapi.

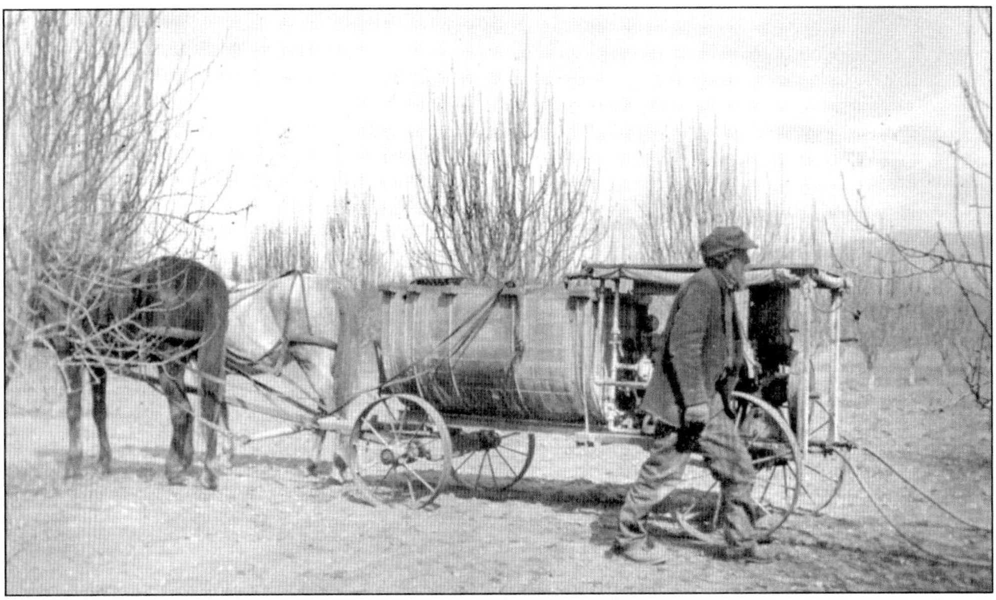

A horse-drawn water tank and buckets helped solve the problem of watering trees in Tehachapi's newly established town park. Trustees paid $750 to purchase Block 33 and two adjoining lots to create the park. Planting trees was delayed until 1914 when trustees hired a man for the job. Each morning, he would fill his horse-drawn tank with water and drive into the park where he watered each of the 160 trees with a bucket. Today's residents and visitors enjoy the large shade trees and facilities of Phil Marx Park.

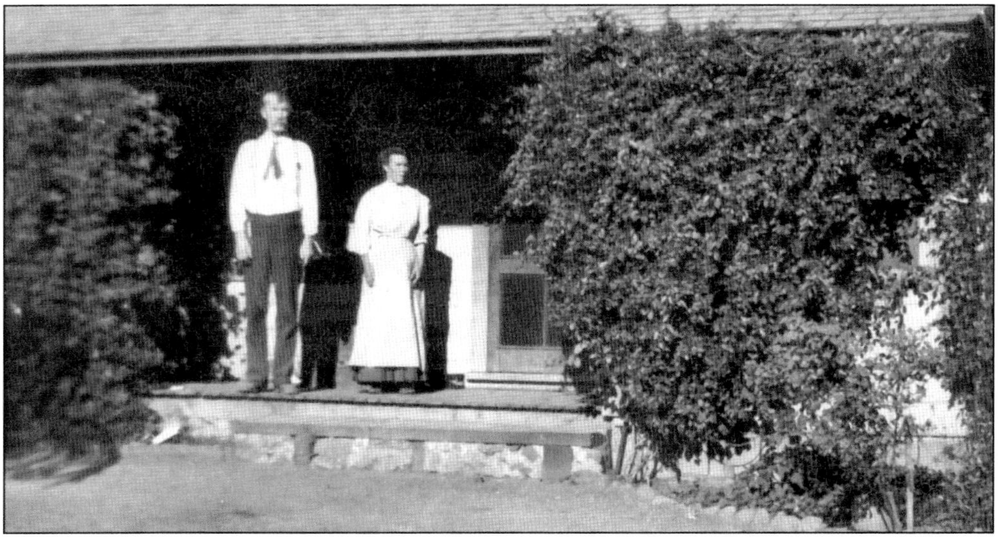

With each year of the new century, Tehachapi slowly shed its raw frontier image. In its place were many new residences with lilac and rose bushes framing the front porch and yards showcasing trees, lawns, and flowers. Inside were such modern inventions as kerosene cooking stoves, hand-cranked washing machines, and gramophones.

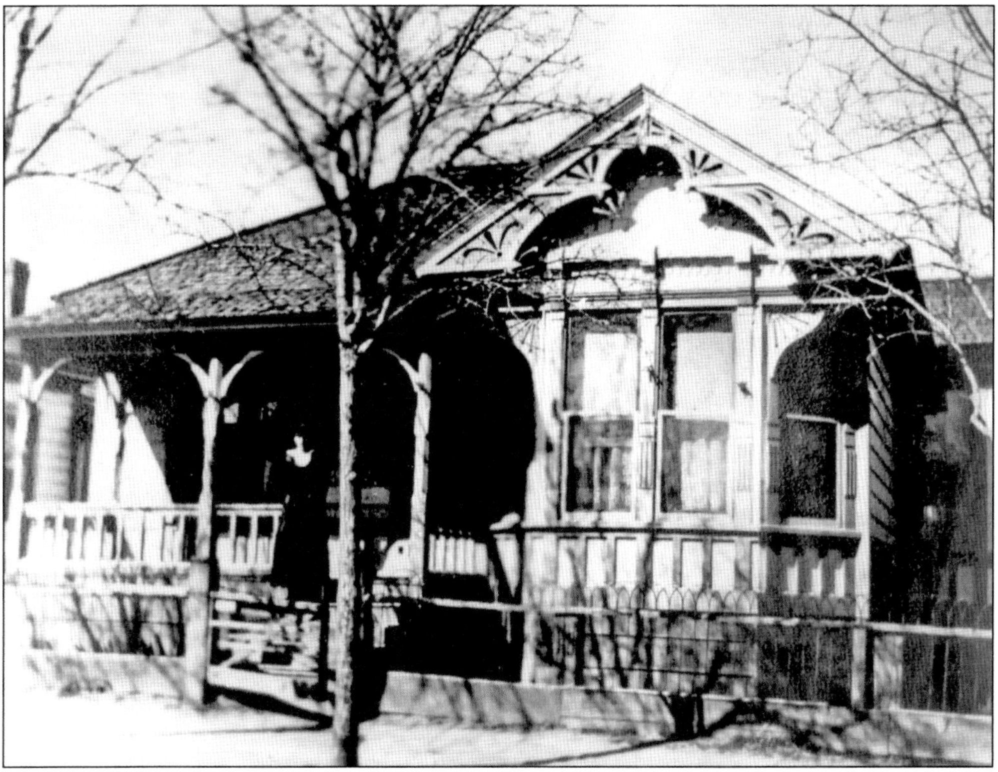

Many of Tehachapi's residents had first settled in Old Tehachapa/Williamsburg. When they moved into the new Tehachapi, it was not with just clothes and furnishings, but also with their house. The structure was jacked up onto a low-bed wagon or a set of logs and then pulled to its new location by a team of stout mules. Many of these old homes are still occupied as private residences.

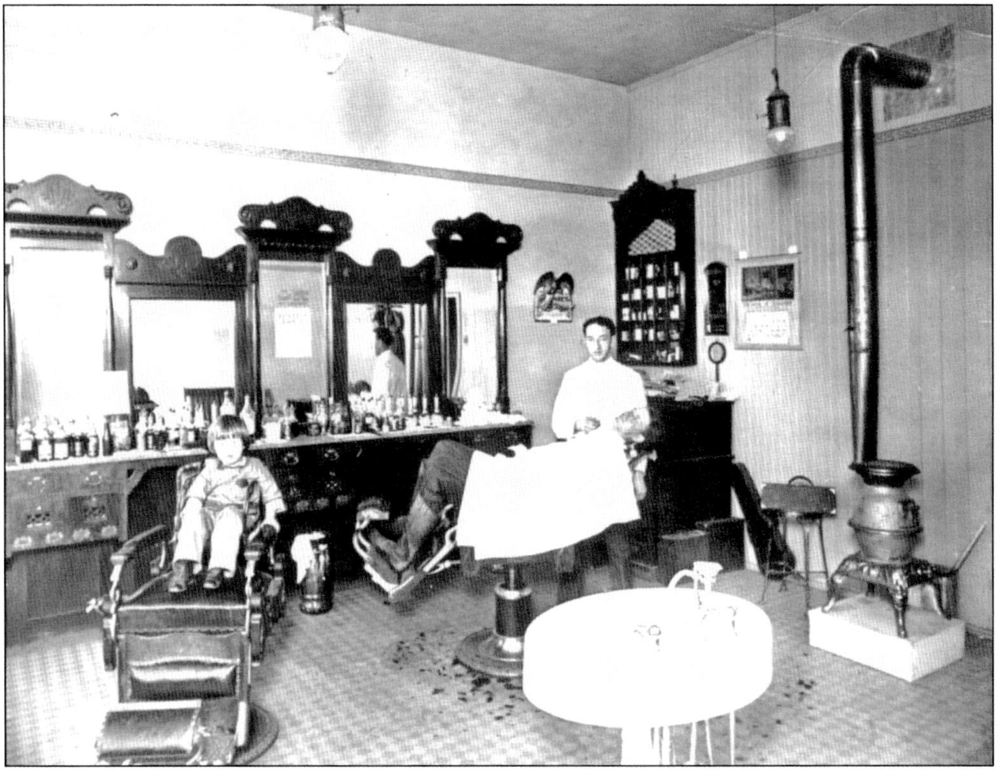

This barbershop was but one of many new businesses opening on Green Street as Tehachapi entered a period of growth and change. In addition to the hotels and restaurants, there were now two general merchandise stores, two barbershops, one drugstore, one butcher shop, a grocery store, one harness and shoemaking shop, a flour mill, and an icehouse.

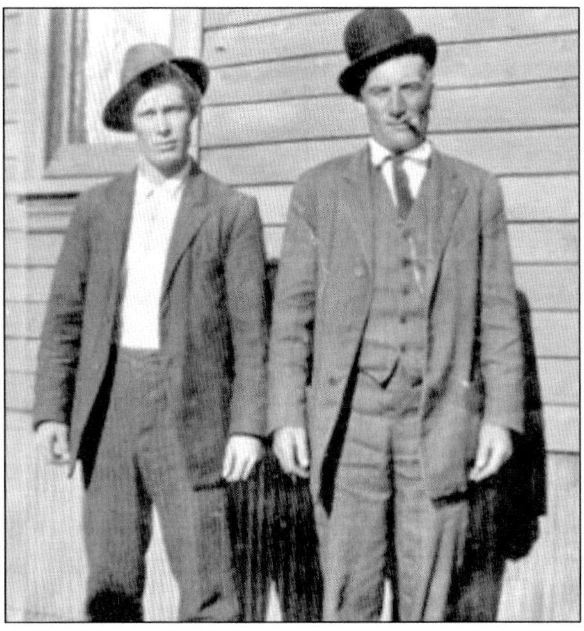

Louis Boden (right) was a hardworking and well-respected member of the community. His father, Fred Boden, opened Williamsburg's first blacksmith shop. Louis gave up farming on White Rock Creek and moved into Tehachapi where he later acted as town marshal from 1915 to 1927. During his years of service in that position and as constable for the 15th Judicial District, he never wore a gun.

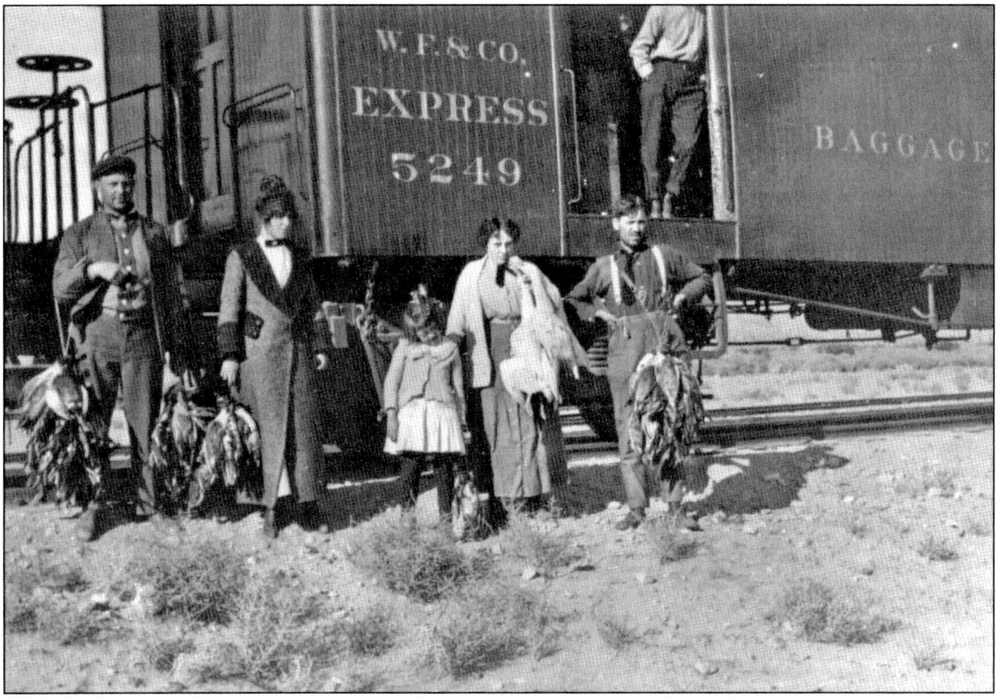

On October 18, 1916, residents flocked to the depot where the Southern Pacific had arranged special cars to Bakersfield for the first annual Kern County Fair. Local businesses and schools closed for the day so people could attend. Their enthusiasm was rewarded: Tehachapi's display and crates of apples and pears took first-place blue ribbons.

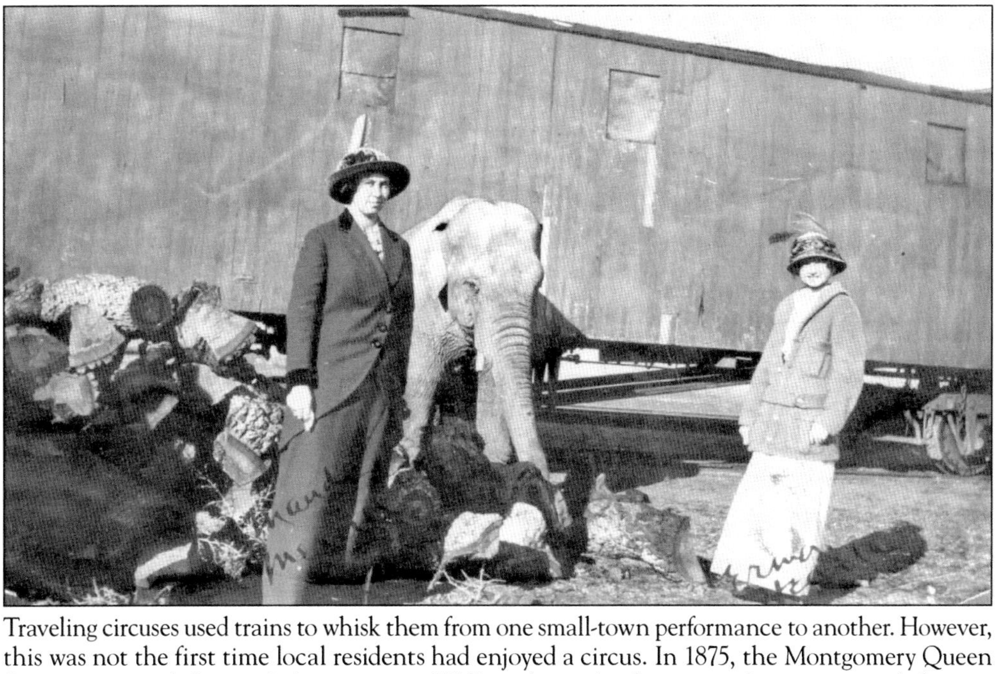

Traveling circuses used trains to whisk them from one small-town performance to another. However, this was not the first time local residents had enjoyed a circus. In 1875, the Montgomery Queen Circus presented the area's first circus in Williamsburg. At that time, the group traveled cross-country in wagons touting the main attraction of a daring female acrobat on horseback.

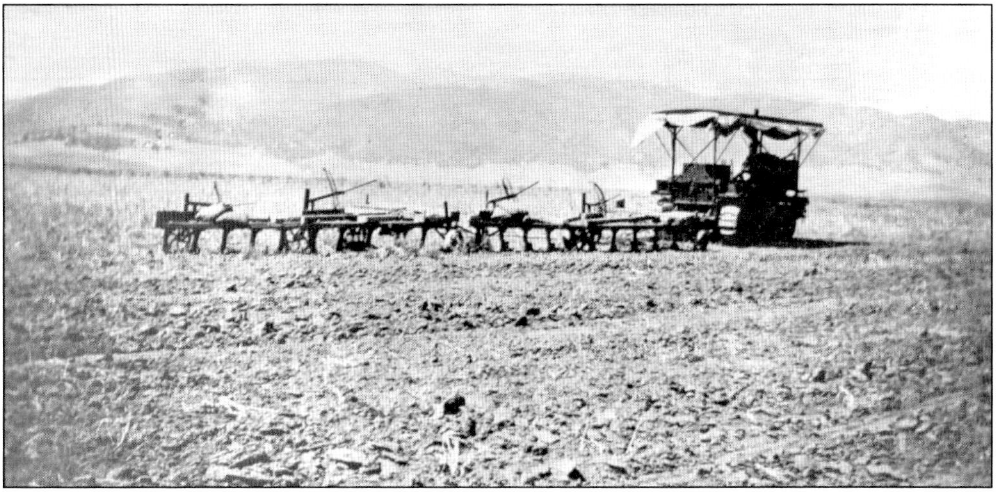

Historians have since credited California farmers for being the most progressive in regards to new equipment. Tehachapi farmers were no exception. Gang plows, wheel plows, rotary spades, steam-powered tractors, and finally gasoline-powered tractors were all in use by the 1900s.

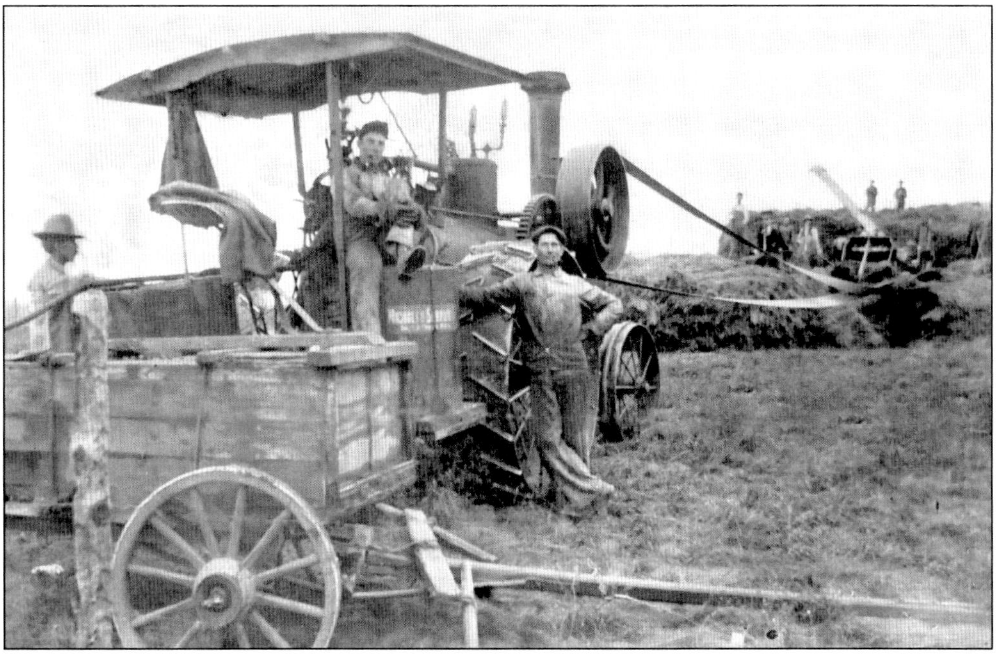

The hay baler was a major improvement in handling and storing hay. The compressed bales were easier to handle, store, and transport. They were also generally more uniform in size and weight than hay sold by the wagonload or stack. By 1900, farmers were shipping baled hay to outside markets where it brought top prices of $20 to $25 a ton.

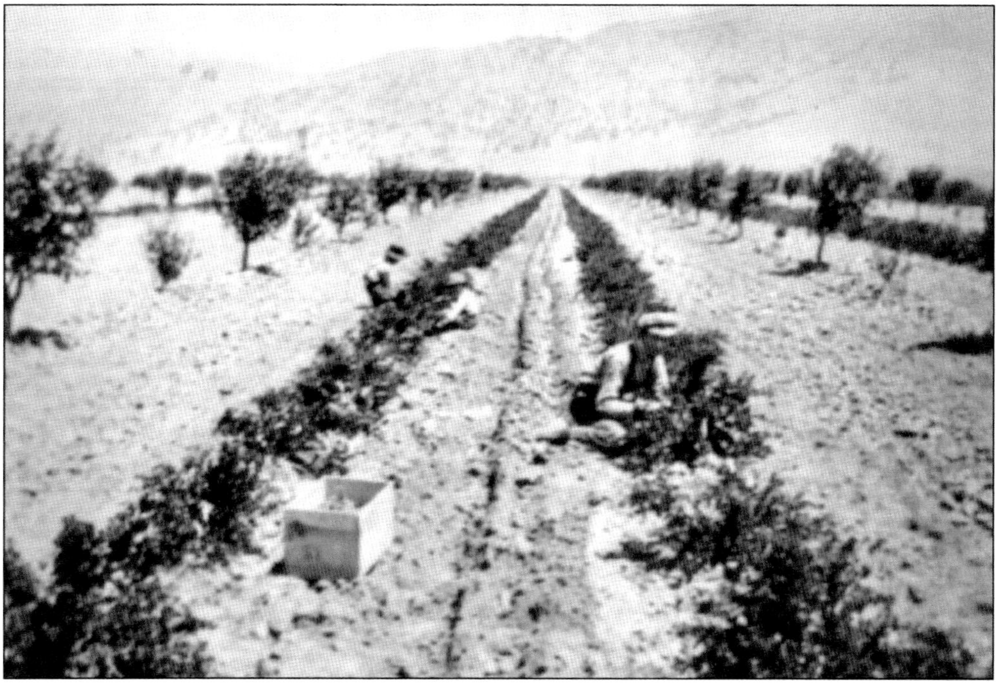

Tehachapi's transition from growing wheat to fruit has been credited to Burt M. Denison, who planted the area's first commercial pear orchard in 1909. Starting with a 40-acre parcel, he soon increased his orchards to 120 acres. His pears were shipped to a Burbank canning factory and marketed under the brand name T-Hacha-P. Others soon followed his lead. By 1922, some 5,000 acres were planted with pears and red winter apples.

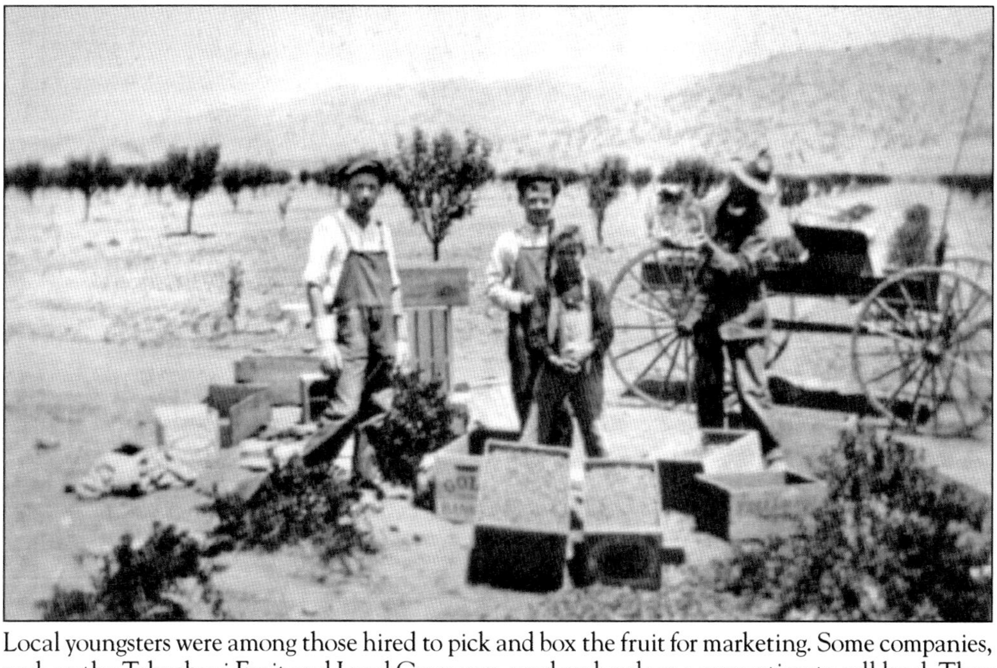

Local youngsters were among those hired to pick and box the fruit for marketing. Some companies, such as the Tehachapi Fruit and Land Company, used orchards as a promotion to sell land. They planted apple trees on small 5-to-10-acre parcels that were maintained until sold to the public.

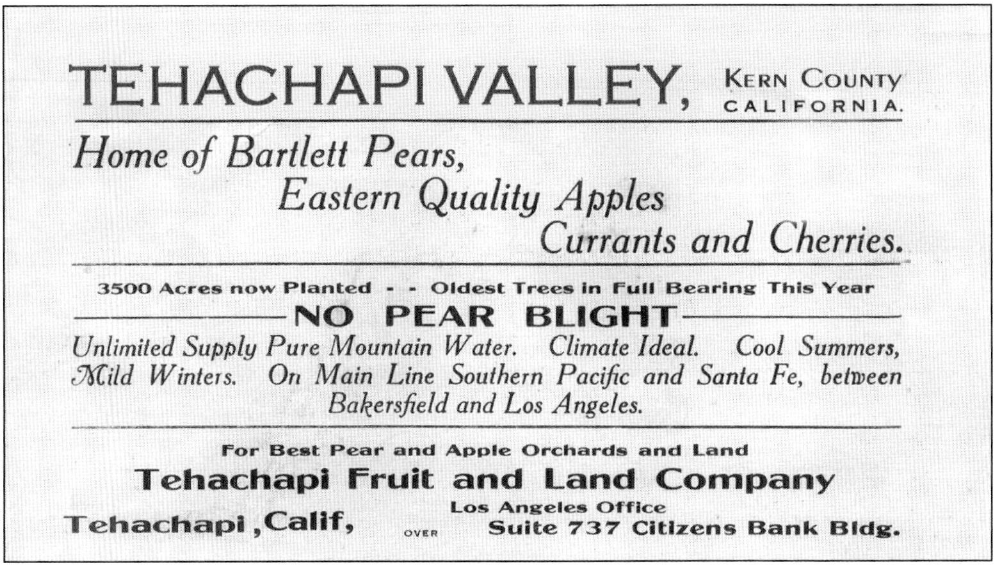

The Tehachapi Fruit and Land Company was the brainchild of Carle Turner McKinnie. In 1910, he purchased 1,600 acres next to town; 500 acres were planted with Bartlett pears and 500 acres with apples. The following year the property was subdivided into 10-acre parcels that were put up for sale. A promotional brochure urged people to "come to the country." McKinnie's sales office was located inside the Clark Hotel near the depot.

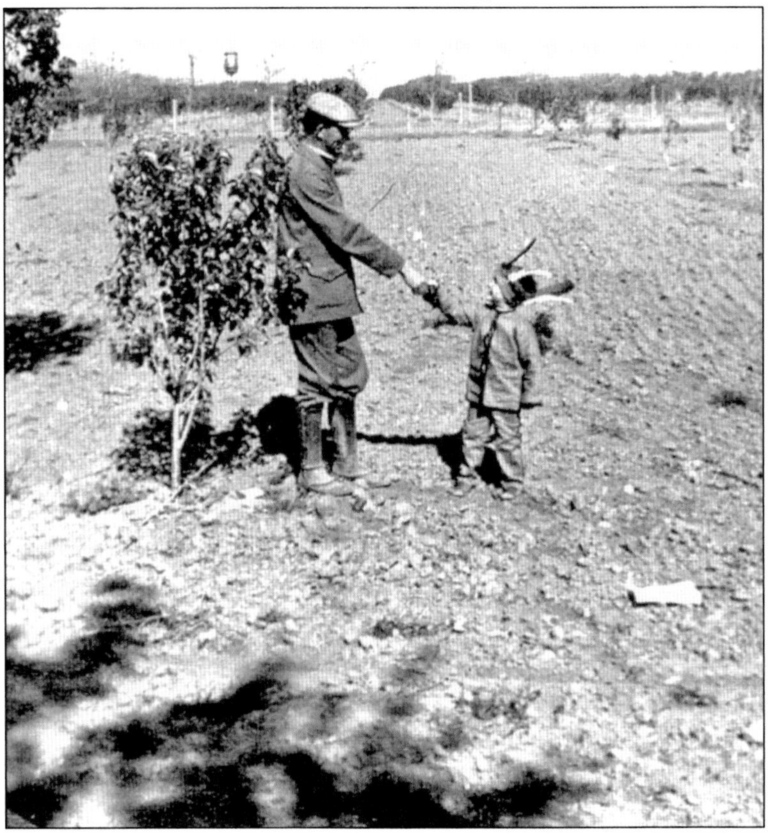

Local orchards were shipping pears to the Los Angeles market where they brought the top price of 6¢ a pound. This encouraged farmers to increase the size of their orchards. By 1917, some 1,800 acres were planted with red winter apples and 1,800 acres with pears. All fruit was shipped to Los Angeles and eastern markets, making Tehachapi orchards famous.

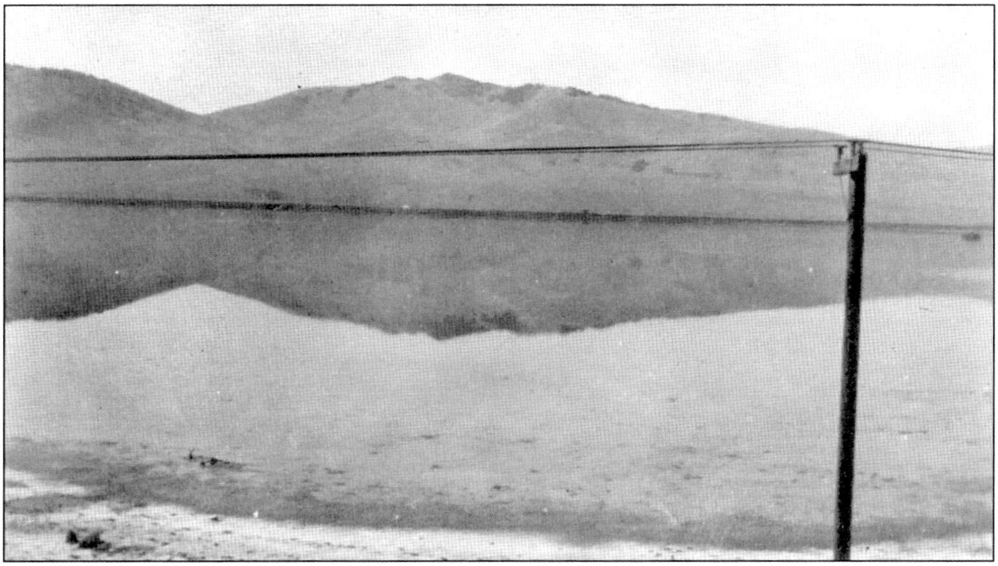

Narboe's Lake continued to produce salt for a variety of owners such as the Cuddeback and Blackley families, the Central Saline Mining Company, the Kern Development Mining Company, and the Tehachapi Saline Development Company. In 1907, the City of Los Angeles acquired the lake and surrounding properties. It needed the clay on the lake's bottom and the surrounding beds of limestone to make cement to build an aqueduct for importing water from the Owens River to Los Angeles.

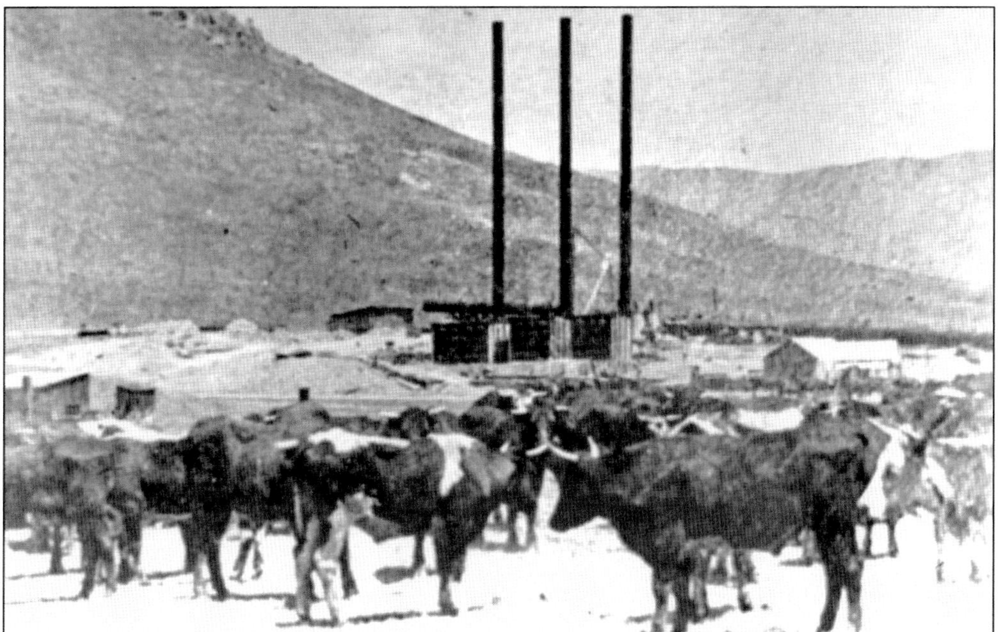

After the aqueduct was finished, the City of Los Angeles leased the plant and accompanying area to a series of operators, including the U.S. Potash Company and the Monolith-Portland Cement Company. The latter ultimately purchased the property. The firm produced a waterproof cement and ran cattle on the land, thus representing the area's two major economies: cattle (19th century) and cement (20th century).

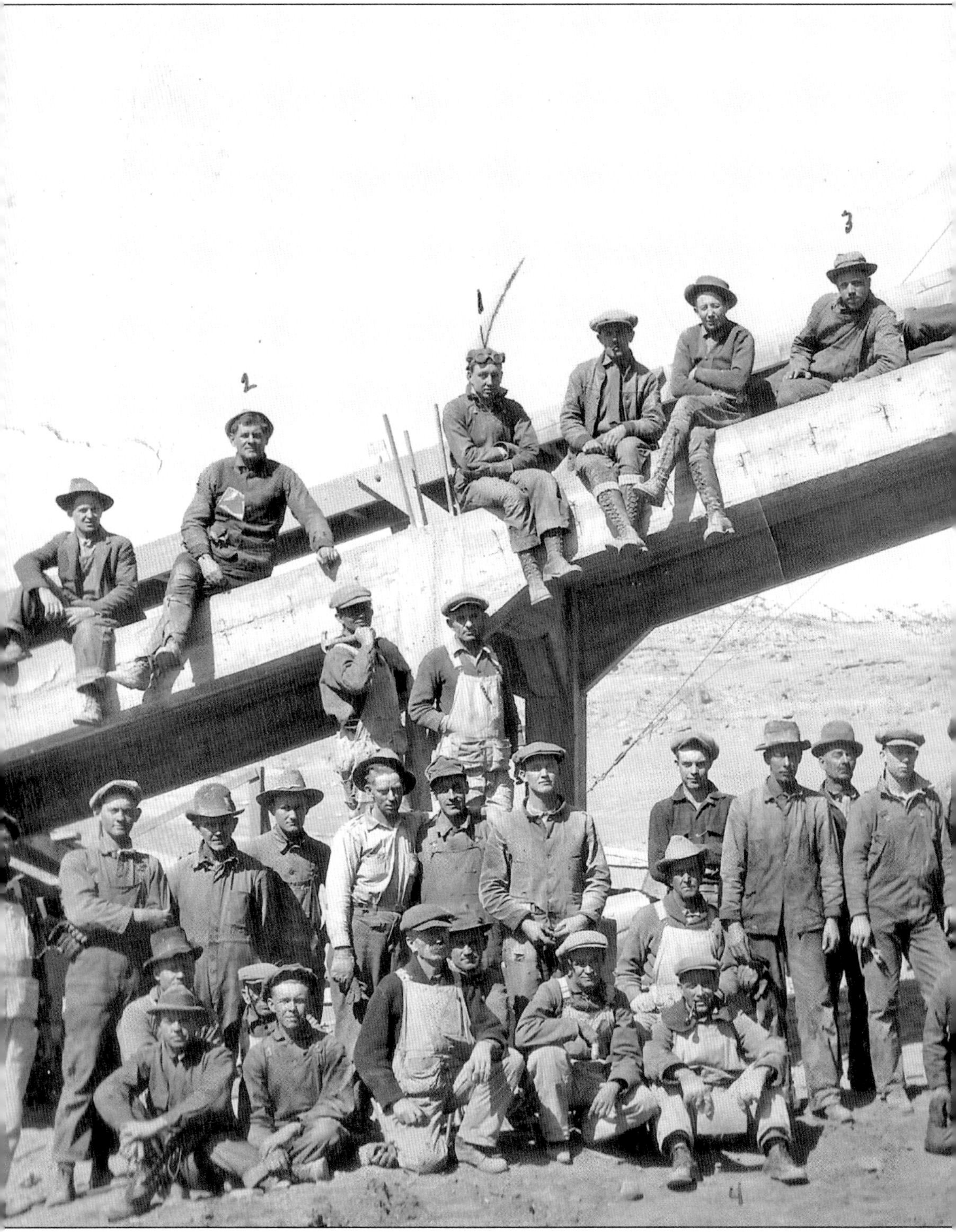

The plant became so large it was called Monolith. By 1909, it included 21 dwellings for employees, seven bunkhouses for the single men, a kitchen and mess hall, a general store, and a hospital. As

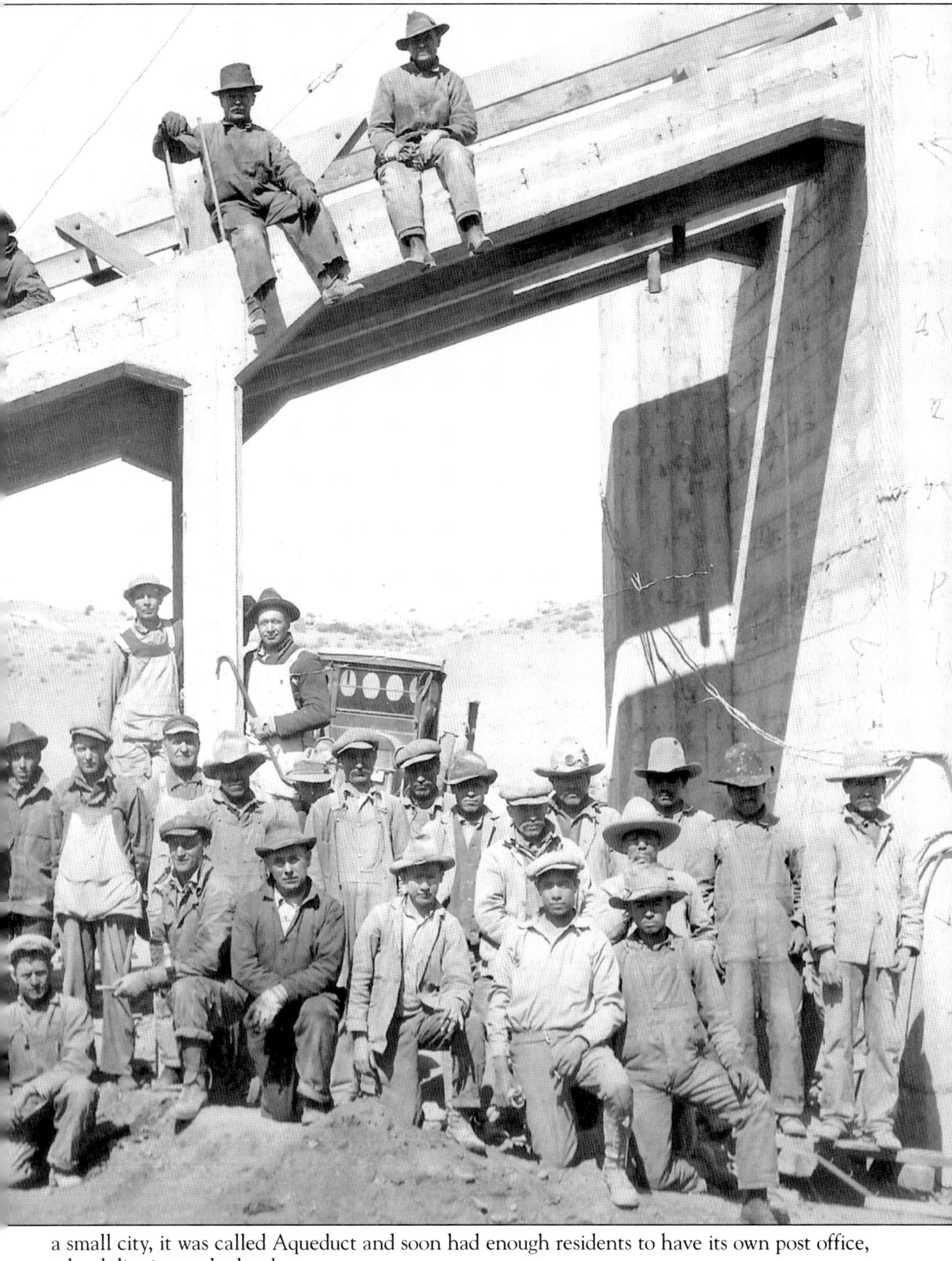

a small city, it was called Aqueduct and soon had enough residents to have its own post office, school district, and school.

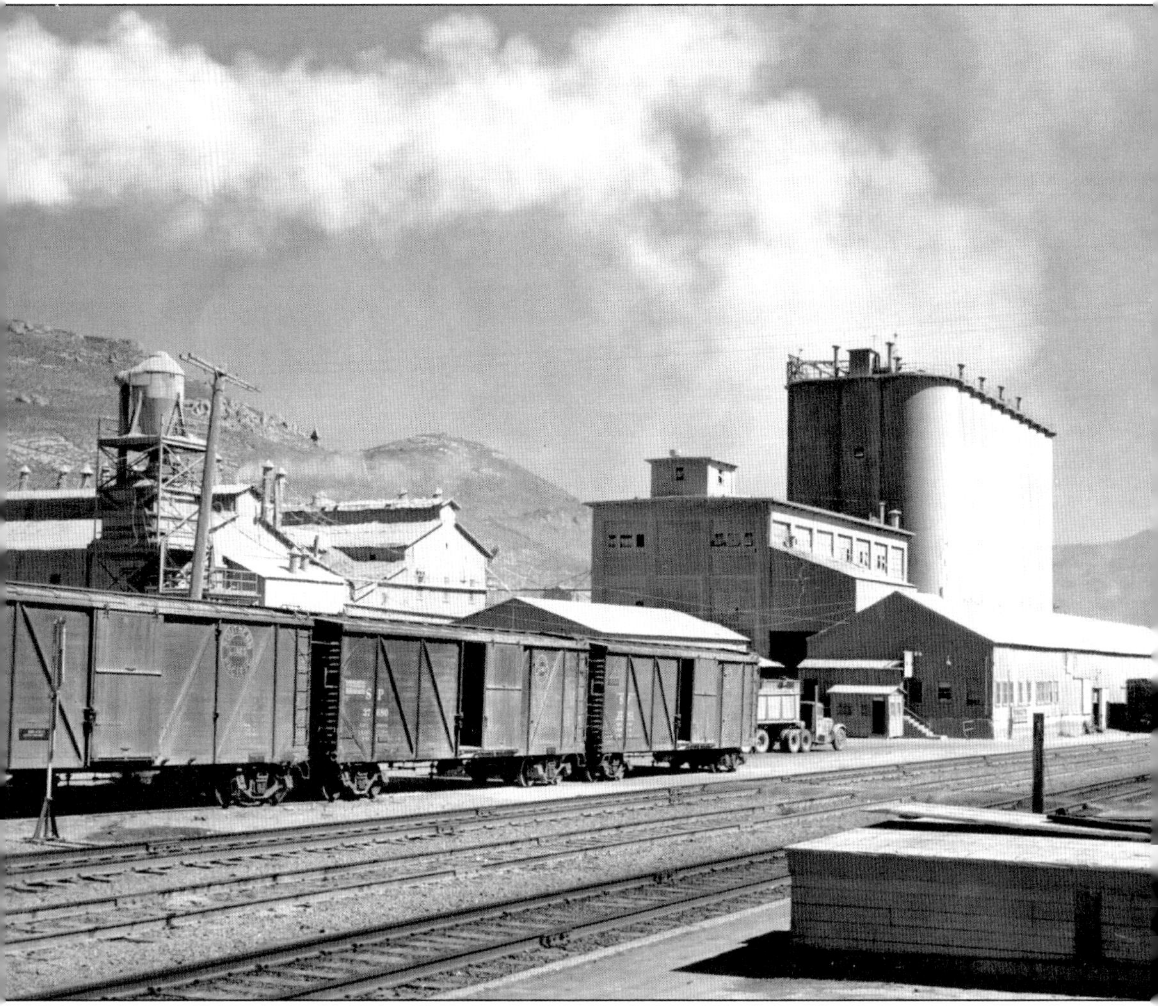

The cement produced at Monolith was top quality. It was so fine that 90 percent of the mixture would pass through a sieve of 40,000 openings per square inch. The firing temperature within the huge kilns was up to 2,700 degrees Fahrenheit. Following the completion of the aqueduct, the plant shut down in 1920. By then it had produced an estimated 900,000 to 1.25 million barrels of cement.

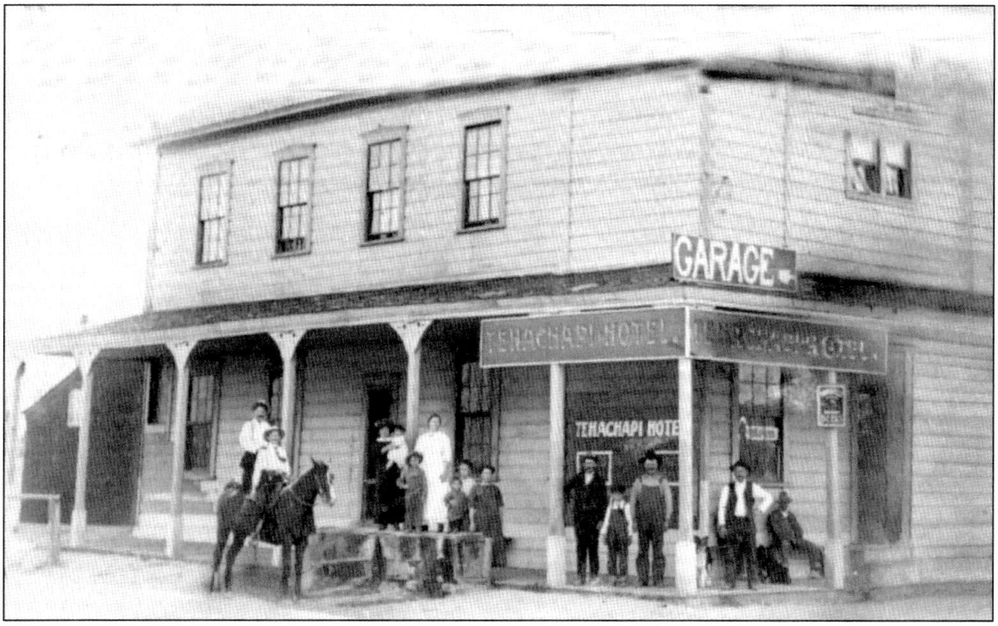

By 1910, the Tehachapi Hotel's visitors were arriving on one of the 10 passenger trains coming through town on a daily basis. Tehachapi's total population was 625 and growing, as were the numbers of businesses and attractions. Asher's Opera House had become the center of entertainment. Many troupes of traveling performers put on such popular plays as *Ten Nights in Barroom*.

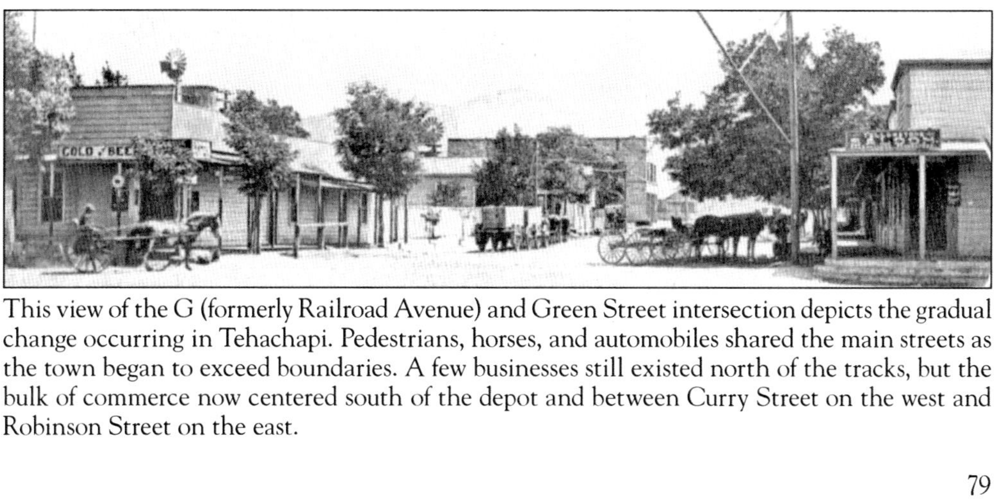

This view of the G (formerly Railroad Avenue) and Green Street intersection depicts the gradual change occurring in Tehachapi. Pedestrians, horses, and automobiles shared the main streets as the town began to exceed boundaries. A few businesses still existed north of the tracks, but the bulk of commerce now centered south of the depot and between Curry Street on the west and Robinson Street on the east.

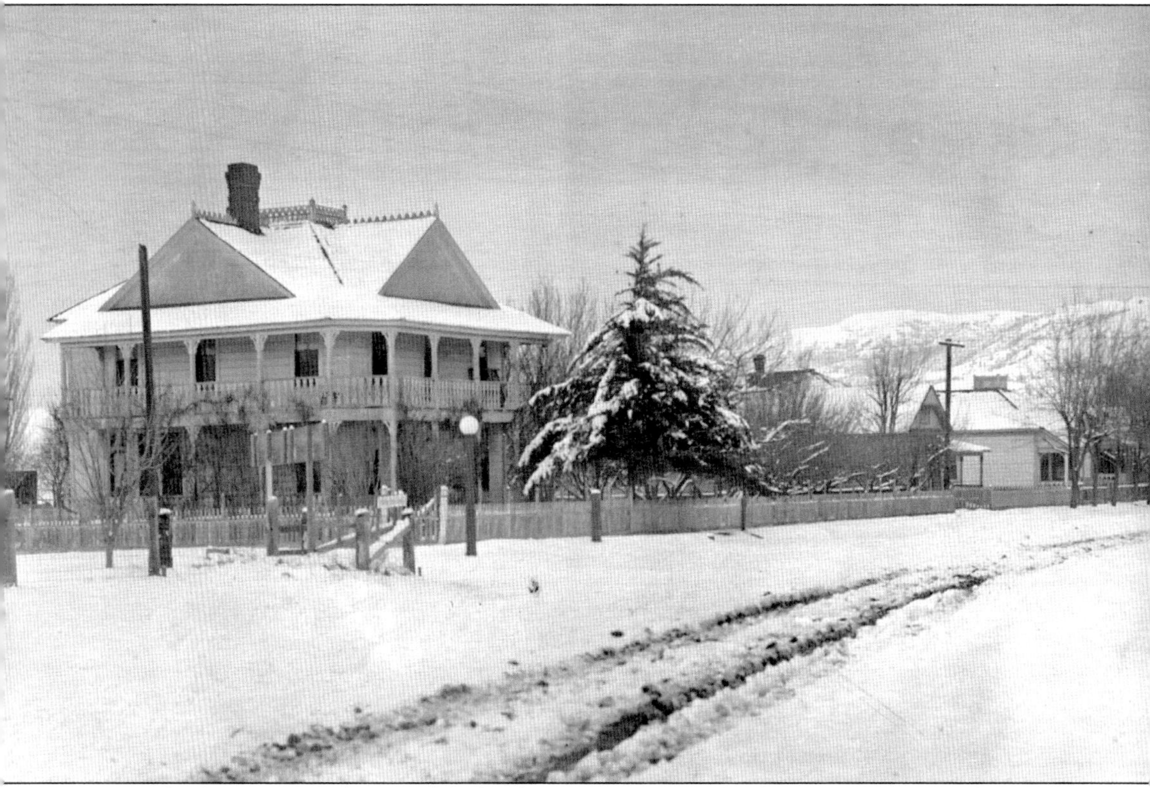

As Tehachapi prospered, many felt the desire to live in "a fine house in town." Andrew Vance reportedly built the first such two-story "fine house" on Curry Street. John Brite's new home was occupied by his widow since John had died shortly before the house was completed. Although the residences were far from the elegant Victorian mansions of San Francisco, they were nice enough to give Curry Street the moniker "Knob Hill."

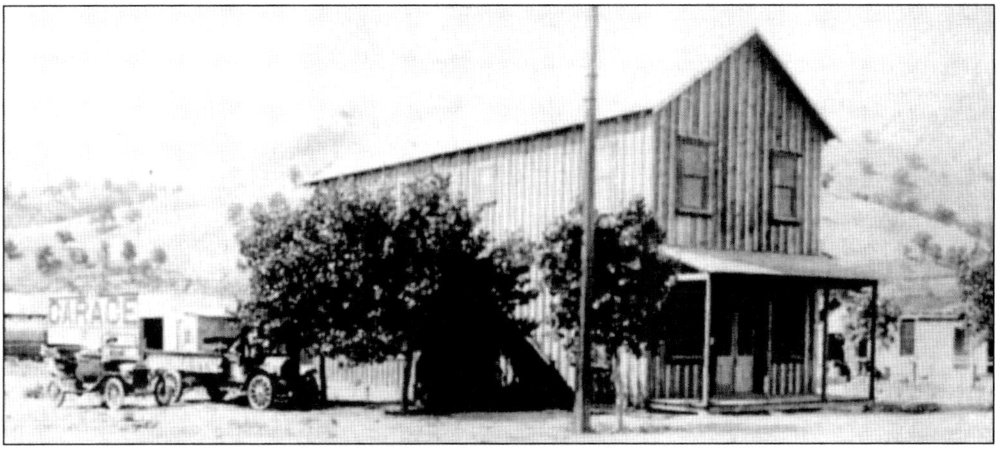

The presence of an electrical light pole indicates that this photograph was taken after 1915, the year Tehachapi voters approved (113 to 11) acquiring and constructing an electrical system. The Pacific Light and Power Company got the bid to bring a line from Monolith to the town of Tehachapi. The cement plant had installed two electrical substations when it began operations in 1910.

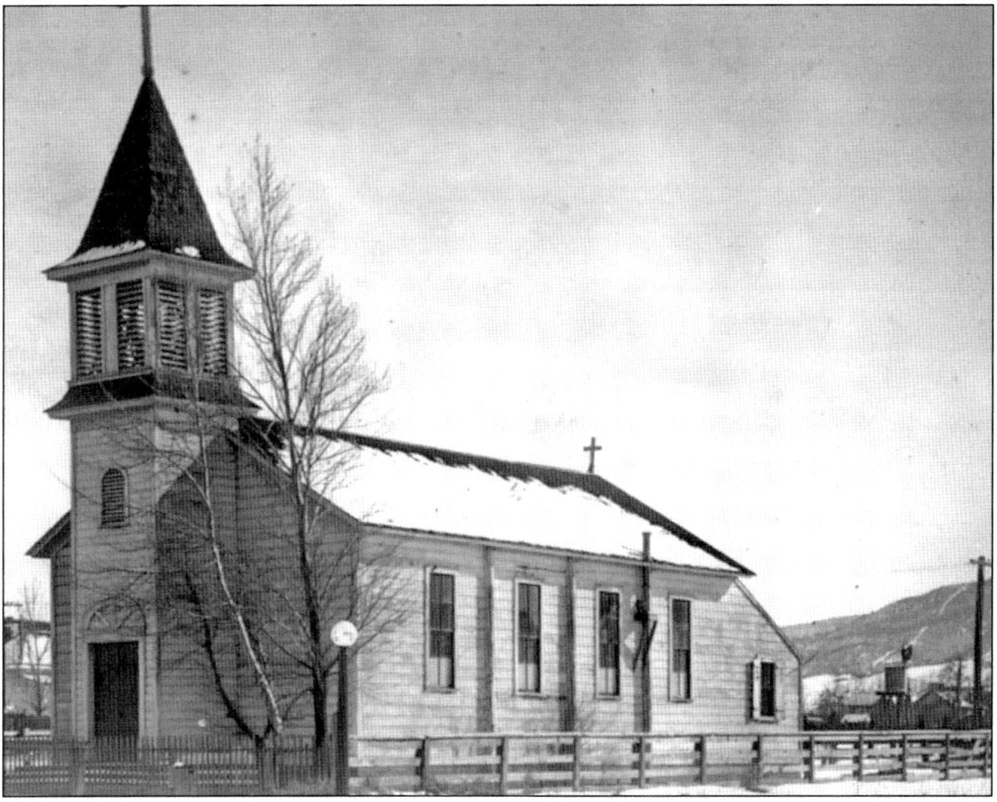

St. Malachy's Catholic Church stood on the corner of F and Pauly Streets in 1916. It was built in 1891 as a replacement for the smaller church, constructed in 1887. The first recorded Mass was held in 1877. Before the original Catholic church was built, Mass was celebrated in the home of Antone Pauly. In 1960, a much-larger and modern St. Malachy's was constructed on the corner of F and Mill Streets.

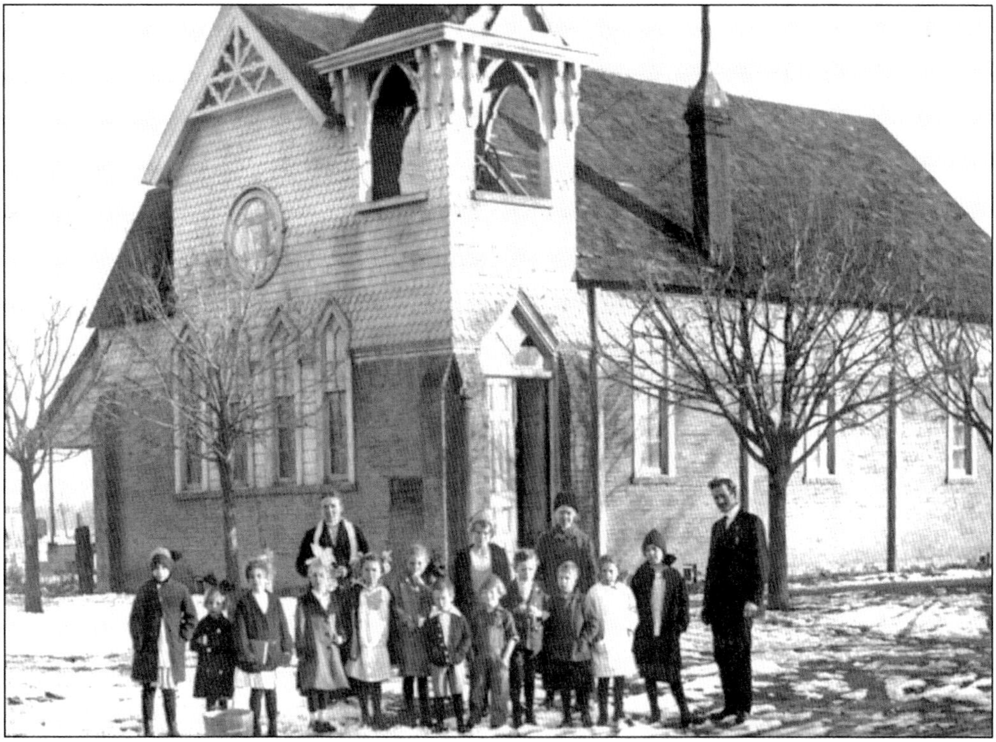

The Tehachapi Methodist Church, shown here in 1916, is located on the southeast corner of D and Green Streets. Protestant services were first conducted in 1871 by Rev. J. L. Bennett, a minister with the Kern River circuit of the Methodist-Episcopal Church. His territory, covered on horseback, included Williamsburg, Havilah, the Kern River Valley, and Bakersfield. In 1888, regular services were held near Old Town (Williamsburg) in a building donated by John Brite.

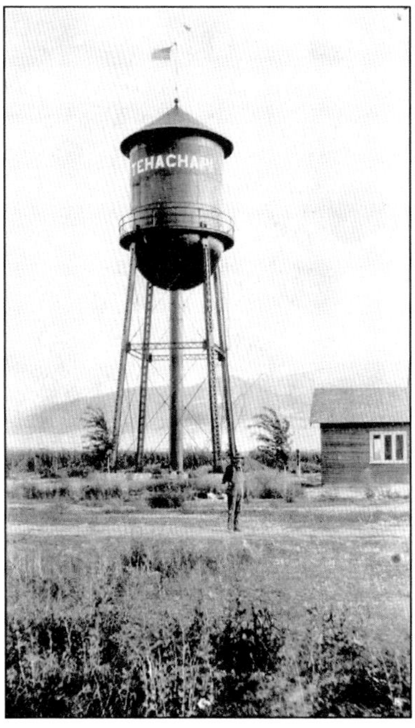

Residents and business owners dug their own wells or bought water from neighbors until early 1911 when trustees voted to install a town well and water system. By August, residents had a 257-foot-deep well, storage tank, and pumping system. Water mains, pipelines, and hydrants came next. By 1914, the town had purchased 141 water meters. One unsung benefit of a town water system was the introduction of indoor plumbing and the subsequent abandonment of outhouses within the business district.

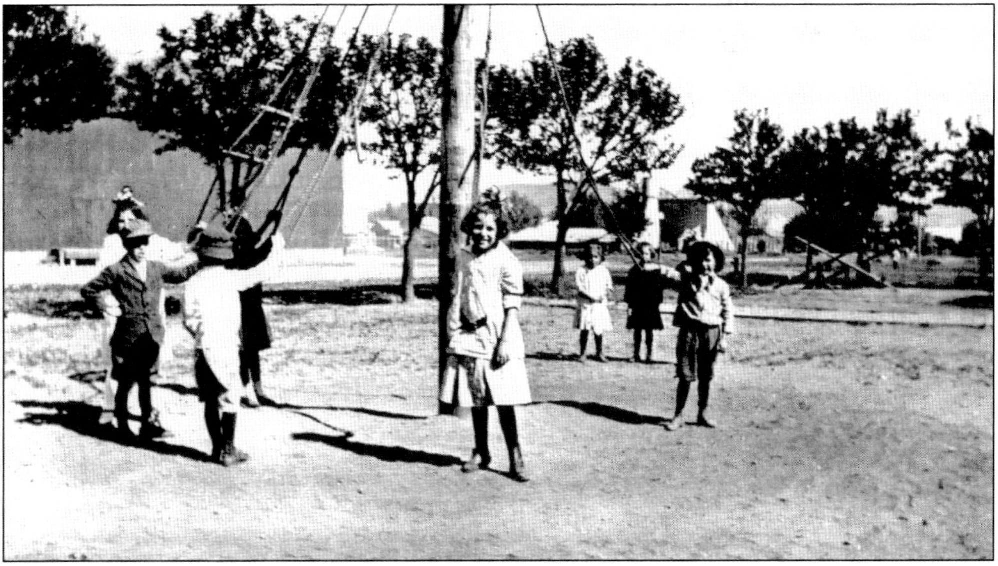

Dancing around the Maypole was but one way schoolchildren celebrated the First of May. They also made paper baskets to hold bouquets of wildflowers and played games. Adults enjoyed this ancient May Day festival as well by holding a community picnic followed by a gala ball presided over by the Queen of May. The celebration, which originated in ancient Europe to welcome spring, was a favorite among local residents.

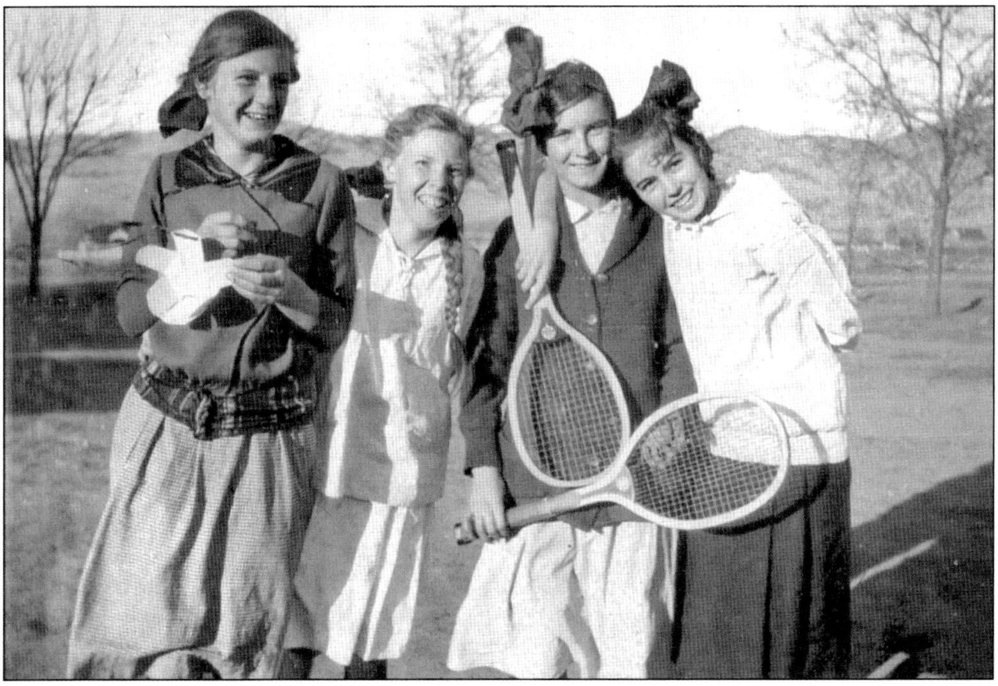

The Tehachapi Lawn Tennis Club formed in 1891 with great success. By now, women were playing tennis and riding bicycles, and local men had started playing baseball in 1890. In 1892, the Tehachapi Athletic Club held boxing and wrestling matches, gave exhibitions on horizontal bars, and provided demonstrations of high jumping, kicking, and fencing.

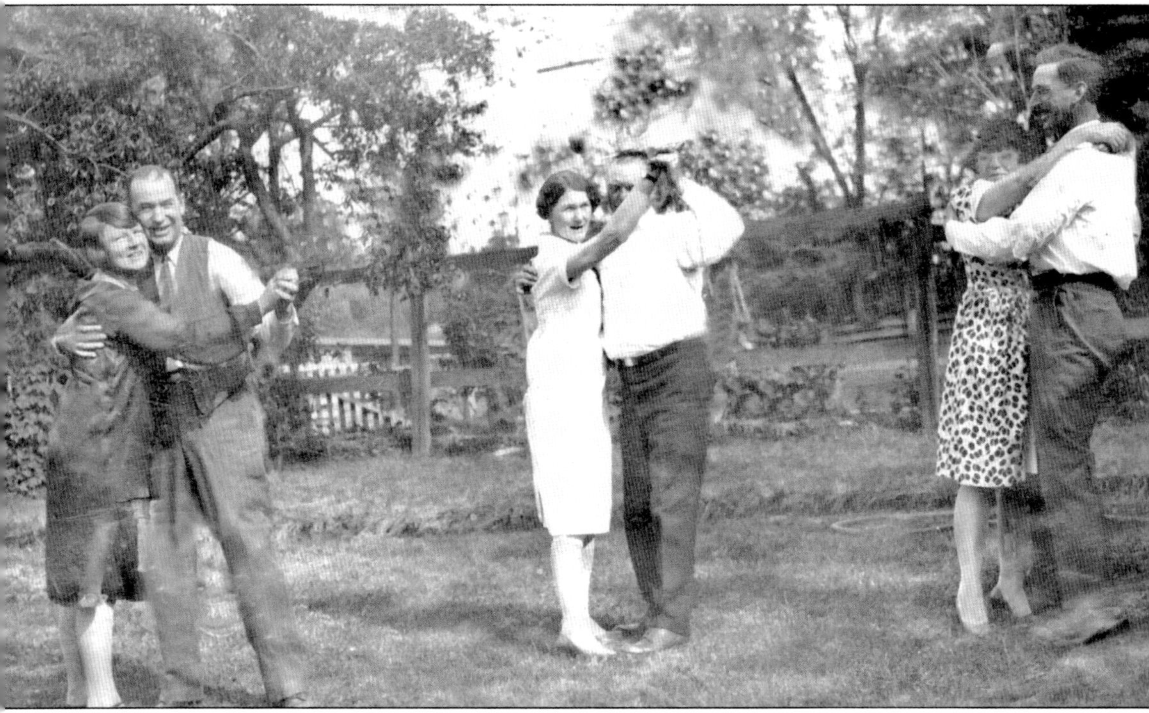

Residents loved to dance. Since the arrival of the first settlers in 1854, dancing was part of any gathering or party. Dances were held in schoolhouses, hotels, or saloons, or outside on swept dirt, lawns, or streets. Tehachapi celebrated its first electric lights with a street dance on July 31, 1915.

Tennis became one of Tehachapi's favorite sports. When plans went forward in 1903 to construct a new three-room Summit School, trustees made sure the budget included money for a basketball court and a regulation tennis court. This was three years before the Davis Cup Tournament created a national interest in tennis.

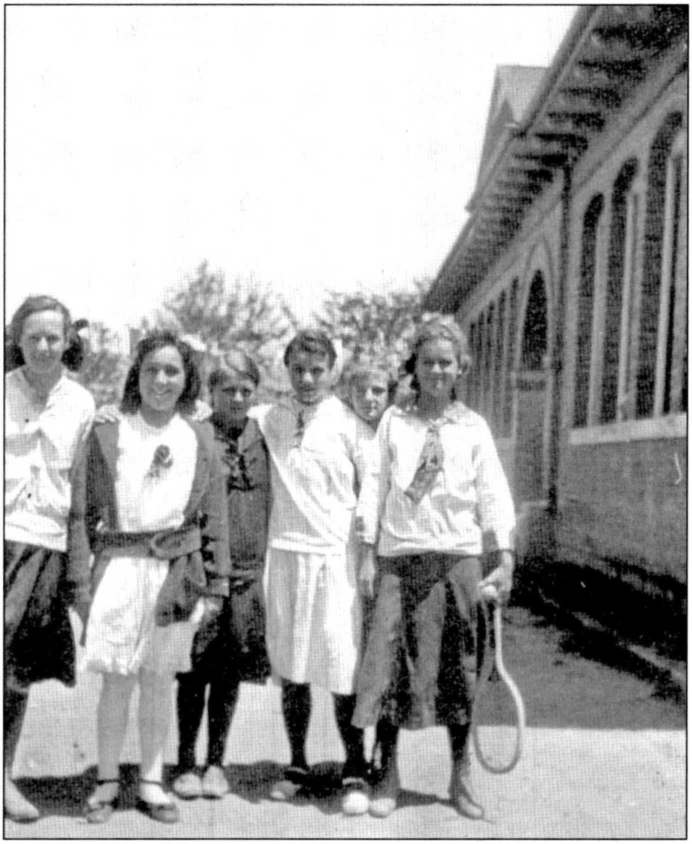

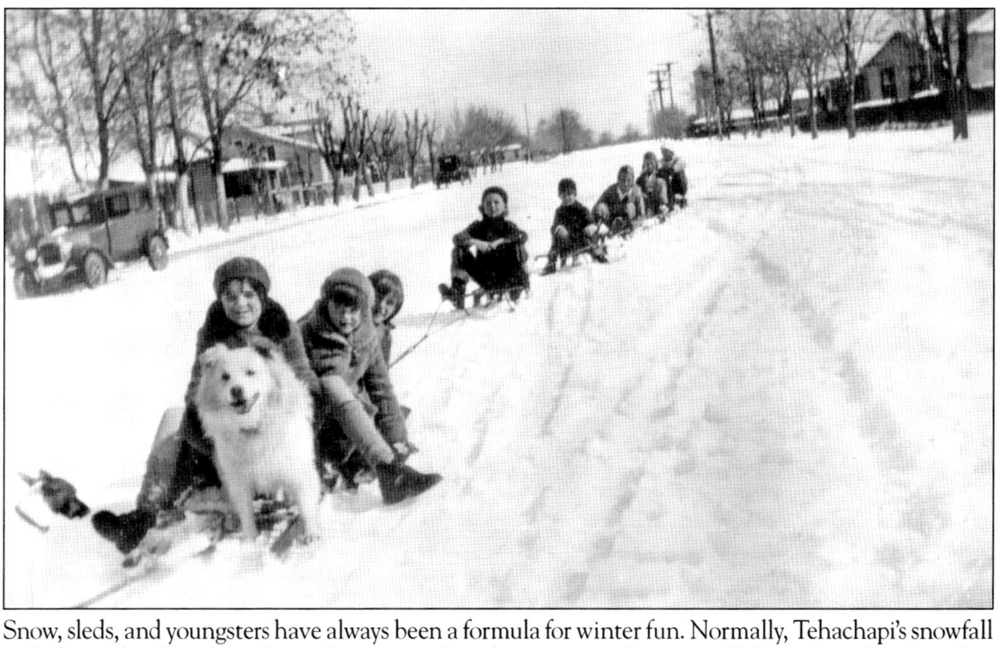

Snow, sleds, and youngsters have always been a formula for winter fun. Normally, Tehachapi's snowfall is slight and will melt within a short time, but the occasional storm will dump 3 to 6 inches that will last for several days. Any slope then becomes a perfect place for friends to enjoy the day.

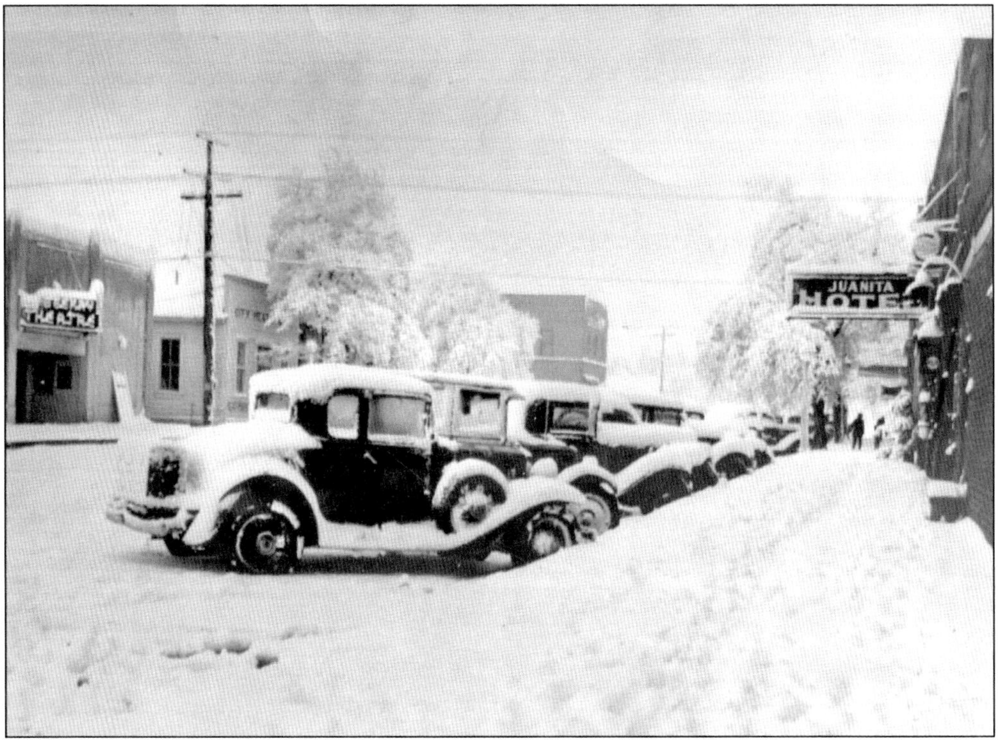

Tehachapi lies quietly under a white blanket of snow. Because it is Sunday, the businesses are closed, activity is scant, and snow does not need to be shoveled away from storefronts. As the morning wears on, the only tracks in the streets will be made by those going to church—or to one of the 14 saloons in town.

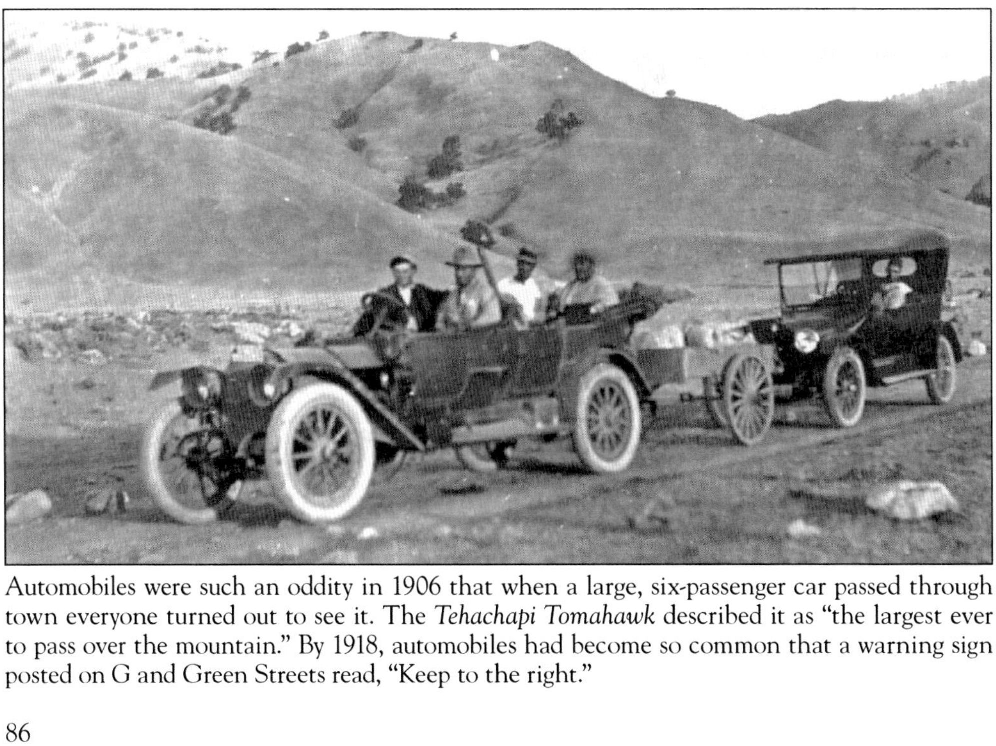

Automobiles were such an oddity in 1906 that when a large, six-passenger car passed through town everyone turned out to see it. The *Tehachapi Tomahawk* described it as "the largest ever to pass over the mountain." By 1918, automobiles had become so common that a warning sign posted on G and Green Streets read, "Keep to the right."

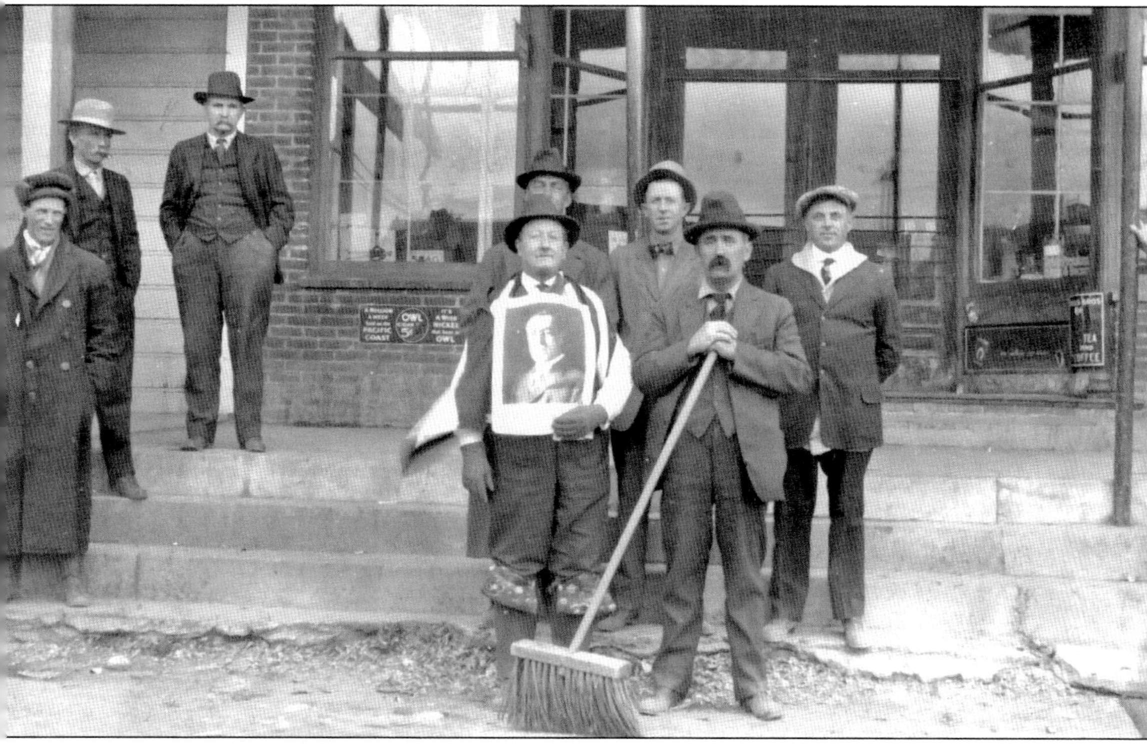

In 1916, a festive crowd gathered to watch popular business owner Harry Downs (holding the poster) fulfill a political bet. Downs had promised that if Pres. Woodrow Wilson was reelected, he would roll a peanut down the main street with a toothpick. Supervisor Lucas "Gabe" Brite (right) used a push broom to clear a pathway for Downs.

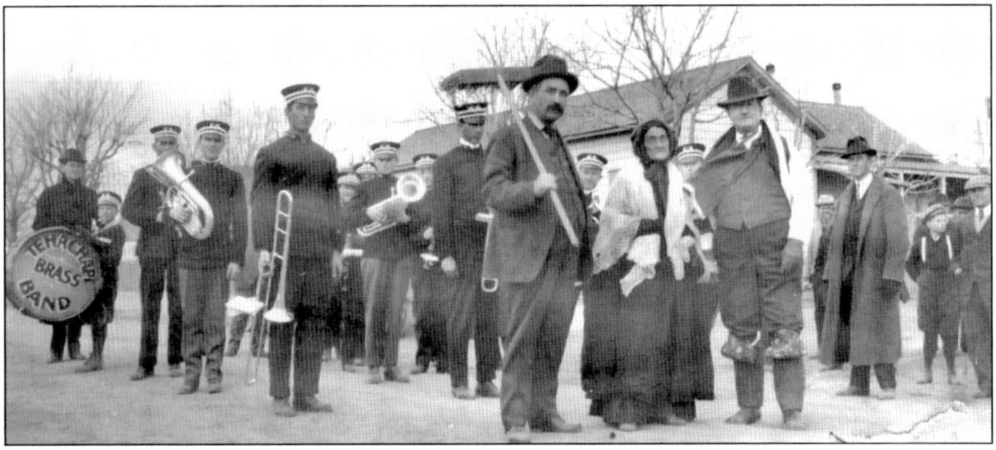

A large delegation arrived from Bakersfield, Mojave, and surrounding areas to witness Harry Downs's peanut-pushing event. As the laughing crowd gathered and shouted encouragement, the Tehachapi Brass Band began to play. To the music of "Tipperary," a men's quartet sang, "It's a long way to roll a peanut when you crawl upon your knees." It was a memorable day.

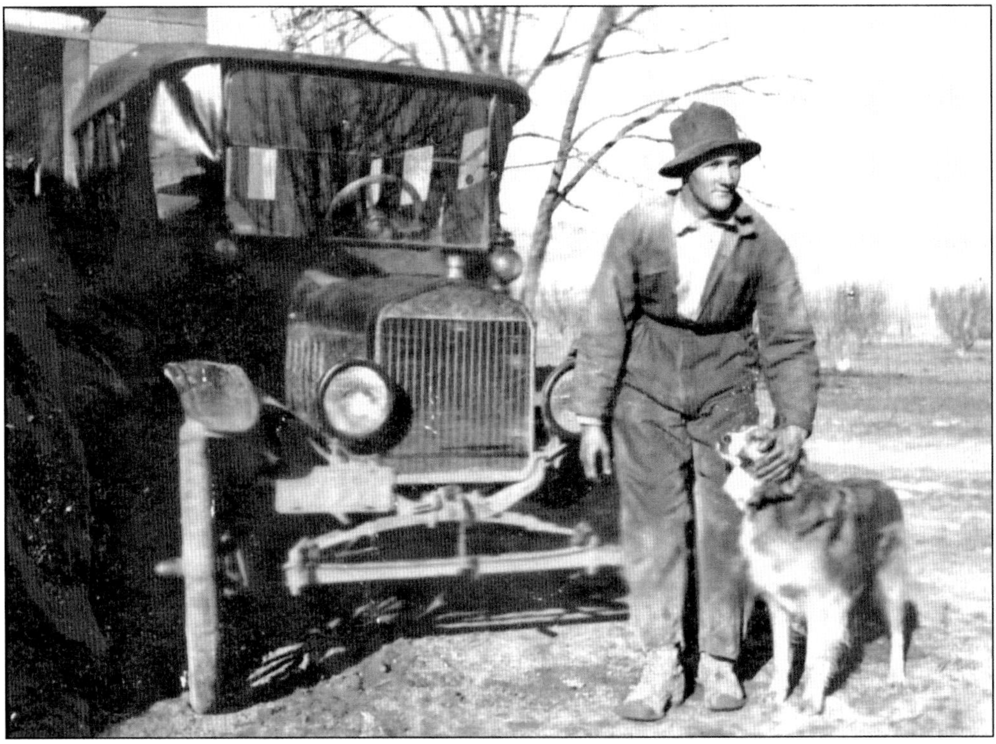

The familiar western trio of "a man, his horse, and a dog" was soon replaced with "a man, his car, and a dog." Despite many faults (it only went uphill in reverse gear; it rattled and overheated), the Ford Model T caught on with the public, especially when the price dropped from $850 to $290 in 1924.

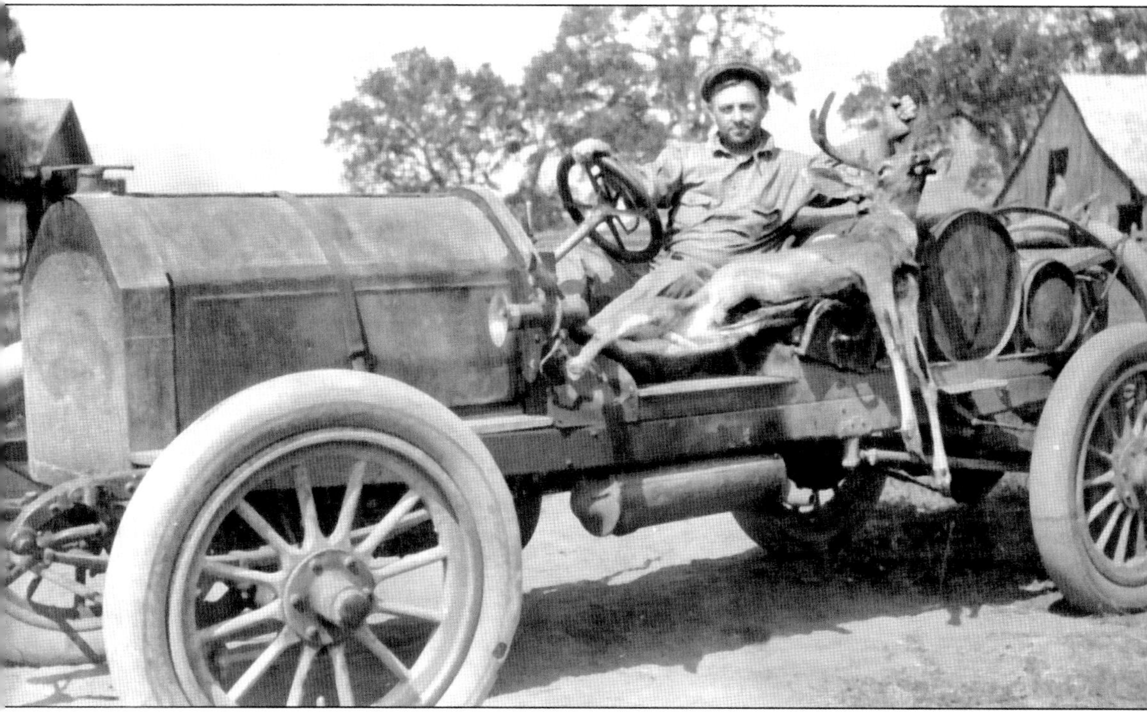

Transporting the results of a day's deer hunt was but one of the ways local residents used their automobiles. Several farmers preferred the Model T for its versatility. Not only could it haul supplies and transport family members on an outing, but after the rear tires were replaced with tractor tires, it could pull a plow or other farming equipment.

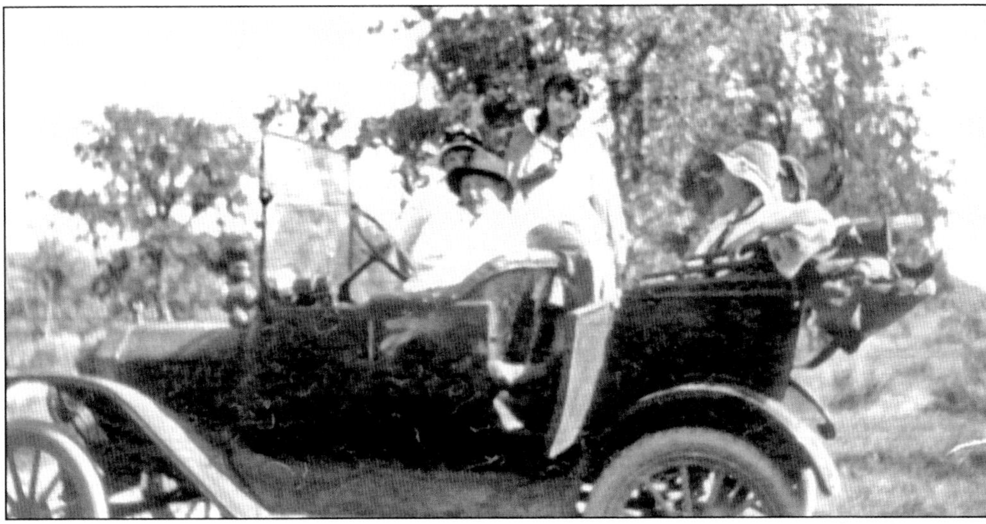

Automobiles soon became so common that a new set of problems was created in downtown Tehachapi. This prompted town trustees to pass a series of new motoring laws in 1912. Speed limits were set at 6 to 10 miles per hour, and loud mufflers were prohibited. Offenders were fined up to $50 or up to 25 days in the town or county jail.

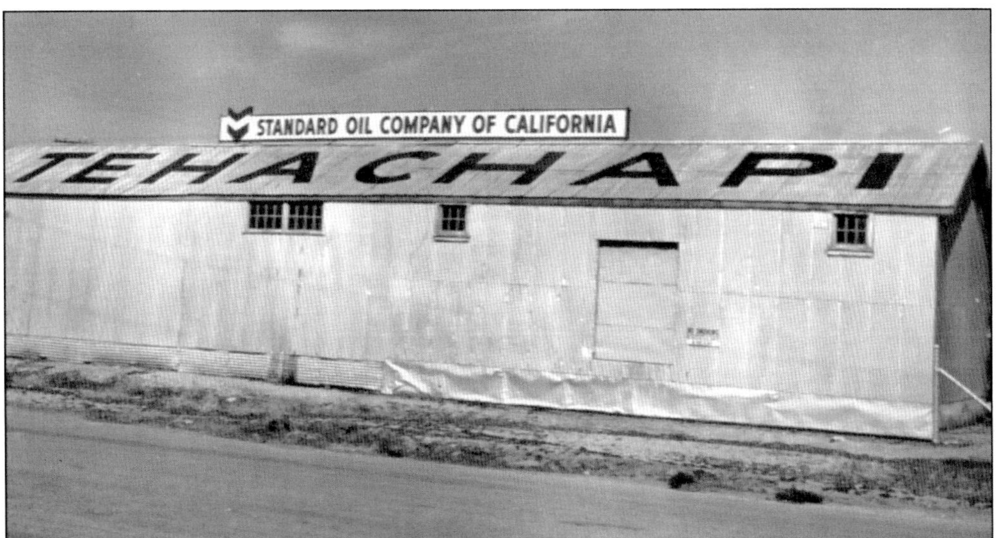

The growing popularity of the automobile prompted the Standard Oil Company in 1918 to open a local plant and storage facility in Tehachapi. The plant, conspicuous with the name *Tehachapi* emblazoned on its roof, included three 20,000-gallon, gasoline storage tanks, a pumping plant, a motor truck, and a tank wagon. The facilities also included a stable for the horses used to pull the tank wagon as it made local deliveries.

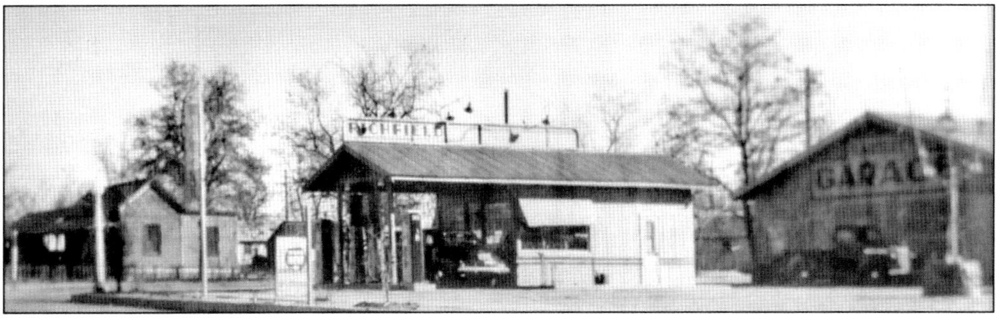

In 1922, Jack Leiva hung up his cowboy spurs and opened this service station in Tehachapi. Antonio, the Leiva patriarch, arrived here in 1880 and, until his death at the age of 84, worked for the Tejon Ranch, first as a *vaquero* and then as cattle boss. While teenagers, Jack and his three brothers were cowboys on the Tejon Ranch as well.

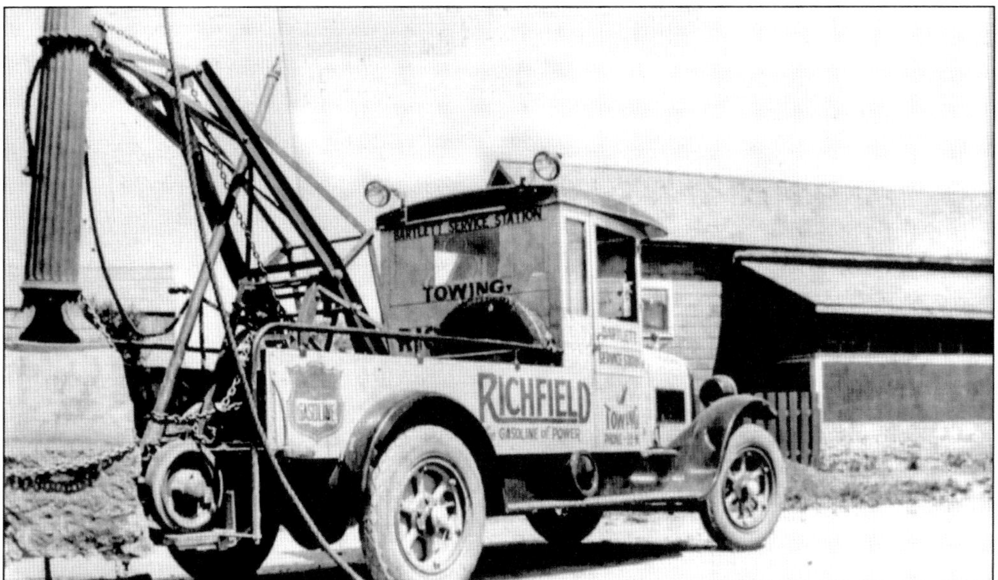

The addition of this tow truck to Jack Leiva's service station was an indication of the growing popularity of the automobile. His transition from ranching to servicing automobiles was but another sign of a changing time. One by one, his brothers Roque, Joe, and Dora quit the cattle business. The family owned and operated this service station and garage for 50 years.

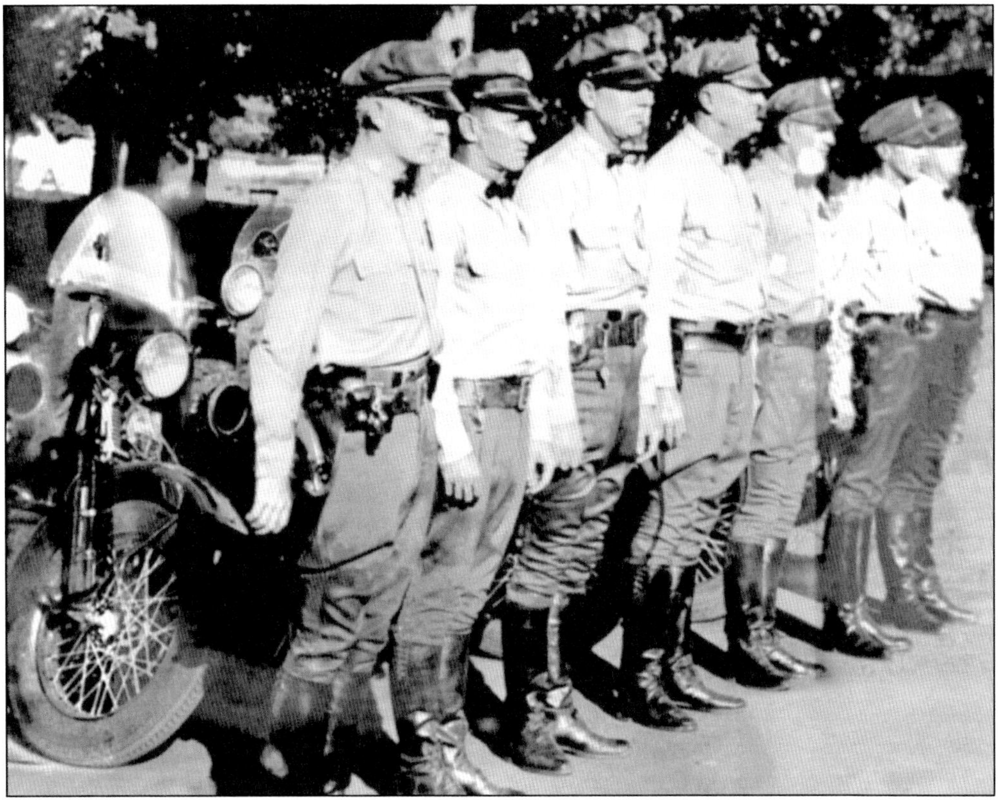

Increased traffic soon brought about motorcycle officers who would patrol the area, and many young men enrolled in training to become such an officer. Motorcycles had already attracted the attention of the more daring, especially after watching the endurance and hill-climbing cycle races held on the slopes of the Tehachapi Mountains, including White Wolf Grade. The favorite cycles of 1910 were the Excellor, the Yale, and the Reading Standard.

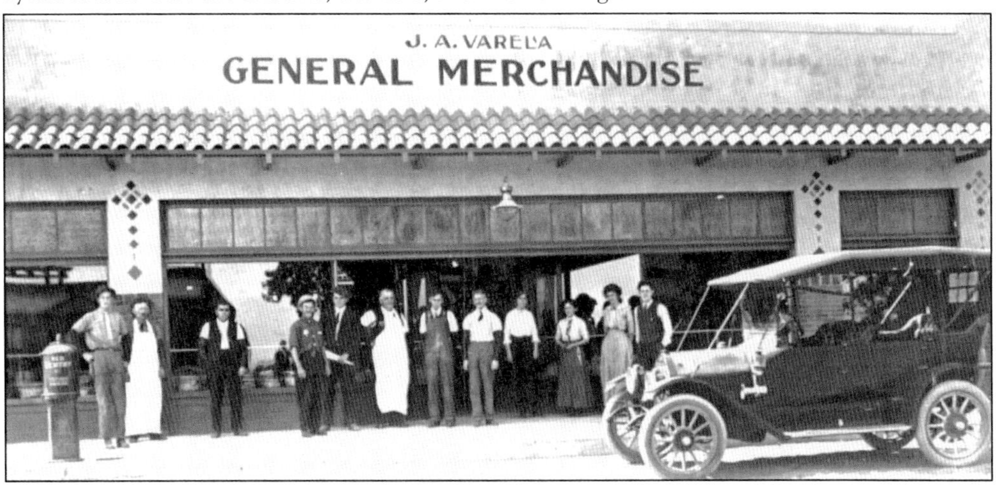

By 1920, brick buildings and sidewalks had replaced the early wooden structures; the dirt streets and horses tied to hitching racks were replaced with oiled streets and automobiles. Although growing, Tehachapi was still one of the smallest municipalities in California. Of the area's general population of 1,323, only 458 people lived within the town limits.

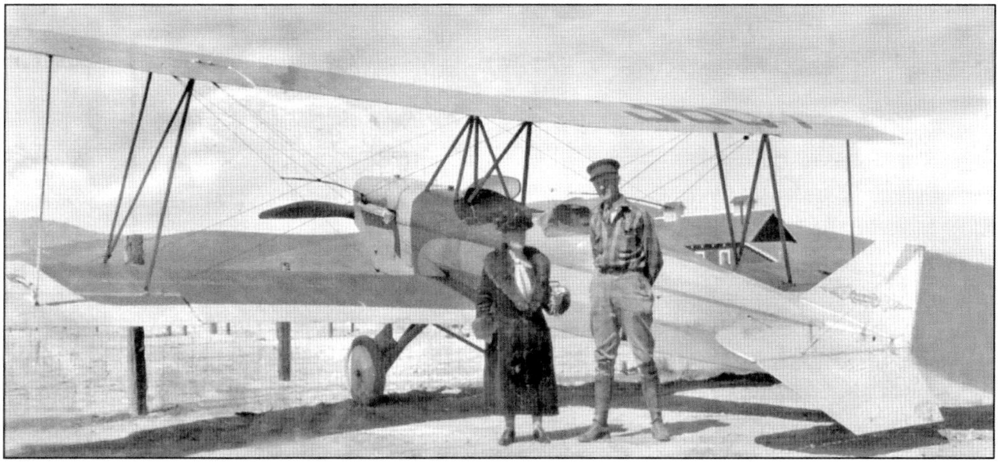

Tehachapi welcomed an airport during the 1920s. The area's introduction to the airplane occurred in 1914. Silas Christofferson flew over Tehachapi while demonstrating his long-range ability between San Francisco and San Diego. Christofferson was 800 feet above the valley and could wave at onlookers. By 1921, town trustees were so excited about the prospect of air travel that they discussed the idea of building a field for planes that "needed a place to set down."

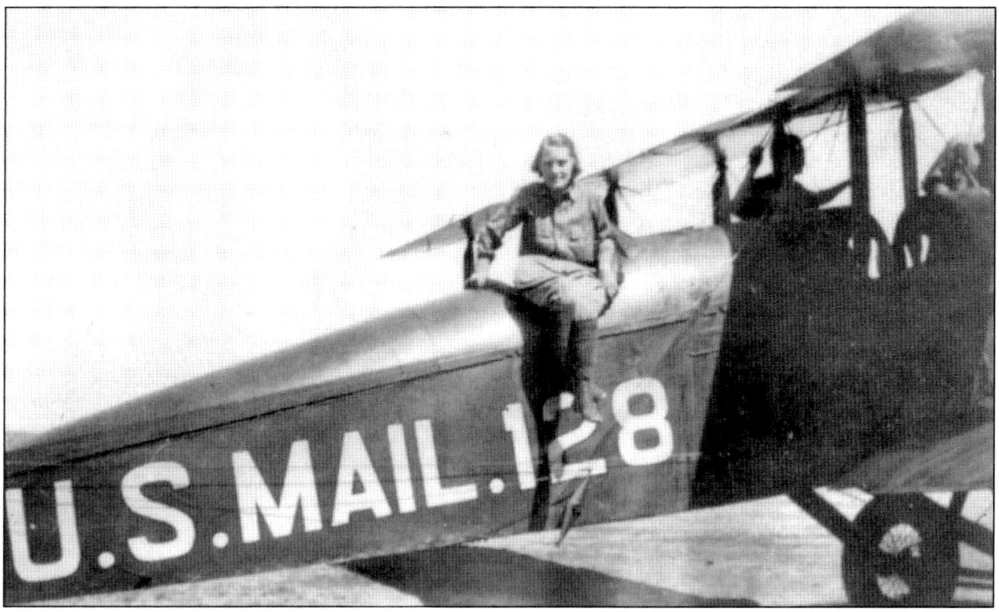

The first airmail letter from Tehachapi was posted by David Pitts in 1924. Addressed to his niece in New York, it went from Tehachapi to San Francisco then cross-country by air to its destination. The letter took 41 hours compared to the 120 hours by rail. Shortly thereafter, Mr. and Mrs. "Butch" Sullivan (pictured here) and their U.S. Mail Plane No. 128 made daily flights to the main post office in Bakersfield.

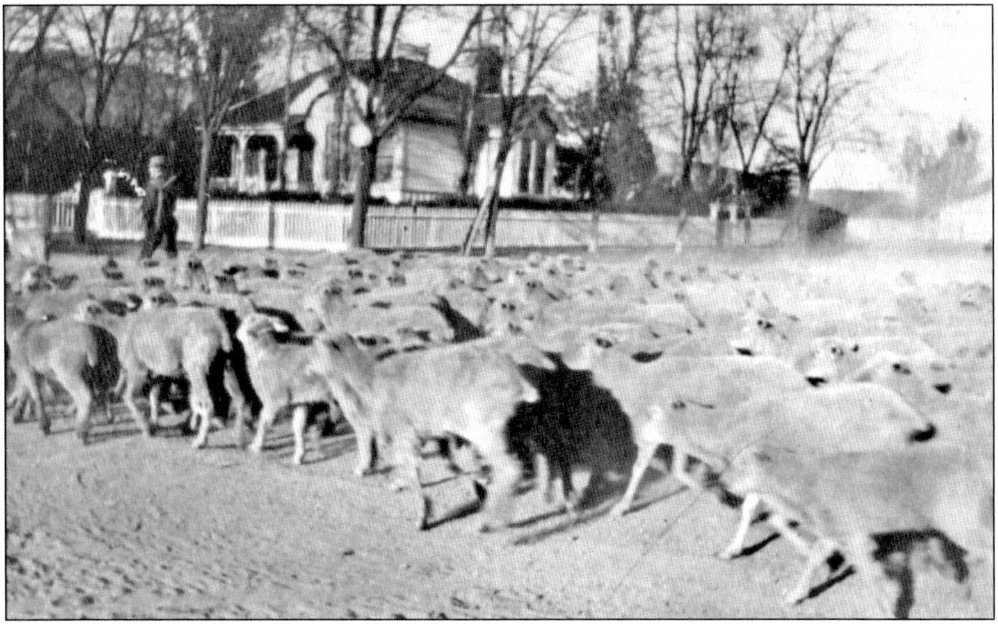

Both sheep and cattle drovers used Curry Street to herd their animals into pens near the railroad and butcher shops. The odor, dust, noise, and broken fences—not to mention trampled gardens, impromptu fertilizer, and disrupted open-air laundry lines—eventually forced a rerouting of the animals down Mill Street.

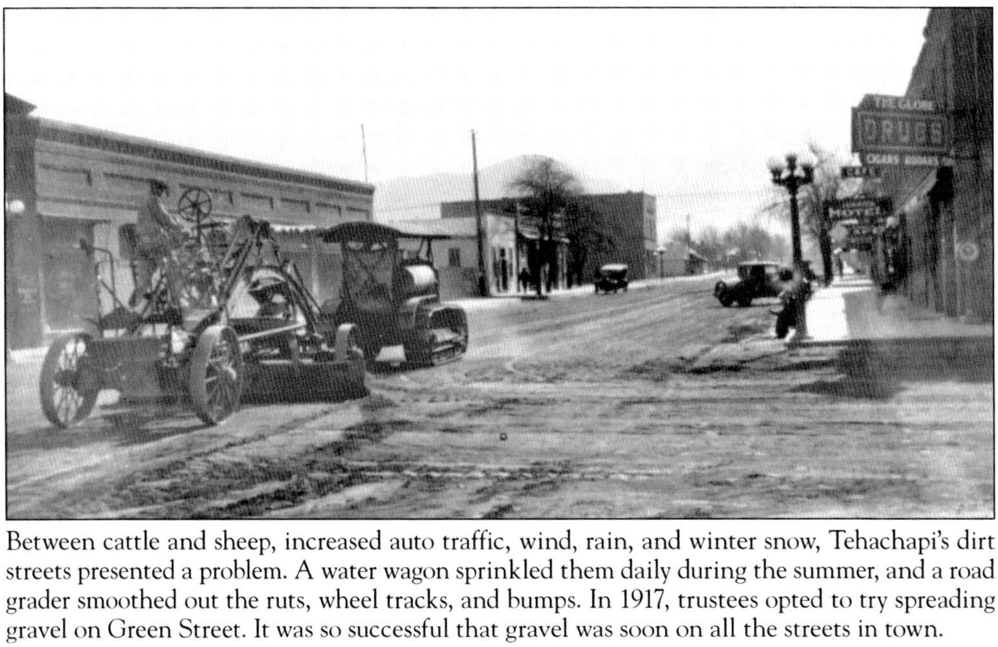

Between cattle and sheep, increased auto traffic, wind, rain, and winter snow, Tehachapi's dirt streets presented a problem. A water wagon sprinkled them daily during the summer, and a road grader smoothed out the ruts, wheel tracks, and bumps. In 1917, trustees opted to try spreading gravel on Green Street. It was so successful that gravel was soon on all the streets in town.

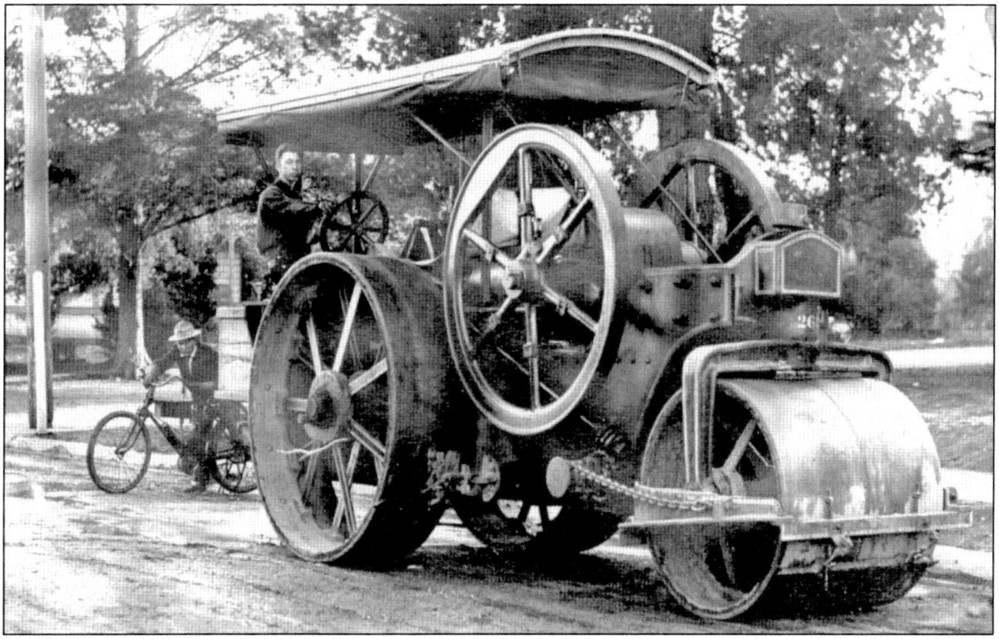

In 1929, the Town of Tehachapi began to replace gravel on the streets with oil. At first, just nine blocks were oiled as an experiment. It was so well received that an additional 19 blocks were included. By 1939, all streets inside town limits were oiled. Everyone knew Tehachapi had entered the 20th century when its water wagon was considered obsolete and sold.

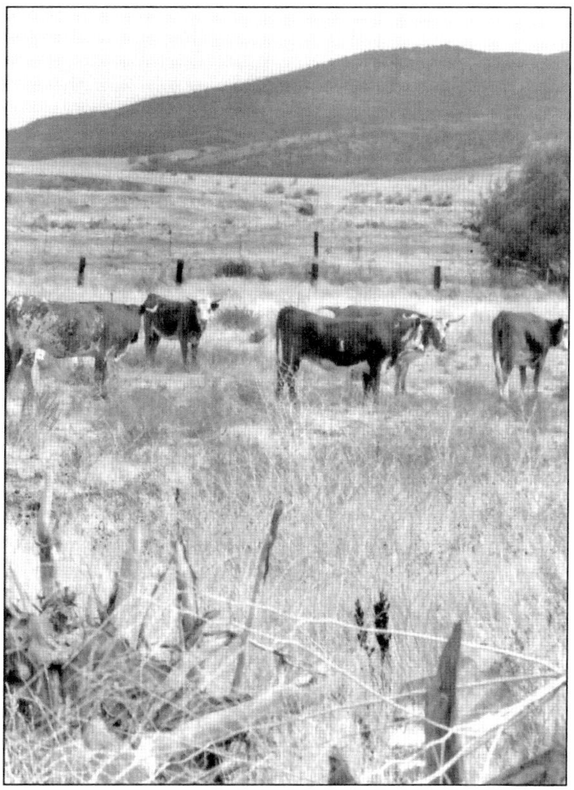

Cows and trains were the ingredients for accidents. Once an engine leaves the Tehachapi station and travels east, the grade between Cameron Station and Mojave is deceiving since it is gradual but steep. One day the engineer of a speeding train spotted some cows on the tracks. The impact caused the locomotive and a second car to derail. The engineer was found some yards away from the wreckage, the brake handle embedded in his chest. He was the only human casualty. (Author's collection.)

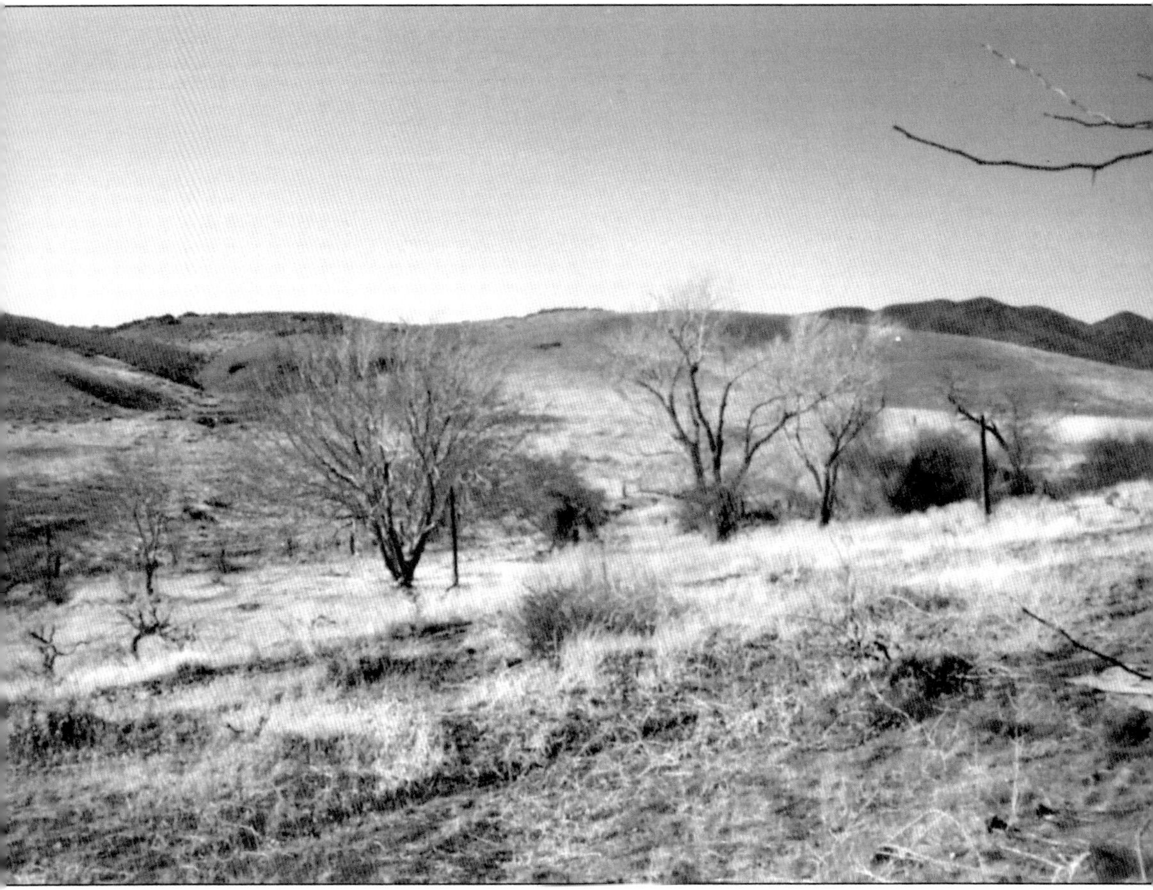

In 1922, local orchards produced a bumper crop. Land promoters anticipated that this would bring more buyers for their 10-acre orchards, but sales remained slow. In 1930, a late-May snowstorm hit the area and ruined a promising crop. At the same time, taxes rose along with expenses, and the boom spiraled downward. By 1932, all but two or three orchards had been abandoned. The Great Depression had crept into Tehachapi. (Author's collection.)

Six

DEFYING THE DEPRESSION

Our town is in excellent financial condition, no bonded indebtedness, and a substantial balance in their treasury.

—W. R. Powell, Bank of Tehachapi cashier, June 1933

In 1933, the nation was still reeling from the effects of the 1929 stock market crash. Some 1,000 banks had closed with investors and private savings accounts wiped out; businesses had failed, and millions were unemployed. But in California, the effects were not so severe. The state was expanding domestic and foreign trade, and new industries and housing were booming. The Bank of America was acquiring a number of small community banks.

Nature had dealt the worst blow. A prolonged drought had lowered the water supply just as taxes were rising. When the rains finally came, floods washed away valuable topsoil, covered streets, and wiped out railroad tracks. Discouraged, many property owners let land go to pay back taxes, and foreclosures became the norm. For many, it was the worst of times.

But Tehachapi mirrored the state and, in fact, experienced the best of times. The privately owned cement plant and the new county sanatorium had payrolls totaling over $500,000. The state had just purchased 1,700 acres from Lucas Brite to build a women's prison and was planning to add a highway road camp nearby. Town trustees had $100,000 to spend on civic and business improvements. Farmers reported success with alfalfa and sugar beet seeds. The potato harvest required at least 300 harvesters, allowing opportunities for work.

"Our citizens are sturdy and substantial," W. R. Powell stated. "These qualities . . . have made the Bank of Tehachapi a profitable institution throughout the many years of the existence of the bank." Powell's report was formed in response to the Bank of America's interest in acquiring the Bank of Tehachapi, whose trustees saw no need to be under the larger institution's umbrella. They rejected the offer.

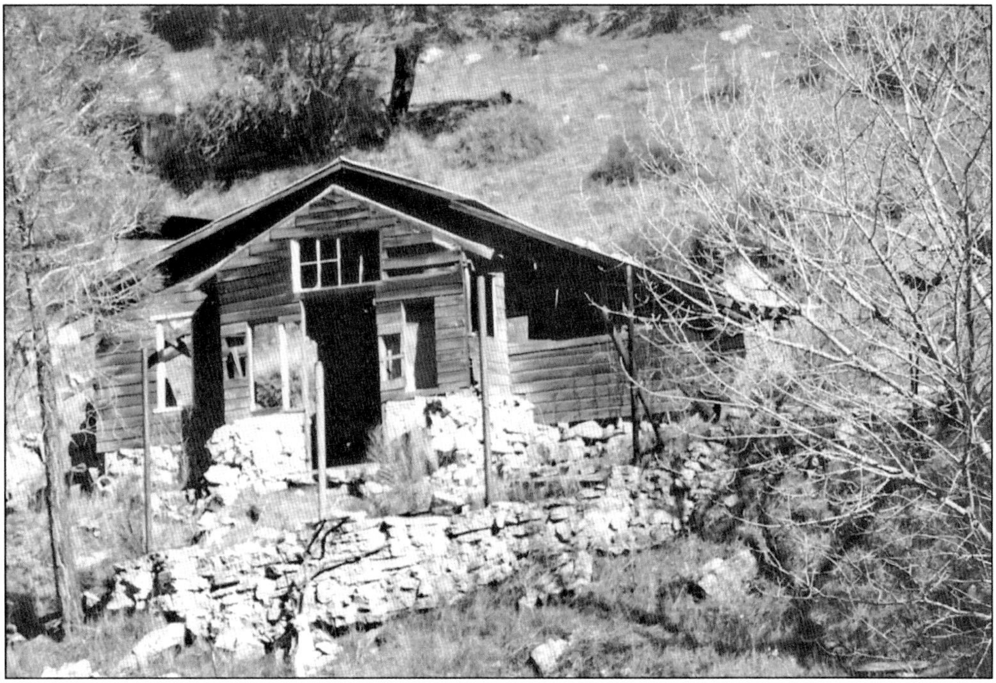

Rising taxes, high mortgage payments, higher operating costs coupled with below-average rainfall, lower water levels, and late frosts were too much for many. For Sale signs were vying with For Rent signs on properties owned by residents and non-residents alike. Many were so discouraged they just boarded up their homes and walked away. (Author's collection.)

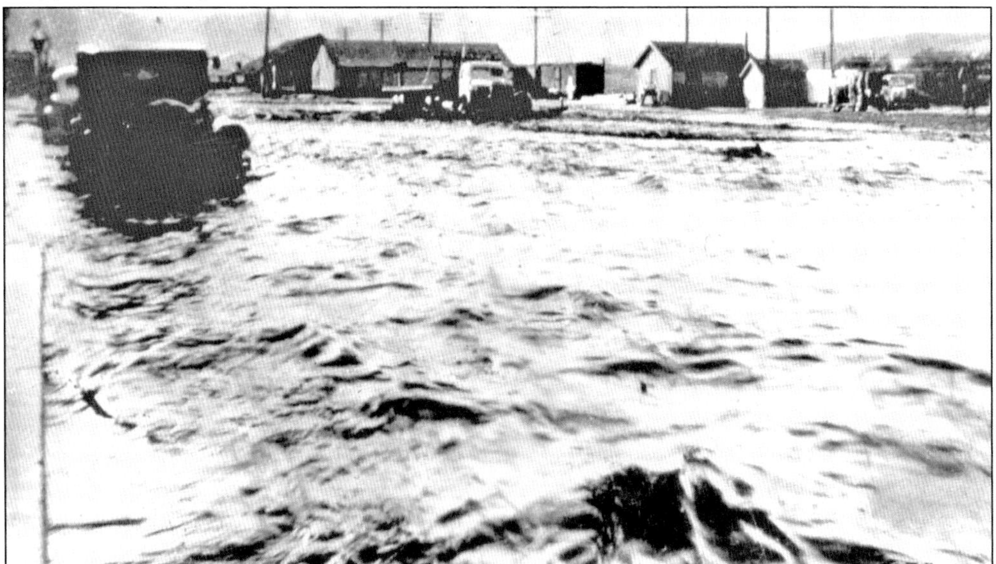

After a prolonged drought, the rains finally came—not as welcome precipitation, but as a series of storms in 1931, 1932, and again in 1938. The winter storm of 1931 carried into 1932, then rain came again in September. Older residents called it a "once in a hundred year" storm. Four inches fell within 24 hours, or 1 inch above an entire year's total. Flooding occurred, washing away valuable topsoil.

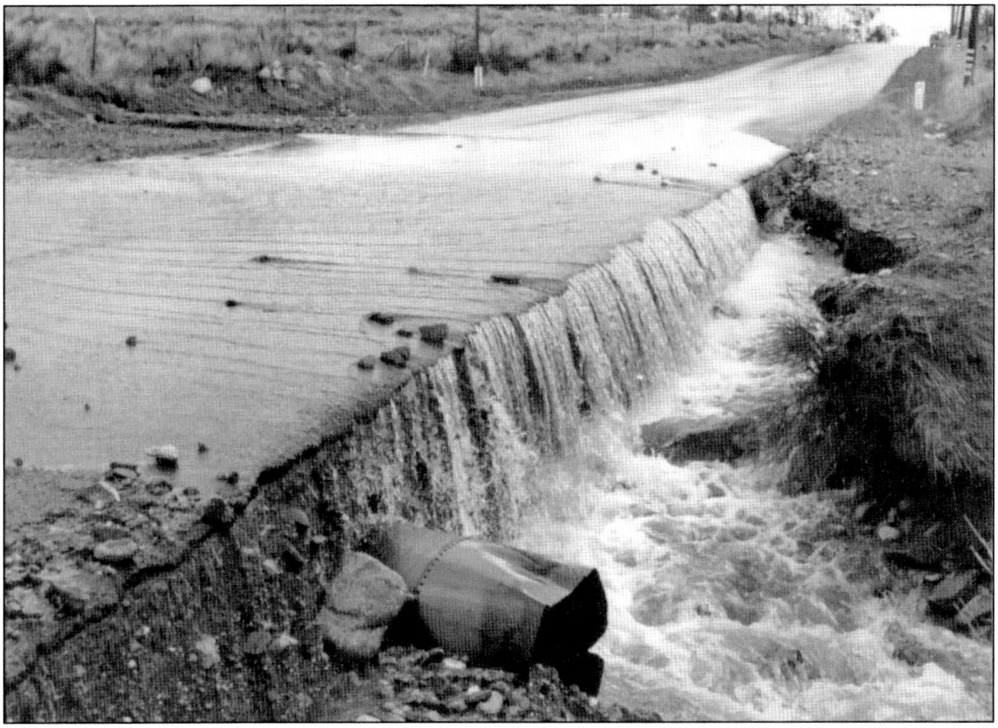

Streets in Tehachapi resembled shallow rivers. Earlier settlers had cautioned that such flooding could happen since Tehachapi was situated nearly at the base of an alluvial fan. This had been created eons ago by the merging flow of four mountain-fed creeks. It took the storm of 1932 to prove their prediction correct. Years later, a watershed program would install catch basins at the canyons to help alleviate the problem.

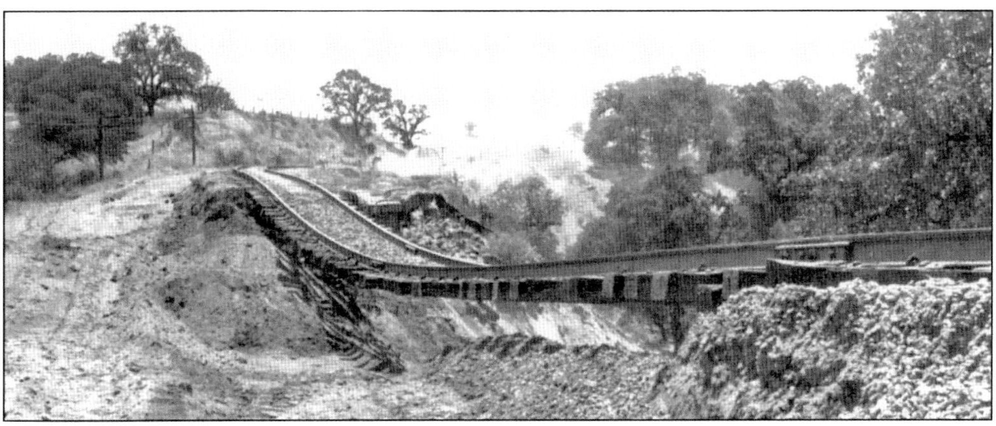

The railroad received the brunt of the 1932 flood. Tehachapi Creek became a raging torrent of churning water and debris, which piled up against railroad crossing No. 7 and then suddenly gave way. Floodwaters first hit a café at Keene, the rail station near the foot of the Tehachapi Pass. Many inside the café had sought refuge from the storm and were unaware of the flood coming their way. Only a few managed to escape.

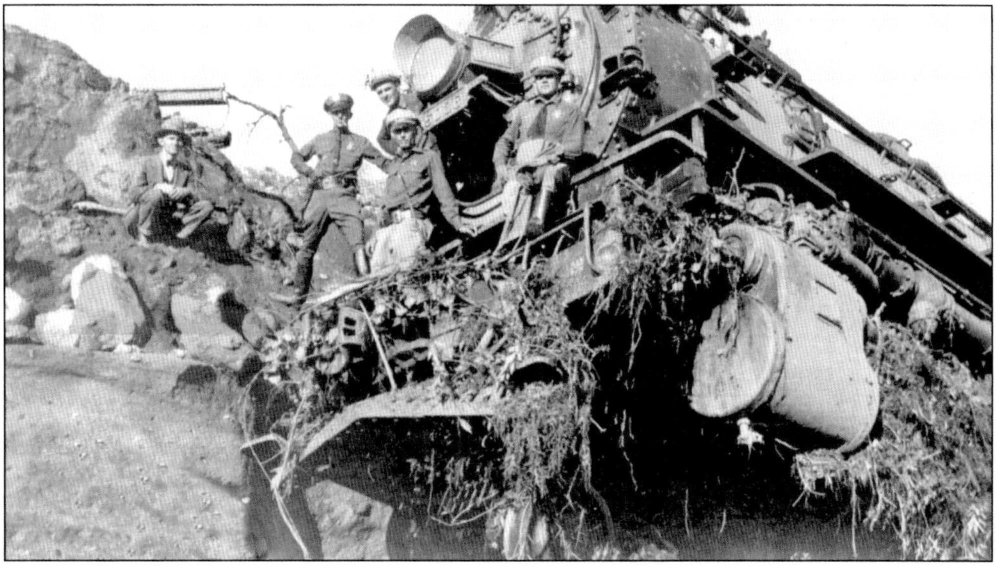

Fortunately, no one was inside this engine when the flood swept it off the track and carried it some 150 feet downstream. By the time the waters reached Caliente, their force was estimated at 37,000 cubic feet per second. All crossings and 31 miles of track were undermined or washed out. An estimated 75 people were killed, injured, or reported missing.

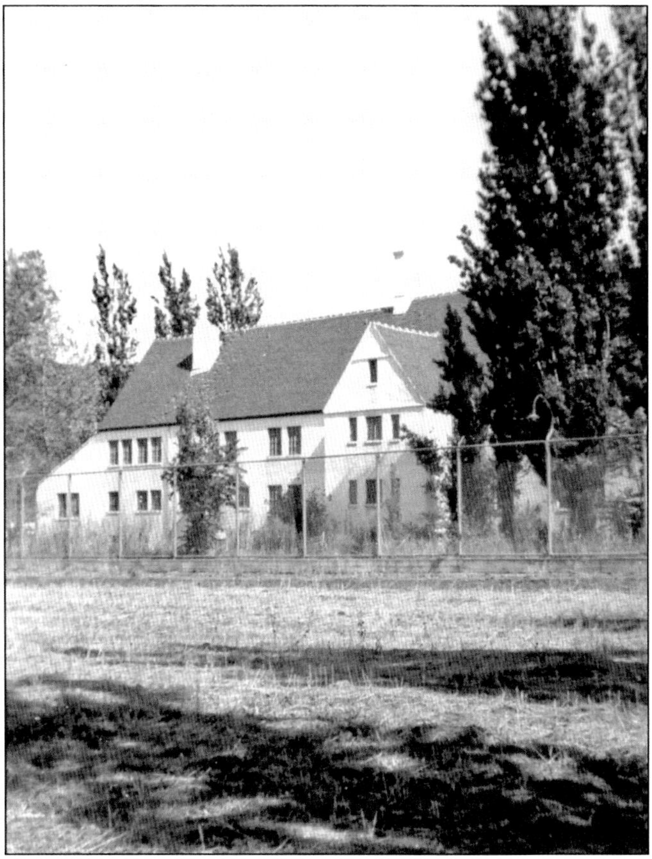

Despite freak storms and the Depression, Tehachapi's progress continued into 1932. The State of California had acquired the 1,700-acre ranch of Lucas Brite two years before and was now turning it into the state's first correctional facility for women with Norman-style buildings in a pastoral setting. The facility operated until becoming severely damaged in 1952. It was later converted to a male-only prison. Another area institute, the Stony Brook Retreat for tuberculosis patients, operated from 1918 to 1961.

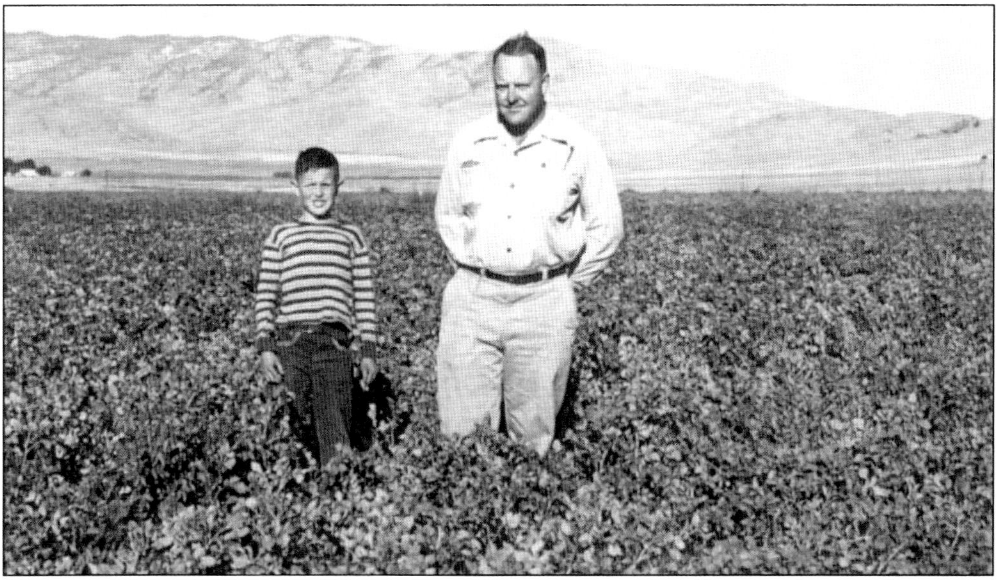

Ed Jacobsen (left, above) and his father, J. C. "Jake" Jacobsen (right, above), were instrumental in promoting local agriculture. Jake arrived in 1940 and raised table and seed potatoes. His farming techniques caught on, and for 10 years, 5,000 acres were in production. Between mid-August and the end of October, 100 rail cars a day transported the crop to outside markets. In 1942, Jake was elected president of the Kern County Seed Grower's Association, which served growers in California and Oregon. He traveled to Washington, D.C., and Europe on the growers' behalf. World War II brought a need for table potatoes, and this machine (below) unearthed them to be bagged by hand. A typical harvest required at least 300 transient workers.

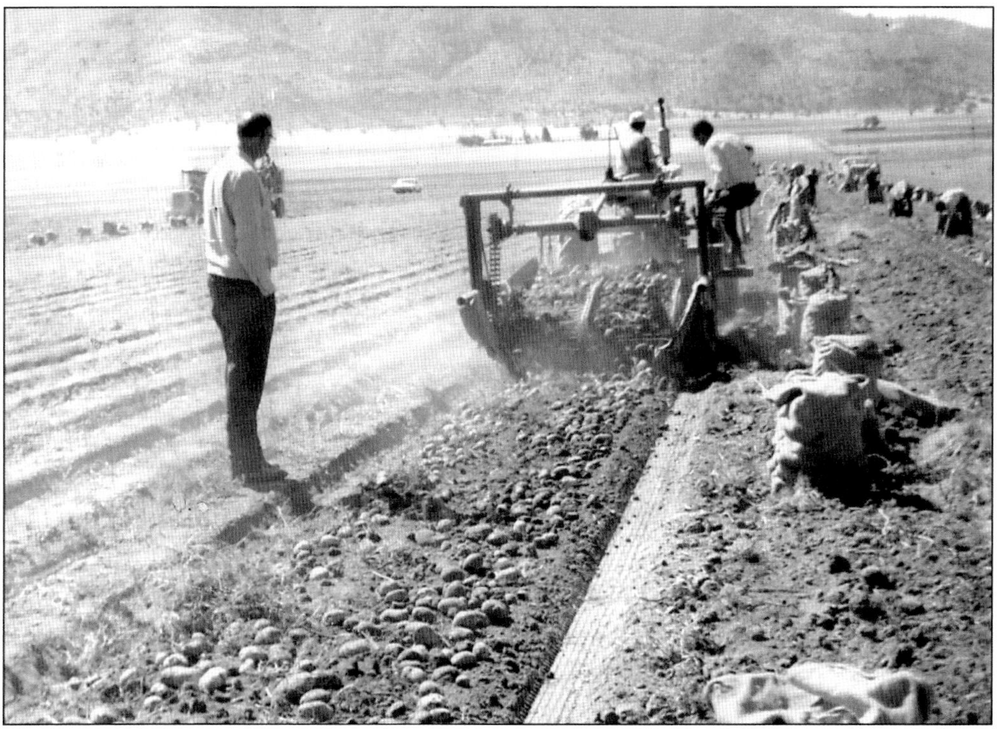

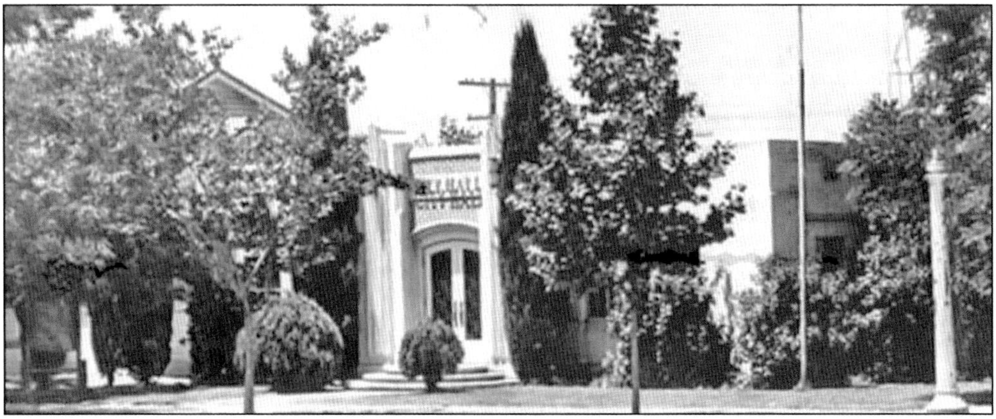

The Tehachapi City Hall was built during the Depression. Town trustees were of the generation that believed in setting aside money for a rainy day. Money from the sale of their electrical and telephone system had gained interest, and $100,000 now sat in the town treasury. Tehachapi was in a position to defy the Depression. It did this by engaging in a series of civic and business enhancements.

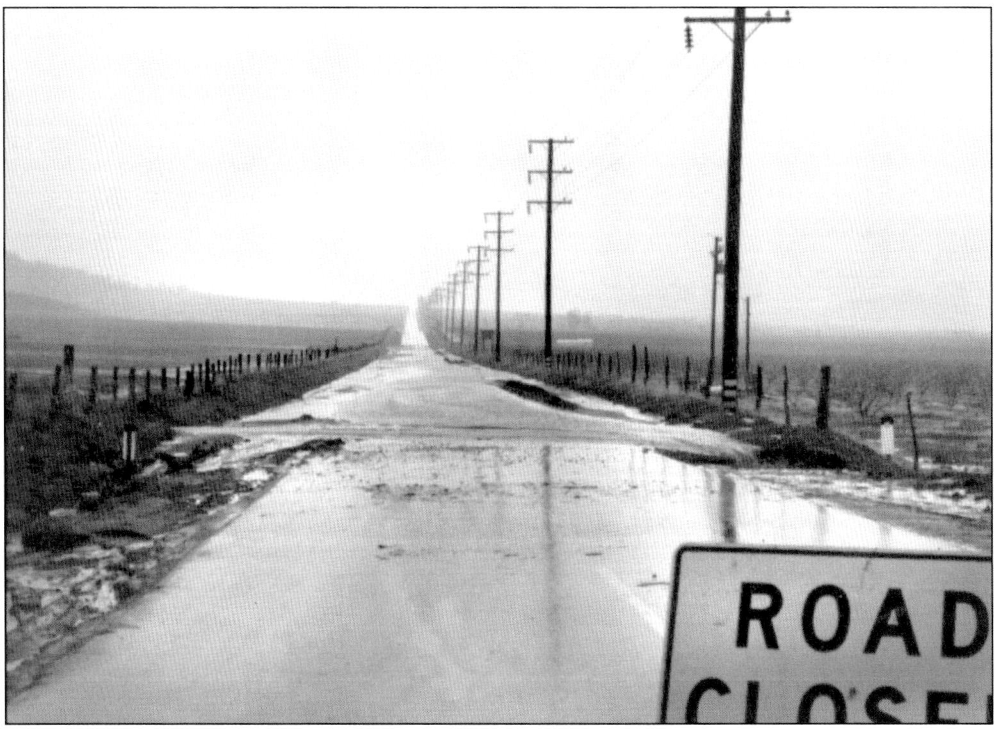

Other major floods occurred in 1938 and 1945. The second storm, like the one in 1932, hit during the late summer, but in 1938, rain fell between February 28 and March 4 in a series of high-intensity and long-duration storms. This flood did not cause any deaths but did cause several road closures and the loss of valuable cropland.

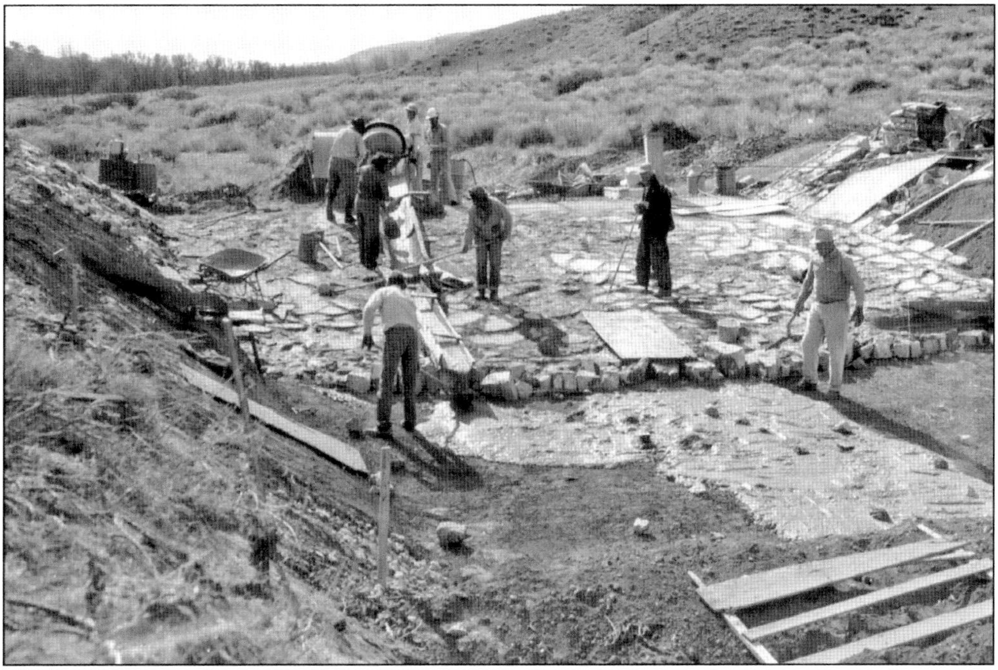

The construction of two flood-control basins was but one of the goals established by the Tehachapi Resource Conservation District (TRCD). After weathering the Great Depression, local farmers adjusted to new crops only to see valuable topsoil washed away by succeeding years of heavy rains and floods. In 1946, they decided to take action and formed the TRCD, which then identified such immediate interrelated issues as flood control, drainage, and watershed protection. Ultimately, water-control basins were constructed at the mouth of Antelope Dam (above) and Blackburn Canyon Creek Dam (below). They have since helped alleviate the flooding problems that once plagued Tehachapi and the surrounding countryside. (Tehachapi Resource Conservation District.)

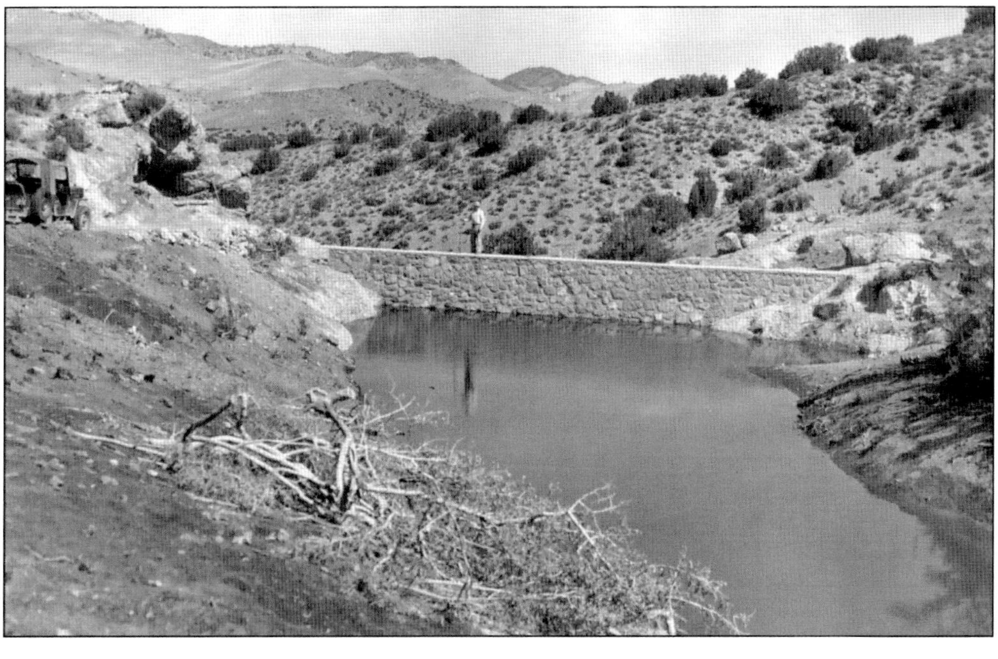

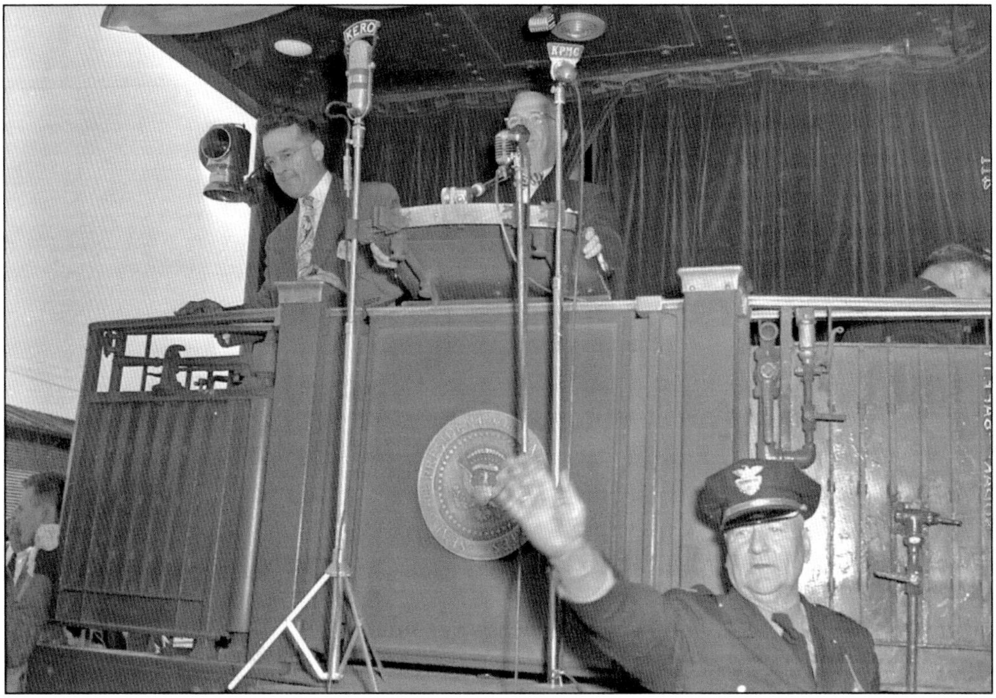

Residents received a special treat when Pres. Harry S. Truman made a whistle stop in Tehachapi on September 23, 1948. The president's wife, Bess, and daughter Margaret were with him during his campaign for reelection. His nationwide, barnstorming trip covered 32,000 miles. Locals say Truman's brief stop in Tehachapi helped sway many Republicans from voting for his opponent, Thomas Dewey. (Kern County Museum.)

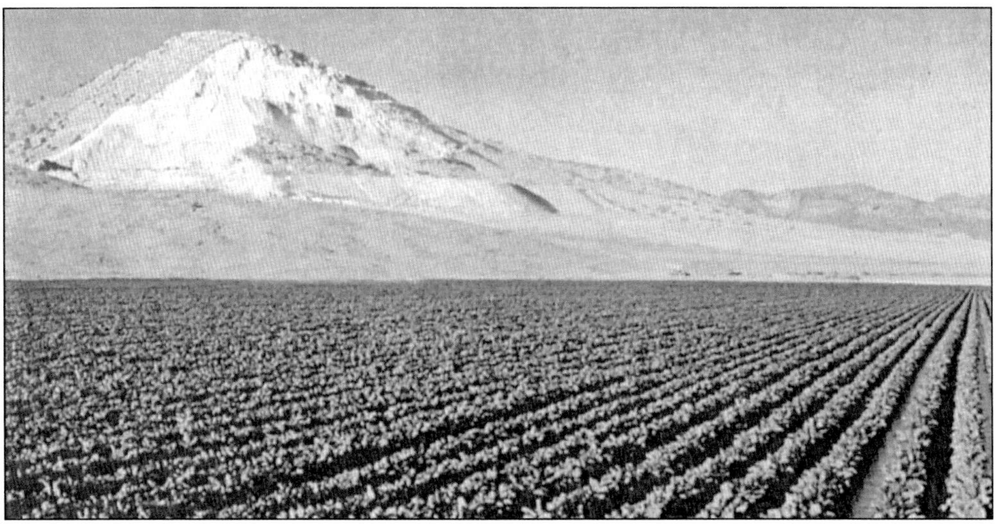

Jake Jacobsen played a significant role in raising sugar beets for seed. He introduced the crop in 1946, and its quality and high yield brought top dollar from the Farrar-Loomis Seed Company of Hemet. Although its peak production lasted just three years, that was enough to help farmers recover from losses incurred during the 1932, 1938, and 1945 floods. Tehachapi became an incorporated city in 1946, a year after World War II ended. Its treasury and local bank were solvent. Business was good, and people were content.

Seven

Rising from the Rubble

American westward pioneers were an independent lot, and they faced their problems accordingly.

—Andrew F. Rolle, *California: A History*

Tehachapi pioneers and their descendants had faced many challenges since first settling here in 1854. But few were prepared for the shock that brought them awake in the predawn hours of July 21, 1952. Later reports said there was no warning, but early risers probably noticed that their animals' behavior indicated something was about to happen. From household cats and dogs, to the horses and cattle in the fields, all suddenly became alarmed and restless. An inner sense had alerted them to the fact that some 10 miles beneath the ground, a long slumbering fault was about to awake.

At 4:52 a.m., the residents of the Tehachapi Valley felt the first and most-severe jolt. The tremor lasted just 45 seconds but registered a 7.7 magnitude on the Richter Scale. A series of aftershocks—50 in all—followed with the rising sun and continued throughout the day. Water tanks toppled, and several wells and springs went dry. Creek beds changed course. Rooftops flattened, steps collapsed, and porches moved inches away from houses. Furniture fell; dishes scattered and broke.

A total of 11 people were killed. Several others suffered injuries of varying degrees. Many were in shock.

Not one building on Tehachapi's main street escaped damage. All rail, highway, and telephone arteries were cut off between Bakersfield and Los Angeles. The railroad's centralized Traffic Control System was knocked out, forcing all operations to a halt. It would be 28 days before any train could again travel through the pass. Even vehicle traffic was affected. Due to several fissures and pavement cracks, the state highway was closed until the highway patrol could escort vehicles through the area.

The situation was so bleak that some predicted it was the end of Tehachapi. They were wrong.

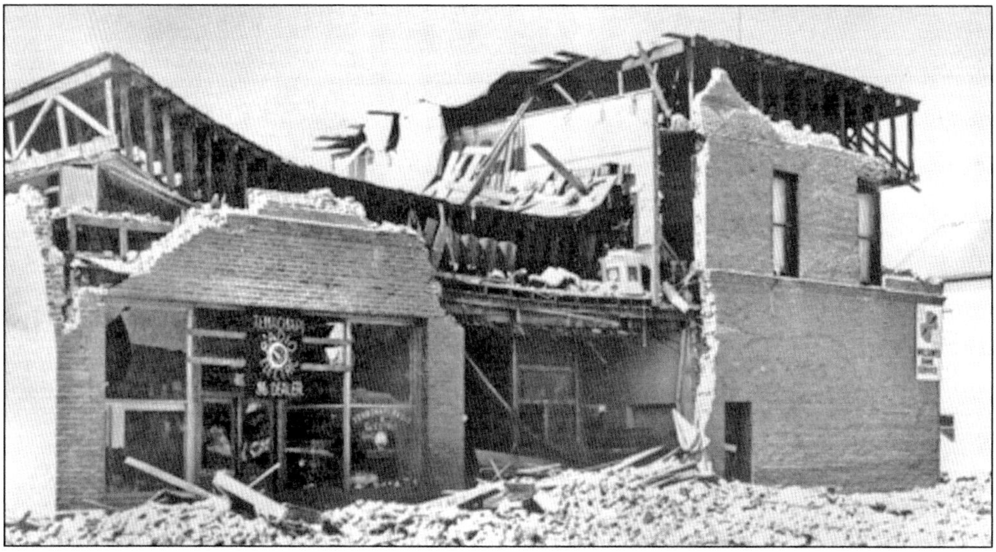

The greatest loss of life occurred to one family who had, on the night before, checked into this hotel on G Street (Tehachapi Boulevard). Mrs. Blance Cantana and five of her nine children took quarters on the second floor. The roof collapsed on top of them; they were unable to escape. Her husband and other four children, who were downstairs, were injured but survived.

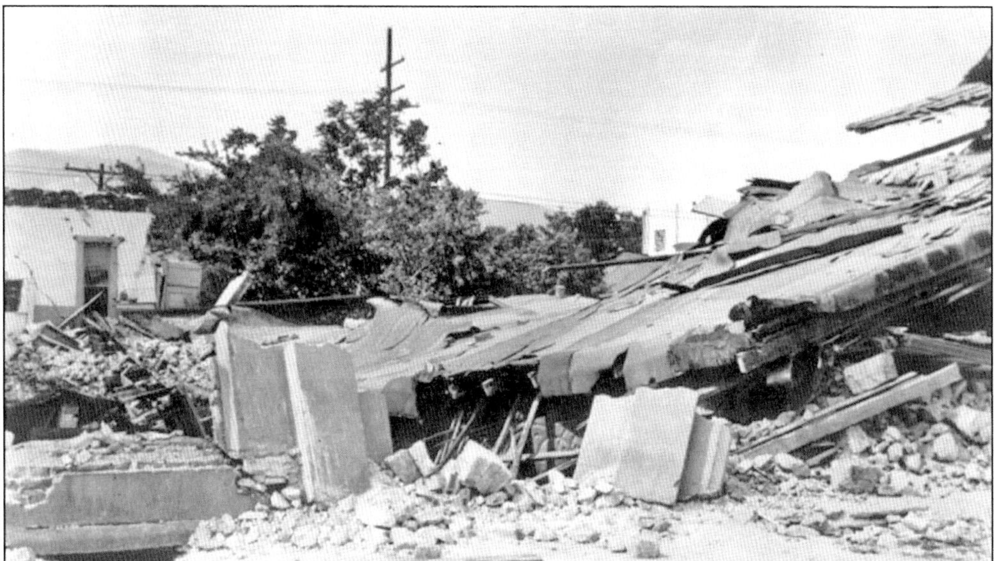

Adjacent to the hotel, Louis Martin's furniture store was a total loss. However, his greatest loss was personal: his three children and their friend. Just the night before, he had acquiesced to their pleas for a sleepover inside the store. Martin never rebuilt.

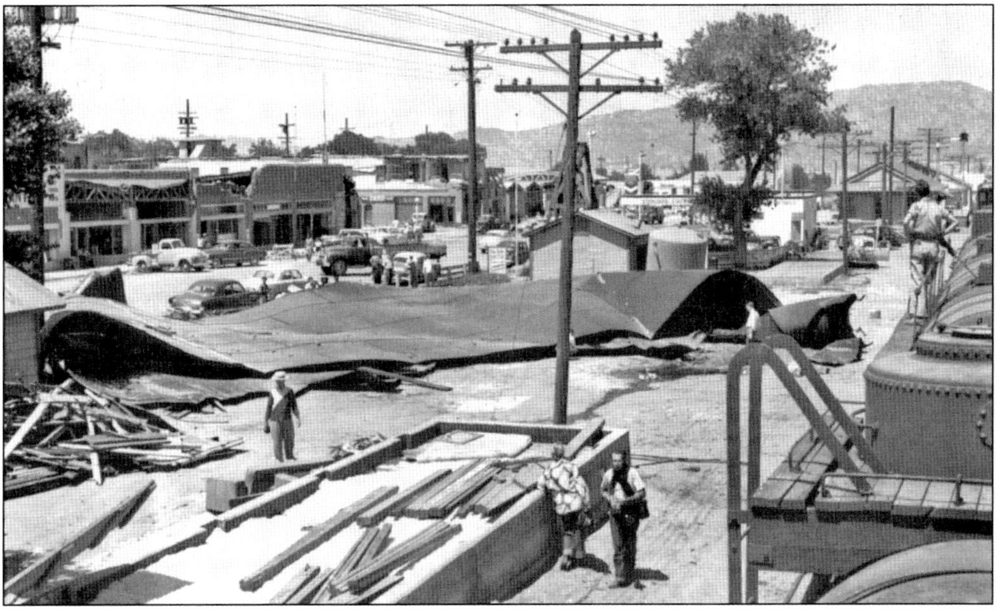

Southern Pacific's giant twin water tanks standing next to the railroad tracks were no match for the velocity of the quake and collapsed. About 1,000 gallons of water spilled over and flooded the businesses across the street.

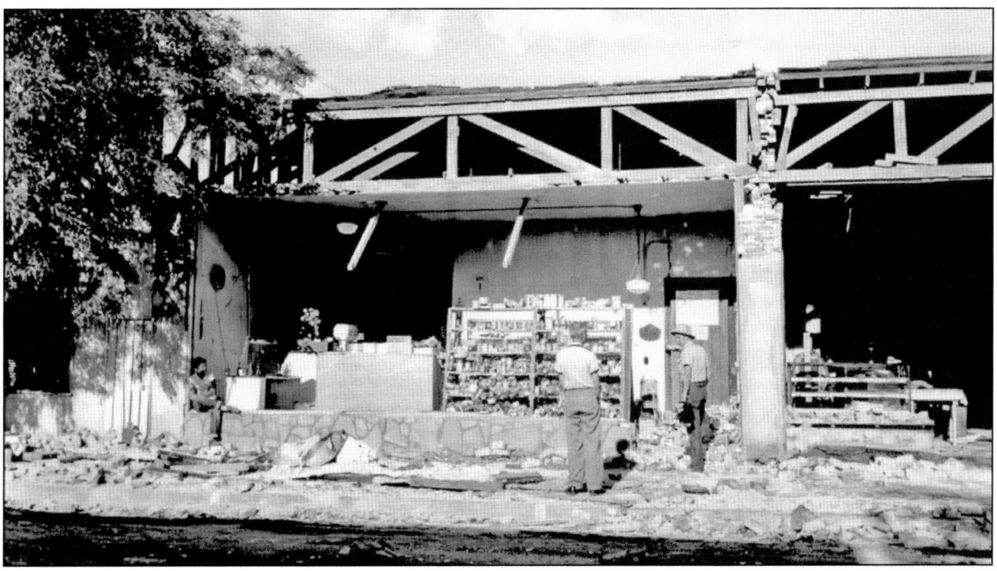

Vern's Auto Supply and Service suffered major damage. The front wall and windows collapsed with the initial shock; stock fell from the shelves. Water from the tanks rushed into the store, ruining its products and fixtures.

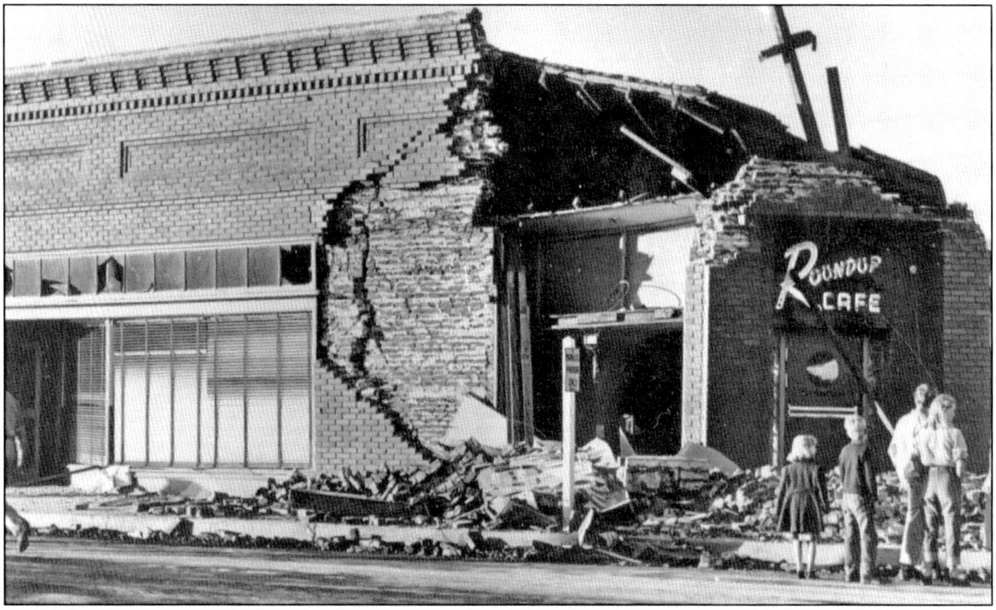

The tenth victim was Walter Nolan, a guest at the Summit Hotel who was unable to escape when the building collapsed around him. The eleventh casualty occurred in Cummings Valley, where a 16-year-old girl was killed by a falling rock wall. She had opted to spend the night inside a stone outbuilding.

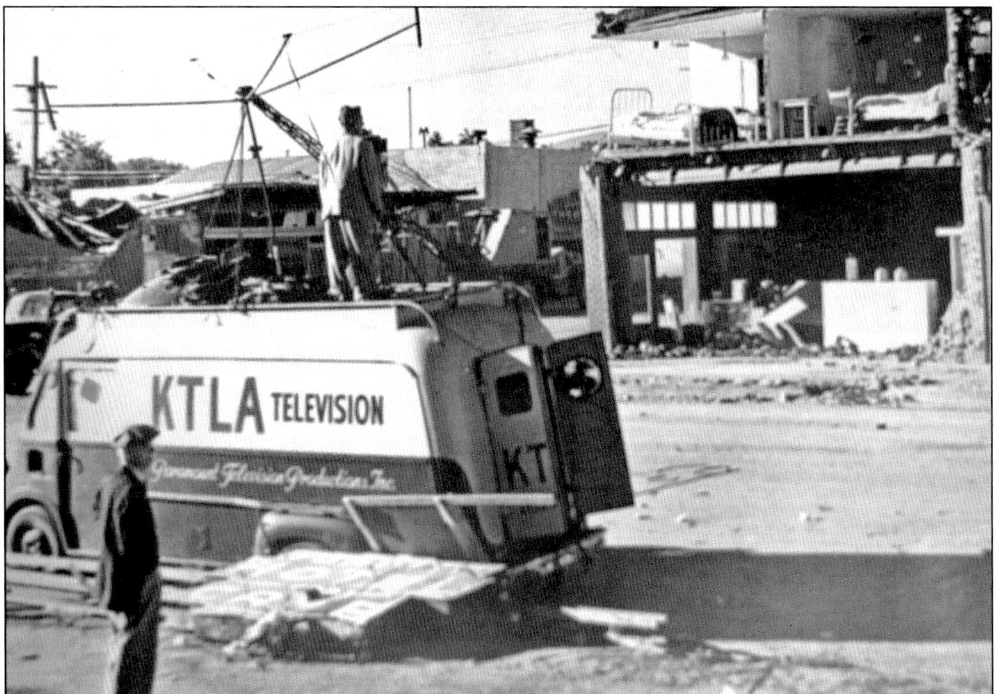

Station KTLA from Hollywood was the first television crew to arrive on the scene. Despite road closures, news teams soon flocked to the area for live reports. Sightseers also managed to slip in and, according to many, kept getting in the way of the rescue and cleanup operations.

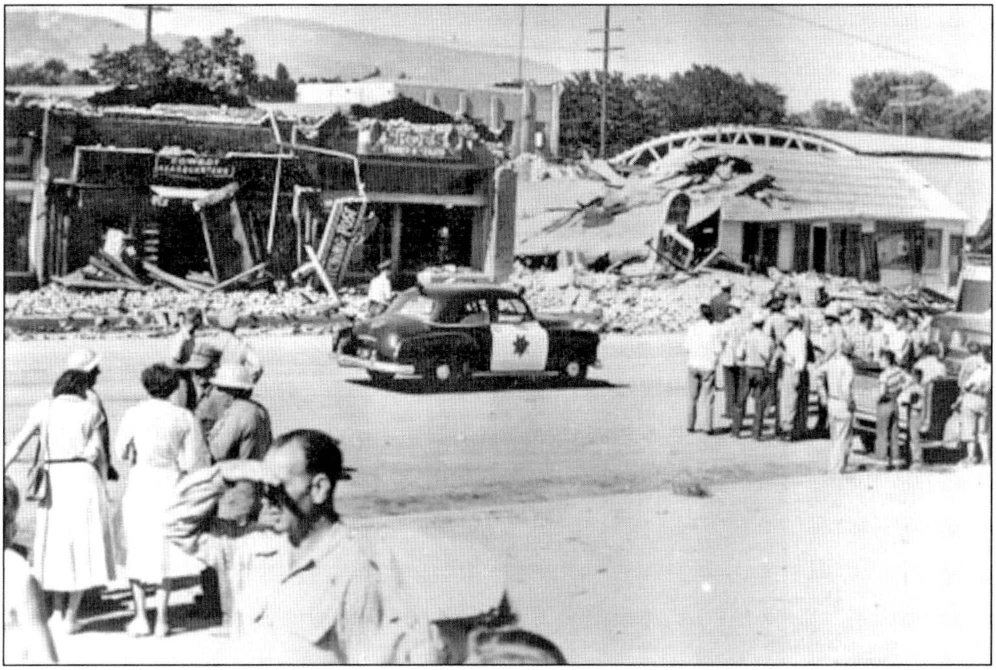

An entire block of G Street (Tehachapi Boulevard) was demolished, including a hotel, café, and drugstore. Many came to survey the damage and to see what could be salvaged. The *Tehachapi News* said Tehachapi looked like "a town God had forgotten."

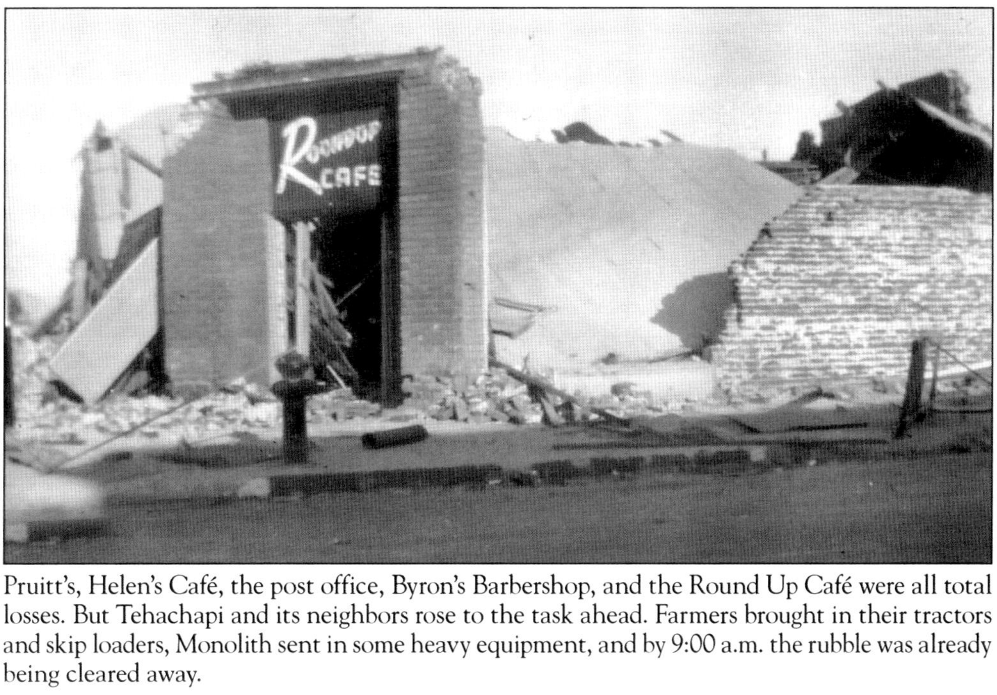

Pruitt's, Helen's Café, the post office, Byron's Barbershop, and the Round Up Café were all total losses. But Tehachapi and its neighbors rose to the task ahead. Farmers brought in their tractors and skip loaders, Monolith sent in some heavy equipment, and by 9:00 a.m. the rubble was already being cleared away.

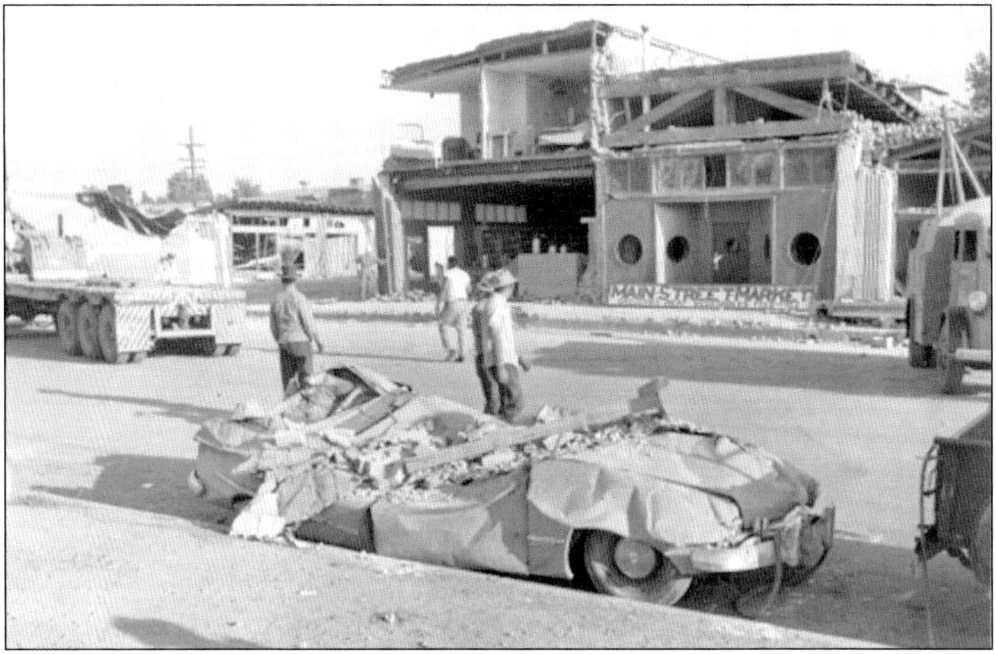

Within minutes of the quake, the city's civil defense system was in motion. Crews shut off gas and water lines to prevent further damage while tow trucks hauled away damaged cars. Army personnel set up barriers to keep sightseers and looters away.

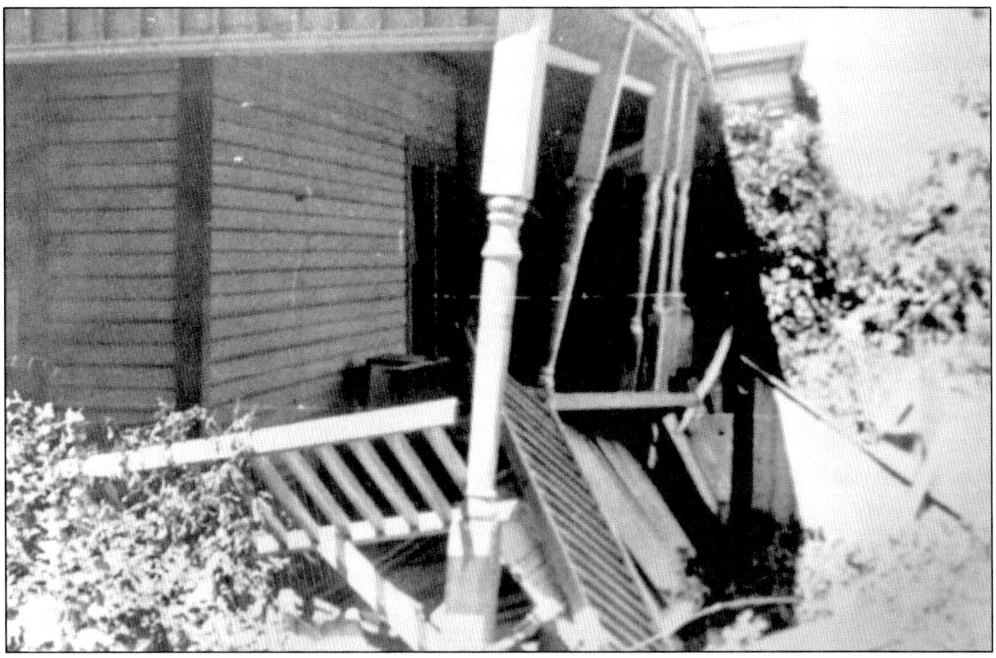

Damage was not confined to businesses. Many homes suffered severe damages. The Brite home on Curry Street was a total loss, as was the two-story hospital on E Street. Prompt action by hospital staff and neighbors prevented any loss of life as patients were evacuated to the front lawn or into neighboring homes until they could be transferred to Mojave. Housewives made sandwiches and boiled coffee over campfires to feed the volunteers.

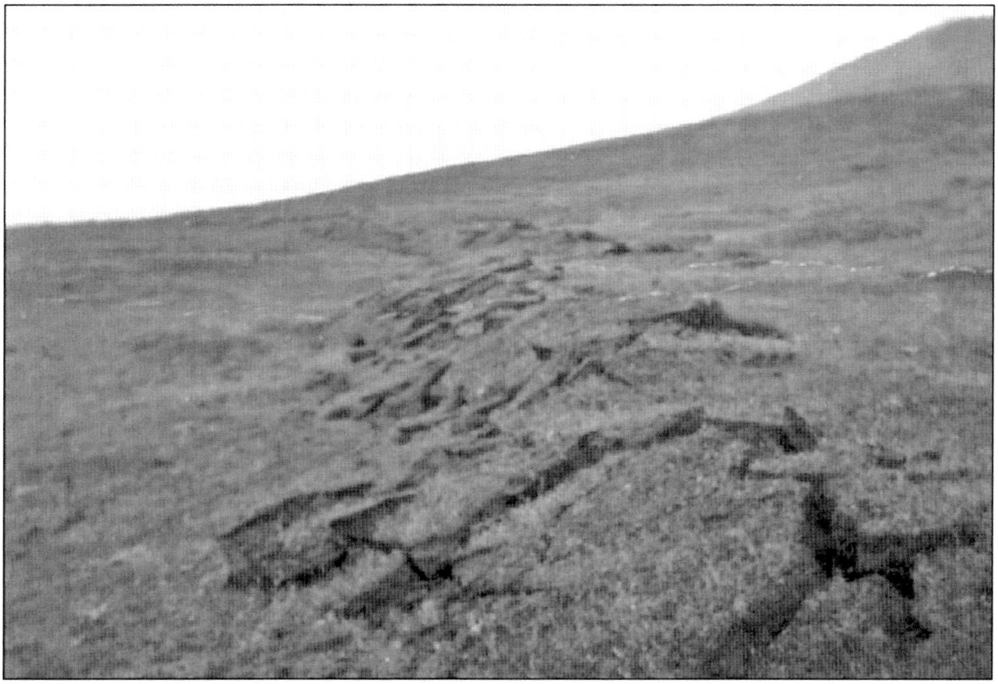

According to the Richter Scale, the earthquake was of a 7.7 magnitude. Its force pushed this ridge of earth several yards long and 1 to 2 feet high. Not since 1856, when an earthquake (later estimated to be around a 6.5 magnitude) caused considerable damage to Fort Tejon, had anything like this happened.

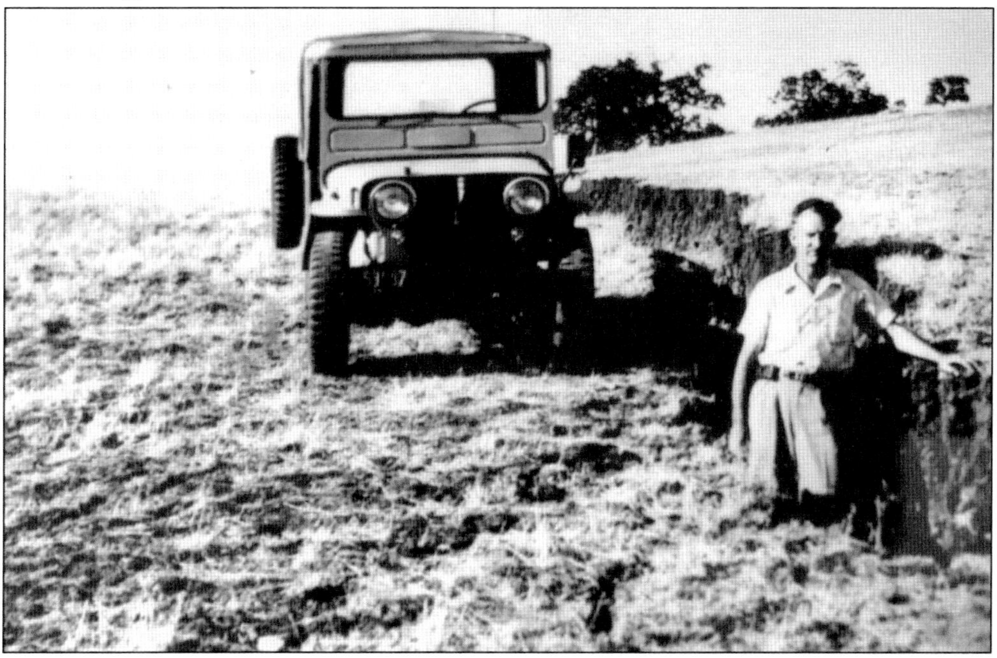

In one place, a fissure opened in the earth that was waist deep on a man. The quake's center was on the White Wolf Fault, which lies west of Tehachapi and extends northeast underneath the Tehachapi Pass.

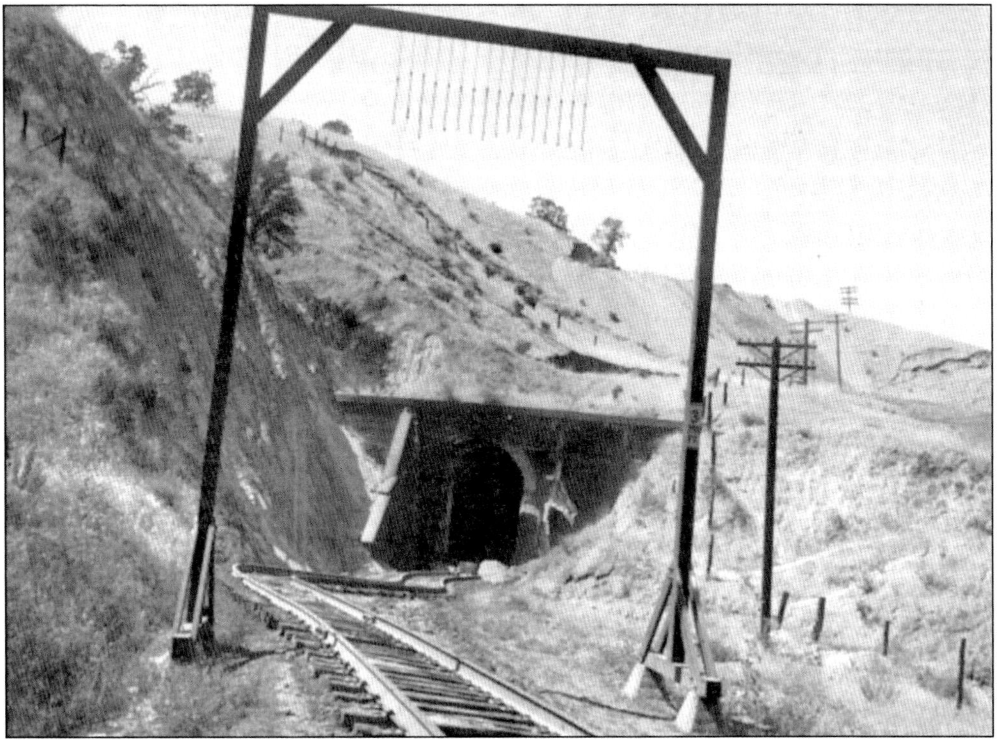

The force caused a three-foot shift in Bear Mountain and had a direct effect on the rail line through the Pass. Tunnel Nos. 3 and 4, initially 300 feet apart, were pushed several feet closer, and the tracks twisted up to 24 feet off center.

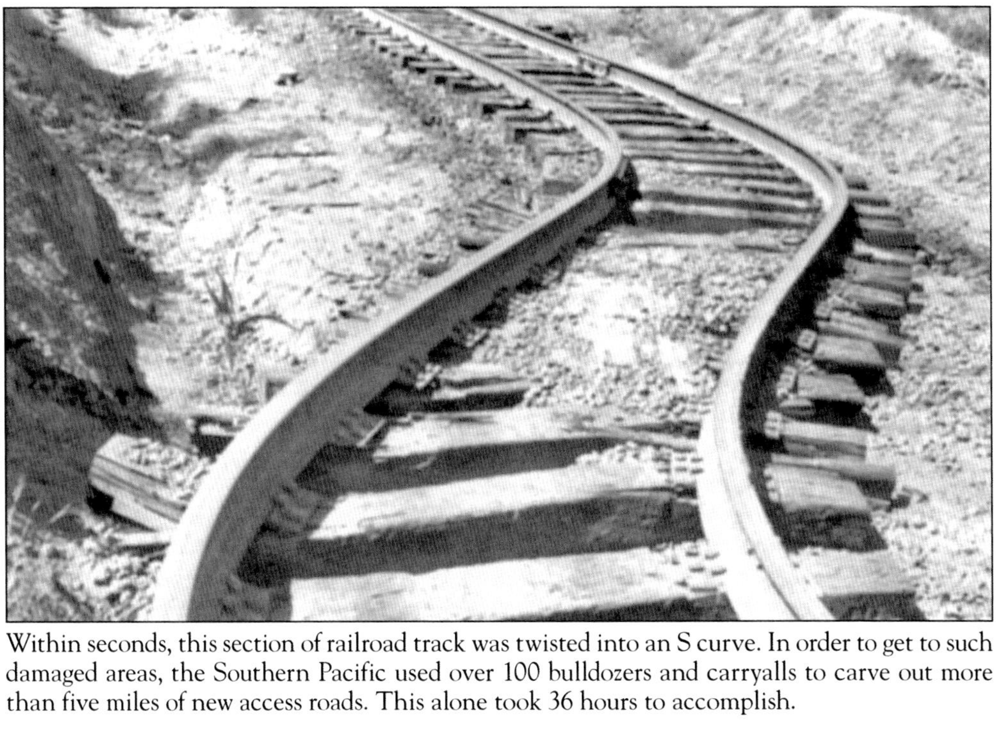

Within seconds, this section of railroad track was twisted into an S curve. In order to get to such damaged areas, the Southern Pacific used over 100 bulldozers and carryalls to carve out more than five miles of new access roads. This alone took 36 hours to accomplish.

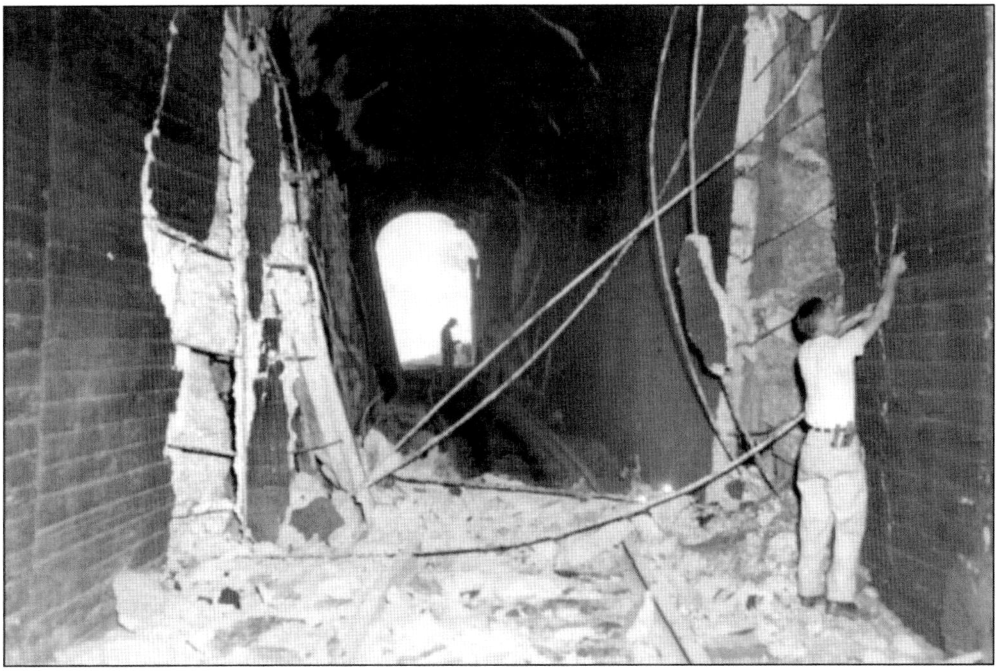

Inside Tunnel No. 3, the heavily reinforced 23-inch-thick concrete walls were pushed up into an arch before breaking. Repair costs, estimated at $2.5 million, consisted of day-lighting (opening at the top) or constructing a shoo-fly (detour) around the mountainside. With the exception of Tunnel No. 5, which received the most damage and took an additional three to four months to repair, the railroad was up and running within 26 days.

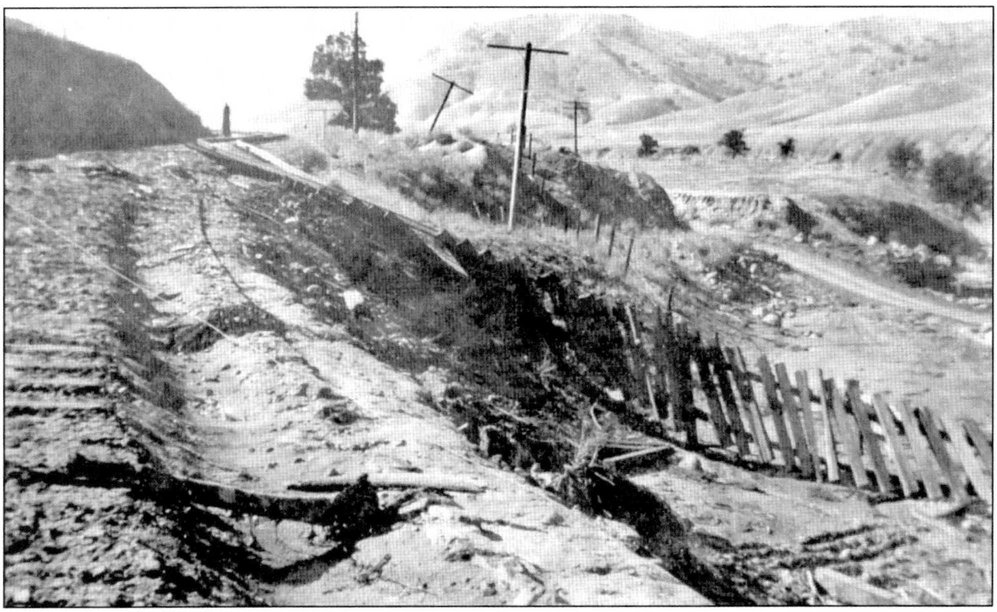

Earth displacements, some up to 10 feet wide, undermined several miles of railroad tracks. Small fissures and cracks in the highway closed down all traffic in and out of Tehachapi. Telephone lines were down and all communication with the outside world cut off—except for the ham radio operators who rose to the occasion.

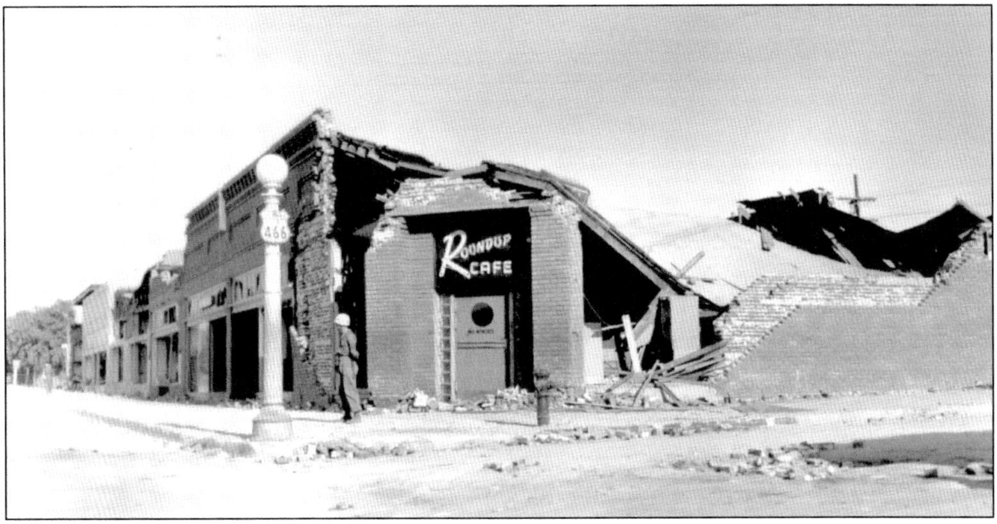

By nightfall, most of the rubble had been removed. On the following day, streets were cleared of shattered glass and scattered debris. Crews began knocking down the walls left standing. The remaining salvage operations were assumed by property owners.

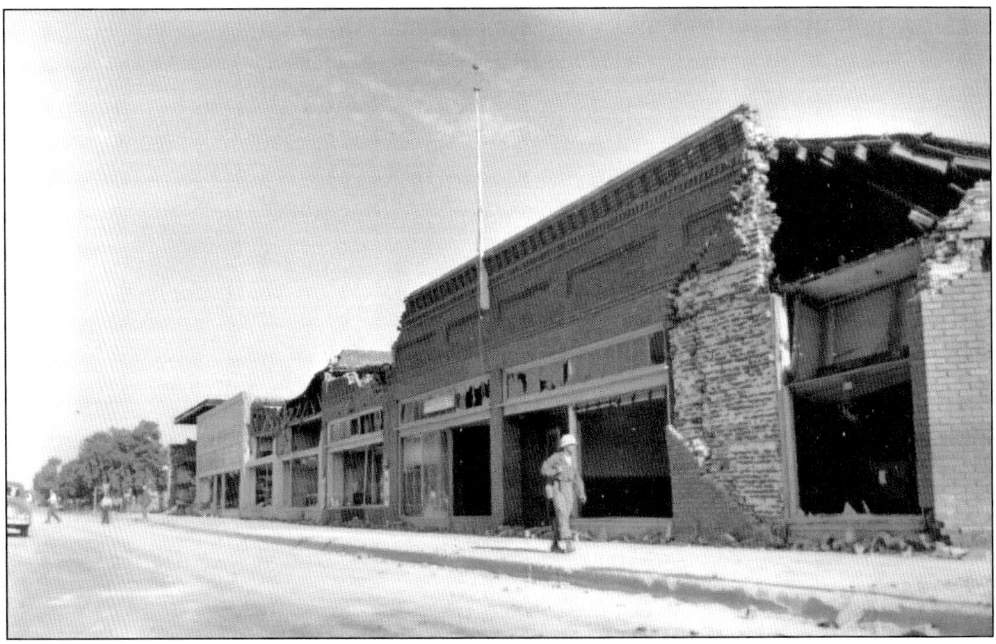

For a while, Tehachapi's main business district was a desolate scene. The rubble had been cleared away, and ruined buildings stood waiting for final demolition. But Tehachapi was far from dead. The Bank of Tehachapi and other businesses on Green Street remained unscathed and open, while owners of ruined stores established temporary quarters. The city council began making plans to rebuild a new and better Tehachapi.

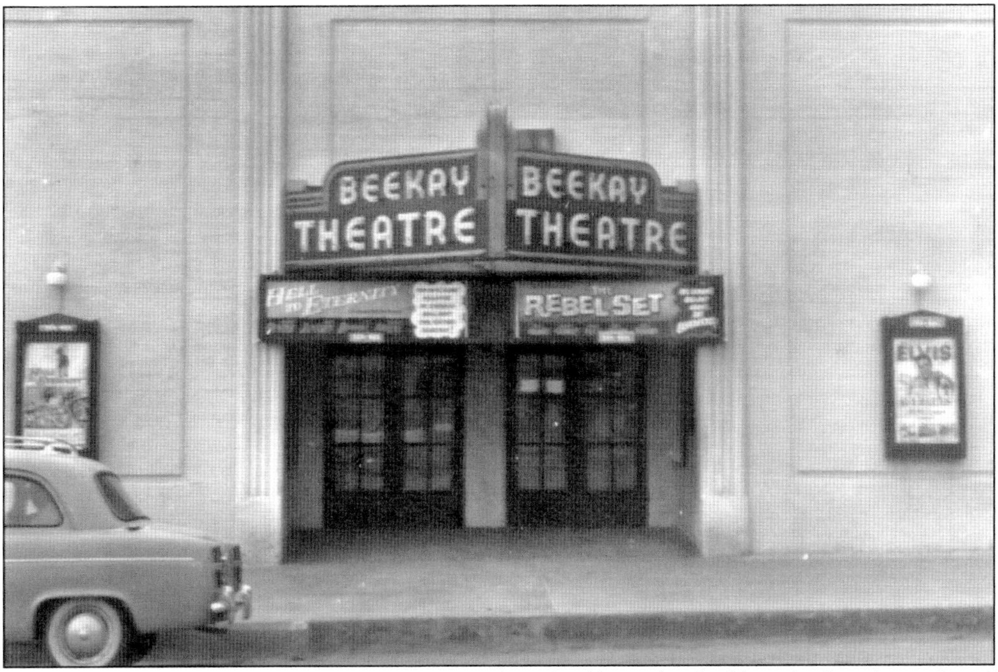

The Beekay Theater on Green Street was among those buildings that had been built with reinforced concrete and managed to survive the earthquake. Others included the Bank of Tehachapi, the IOOF Hall, the Tehachapi Lumber Company, and St. Malachy's Catholic Church. The grammar and high schools, city hall, and the public library also went undamaged.

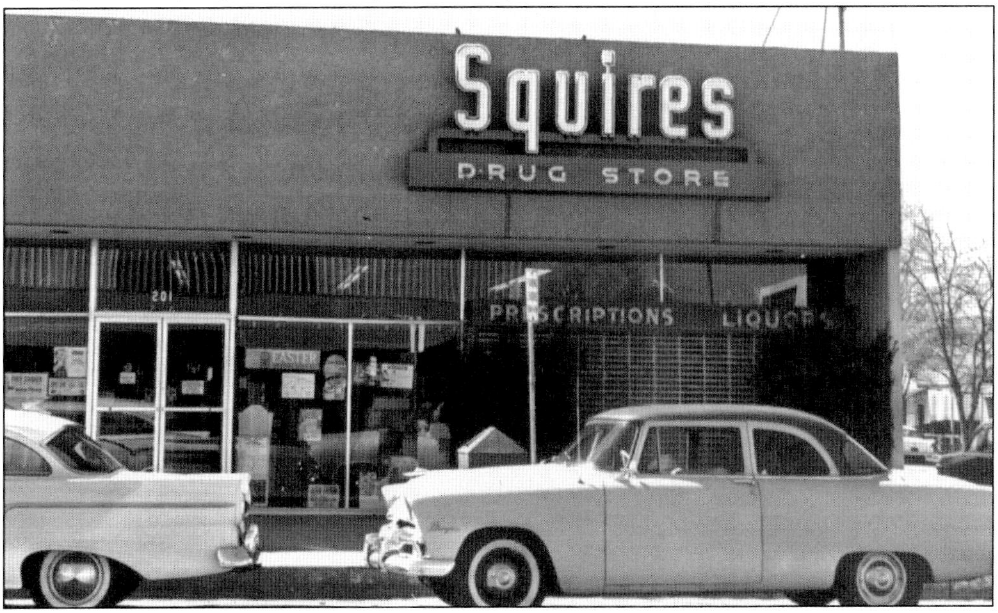

One year after the earthquake, Vaughn Squires, the owner of the damaged drugstore, not only rebuilt his shop in a different location, but constructed a completely new business complex on both sides of Green Street. The all-concrete structures adhered to strict new building codes. Walter Johnson, the publisher/editor of the *Tehachapi News*, called it a rebirth of the business district and added, "This city is far from dead."

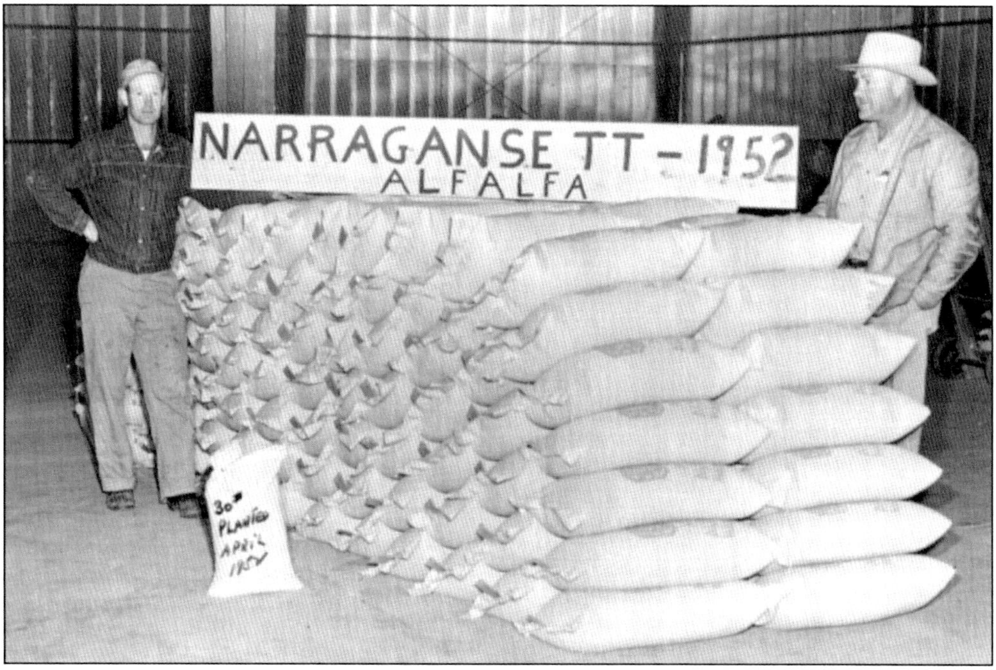

There was also a rebirth in agriculture. Alfalfa fields now dominated the outlying areas. First introduced in 1950, the crop was raised as a legume hay and for its seed. Alfalfa seed was so productive that, within a few years, Tehachapi had achieved national recognition as the center of the certified alfalfa seed industry.

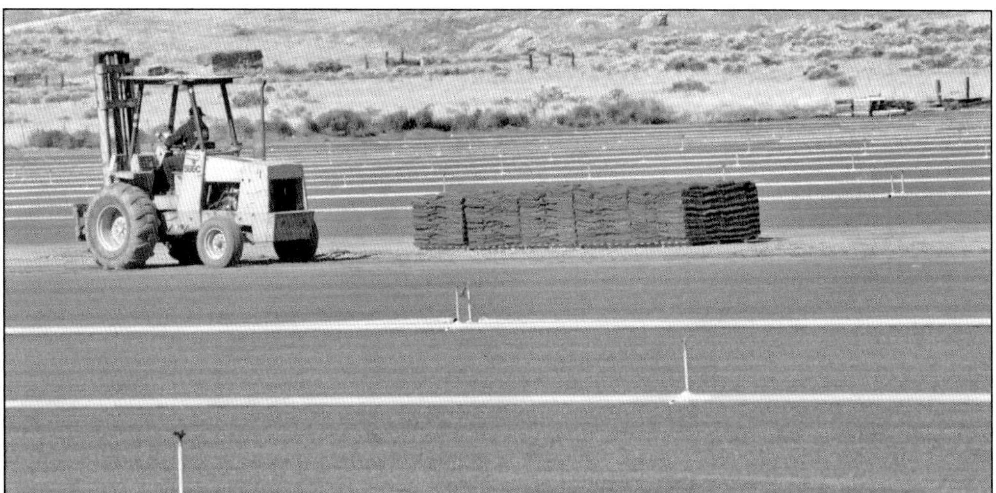

Following the earthquake, Tehachapi underwent many changes. This extended to the agricultural community. The growing of sod found a nationwide market in golf courses, athletic fields, parks, and lawns for the multitude of new housing developments. (Nick Smirnoff.)

Eight

Preserving the Past

When an old man dies, a history book is lost.

—Old Central African proverb

For the most part, Tehachapi residents have retained a sense of pride in the past, including its legends and bits of folklore. Much was originally retained within the memories of early settlers who willingly shared them with family members, neighbors, and friends. In 1894, in order to preserve such memories, an effort was made to form a Pioneer Society. But many felt it was too late. "An old-timer says there are [just] seven men yet living in this country who can be called pioneers of pioneers," stated the *Daily Californian* on March 29, 1894.

It was not until 1976 that a concentrated effort to preserve the past was made with the formation of the Tehachapi Heritage League. It has since become a depository for historical photographs and memorabilia. An all-volunteer staff operates both the Tehachapi Museum and the Errea House. Members have been actively involved in efforts to preserve the winter home of the native Kawaiisus as a California state park and in the formation and support of a native (Kawaiisu) language program.

The nonprofit Friends of the Depot organization is currently working with the City of Tehachapi and the Heritage League to restore the old depot as a railroad museum. The city's Main Street Program has inaugurated a Historical Murals Project, which brings the area's past alive on the sides of businesses and old warehouses. Many of the murals are painted by local artists.

This sense of community is all part and parcel of Tehachapi's small-town atmosphere. And it is not original. The Kawaiisu Indians spent most of the year hunting and gathering food in small family groups. Occasionally, these groups would meet others and gather at a predetermined site. One such site was said to be located where the city of Tehachapi now lies. They called it *Ta-chip-i*, "the place."

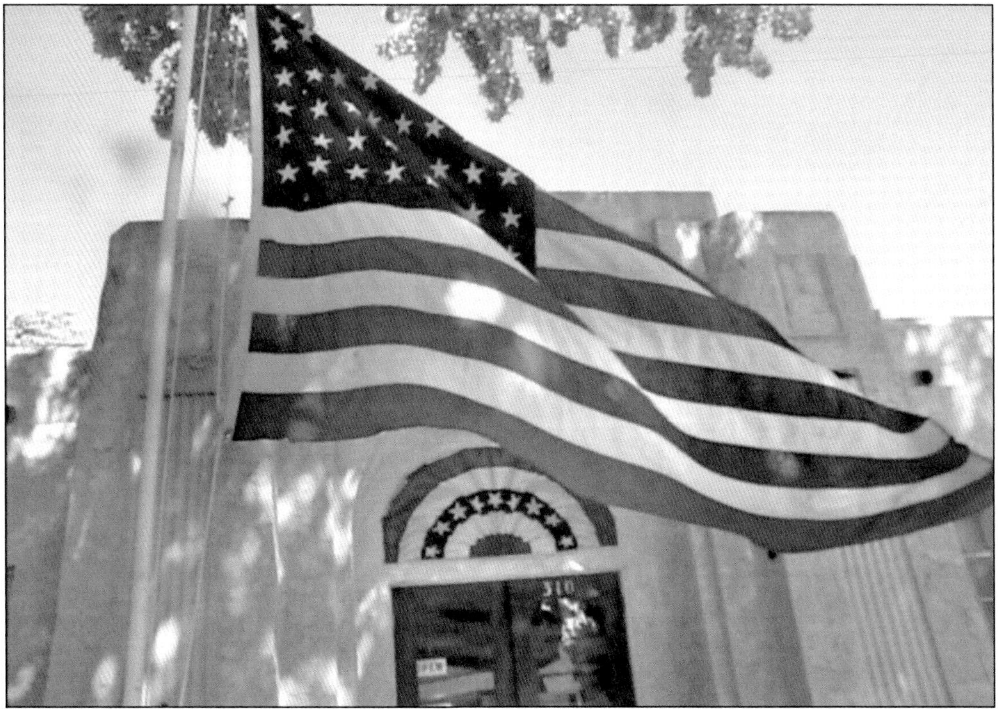

This former library (built in 1932) and the historic Errea House (built in the 1870s) are now maintained and operated by volunteers from the Tehachapi Heritage League. Since its formation on July 4, 1976, the league has worked to preserve Tehachapi's past through photographs, writings, artifacts, and mementos housed in the museum. Special exhibits, displays, and historical events are held across the street at the Errea House.

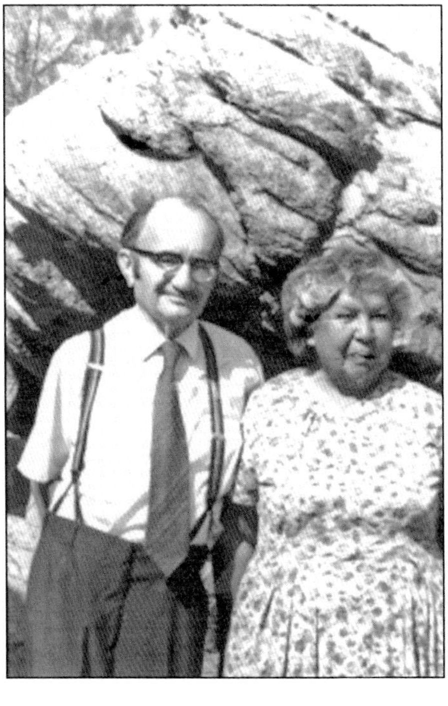

Maurice L. Zigmond, Ph.D., and local Kawaiisu Emma Williams are pictured here. Zigmond spent the summers from 1936 to 1940 living with local families such as the Williamses to further his studies as an anthropologist and ethnologist. He returned again in 1970 and, for the next four years, recorded their language and legends. Zigmond's work, later published, has become the basis for the local language study program.

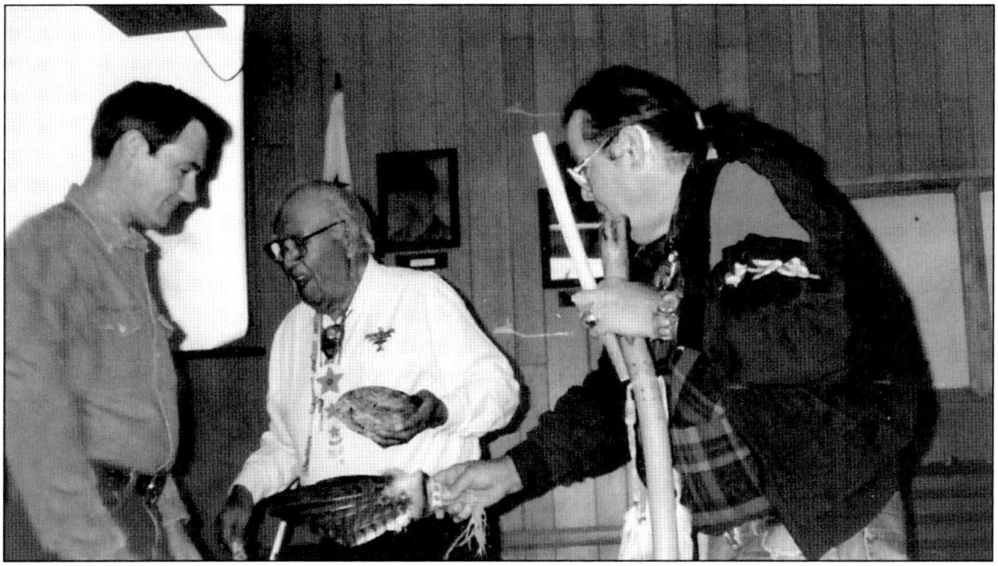

Phil Wyman (left), the grandson of F. O. Wyman; Andy Greene (center), a Kawaiisu elder; and Charlie Cook, an intertribal liaison; are seen during a ceremony to preserve Tomo-kahni. As a state legislator, Wyman worked closely with Greene and members of the Heritage League for the protection of this site. In 1994, the area was officially dedicated as Tomo-kahni State Park, and the 78-year-old Greene was honored as a respected elder.

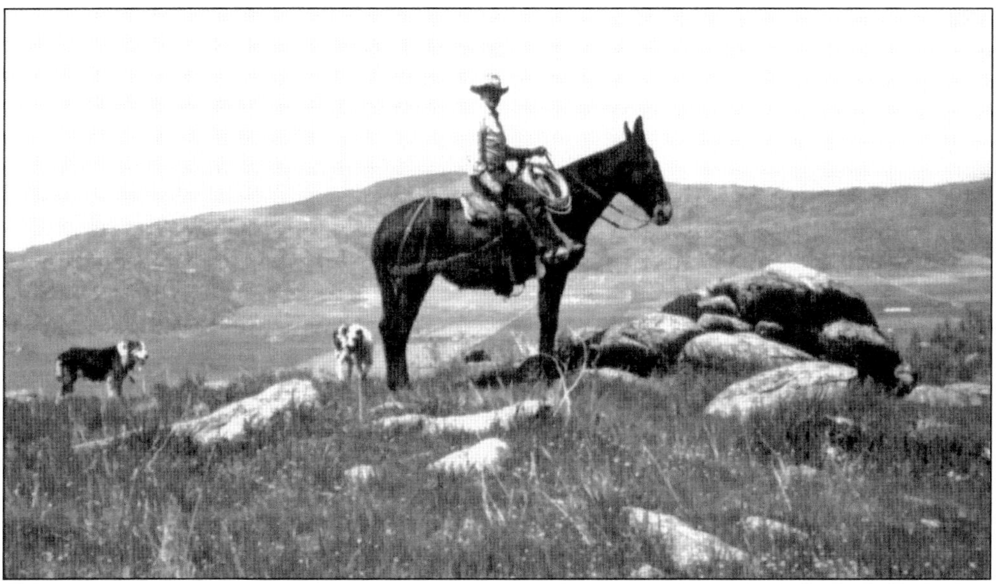

The cowboy is symbolic of Tehachapi's western heritage when large ranches were common. At least two of the early ranches continue to maintain their traditional western roots. Members of the Cummings family still live and raise cattle on the ranch developed by George Cummings in 1854. Cowboys still ride the rugged hillsides of Broome Ranch, which is part of the former Cuddeback Ranch of 1856.

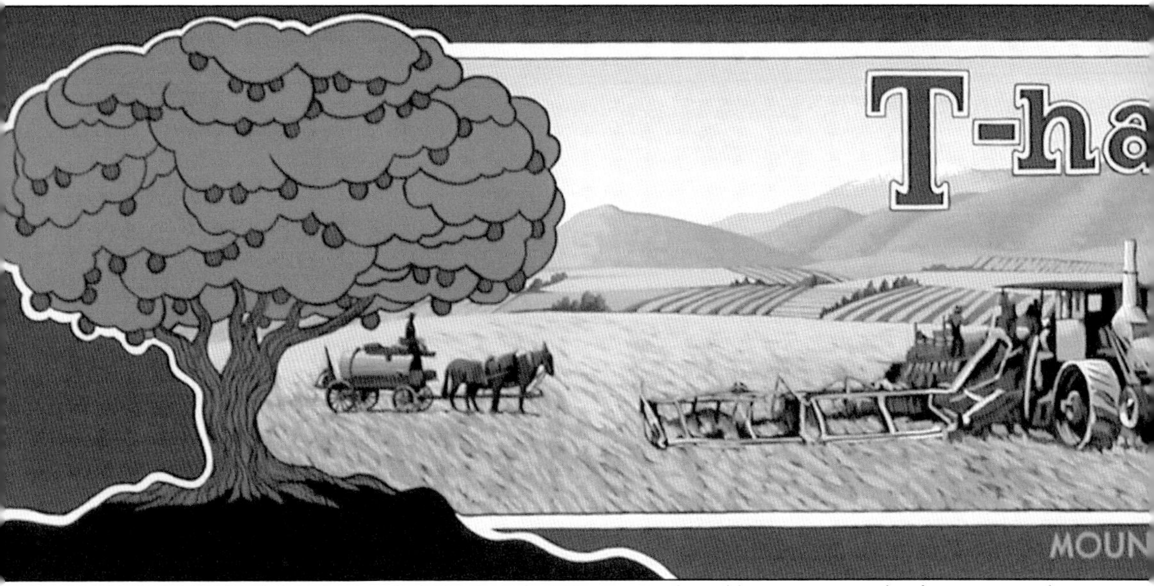

The 2005 *T-hacha-PR-2* mural, depicting the city's agricultural heritage, was the first to introduce local artists into the program. Art Mortimer designed the mural around the logo for T-Hacha-P pears. The portrait is of Jake Jacobsen, a pioneer in new farming techniques, civic leader, and

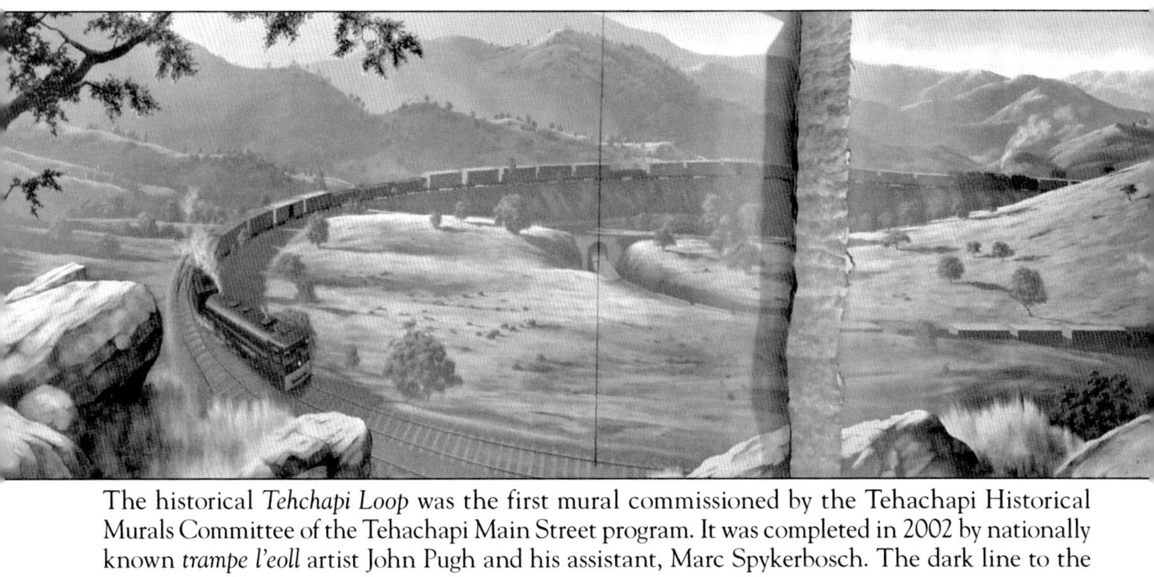
The historical *Tehchapi Loop* was the first mural commissioned by the Tehachapi Historical Murals Committee of the Tehachapi Main Street program. It was completed in 2002 by nationally known *trampe l'eoll* artist John Pugh and his assistant, Marc Spykerbosch. The dark line to the

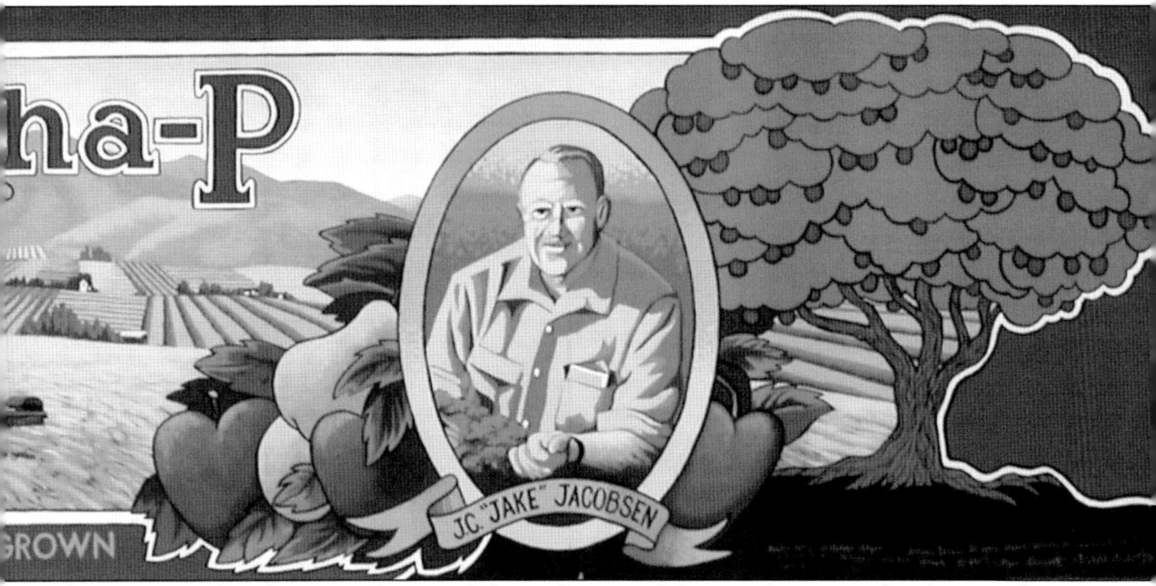

former mayor. Local artists volunteered their talents, and the mural was completed in one day. (Main Street Tehachapi.)

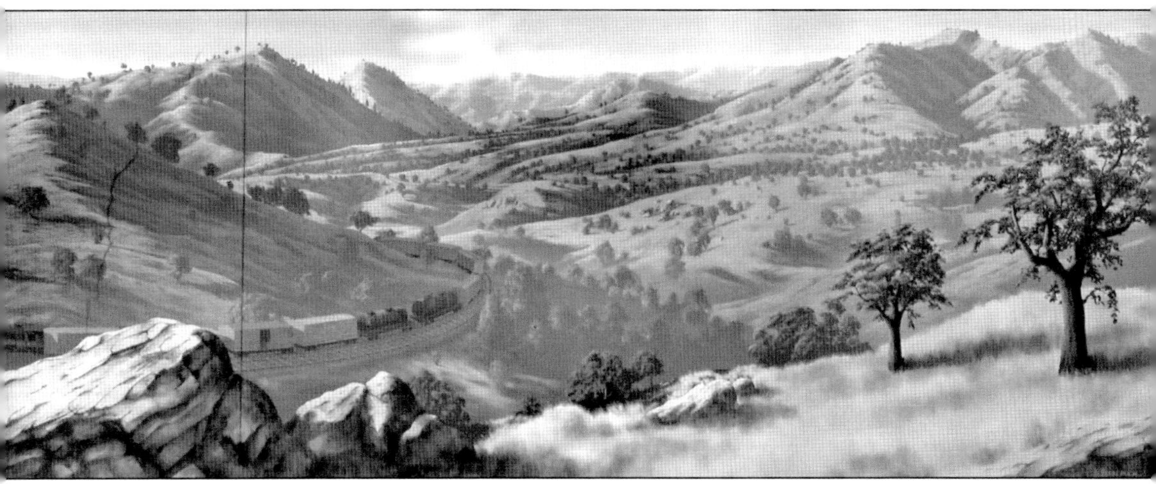

left was devised by the artist to depict damage to the building by the 1952 earthquake. (Main Street Tehachapi.)

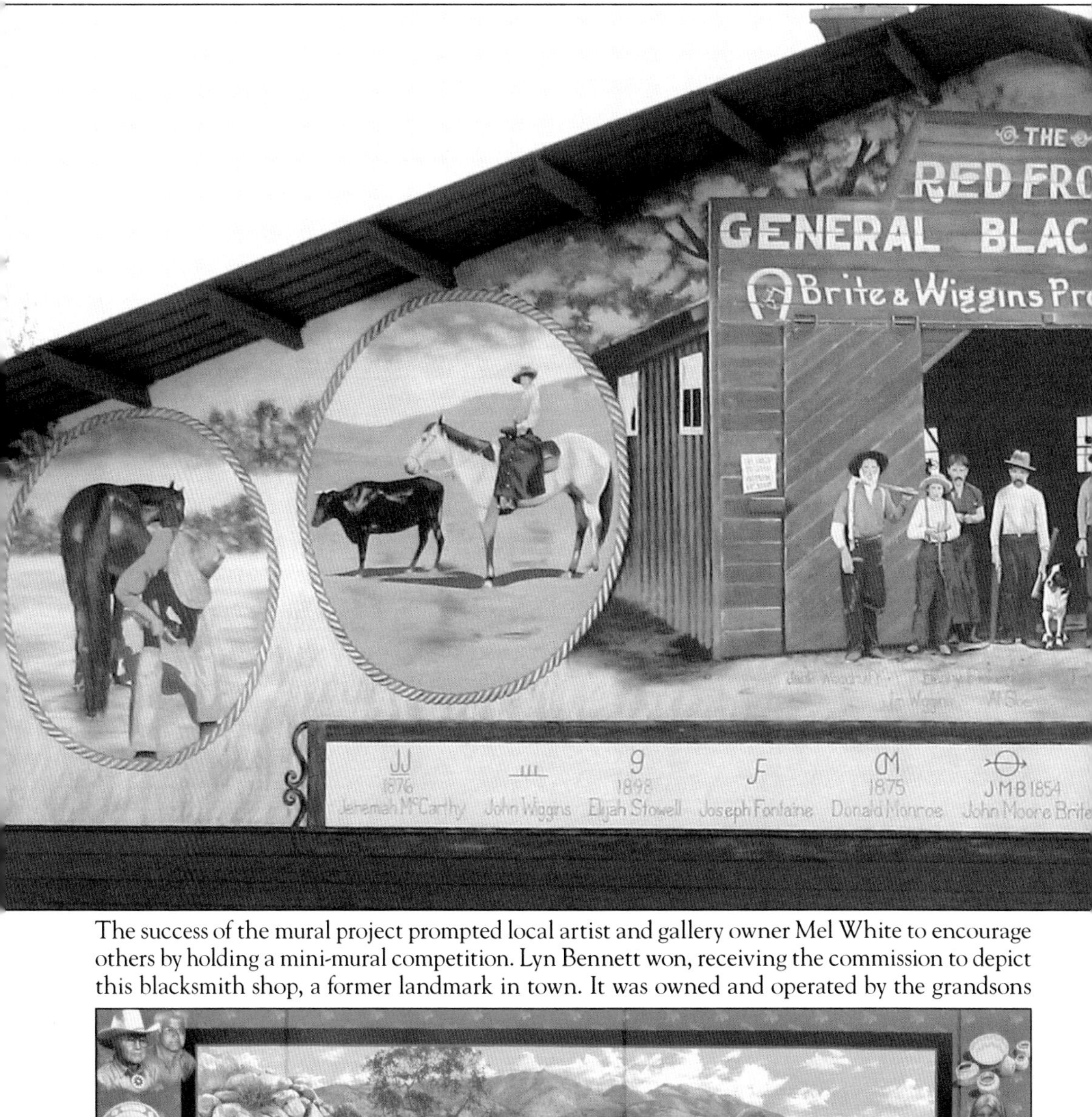

The success of the mural project prompted local artist and gallery owner Mel White to encourage others by holding a mini-mural competition. Lyn Bennett won, receiving the commission to depict this blacksmith shop, a former landmark in town. It was owned and operated by the grandsons

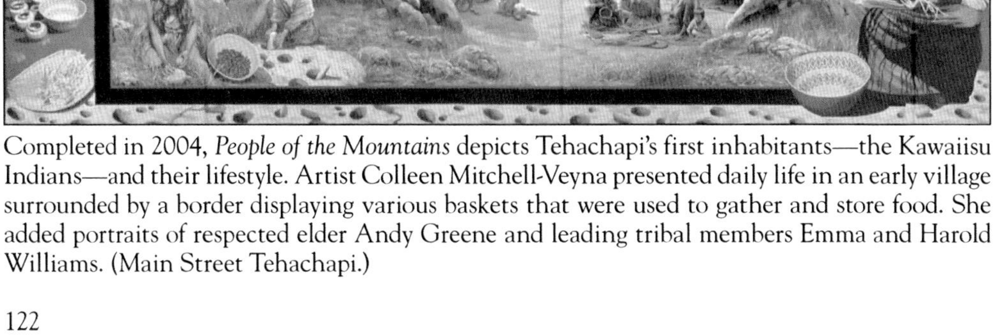

Completed in 2004, *People of the Mountains* depicts Tehachapi's first inhabitants—the Kawaiisu Indians—and their lifestyle. Artist Colleen Mitchell-Veyna presented daily life in an early village surrounded by a border displaying various baskets that were used to gather and store food. She added portraits of respected elder Andy Greene and leading tribal members Emma and Harold Williams. (Main Street Tehachapi.)

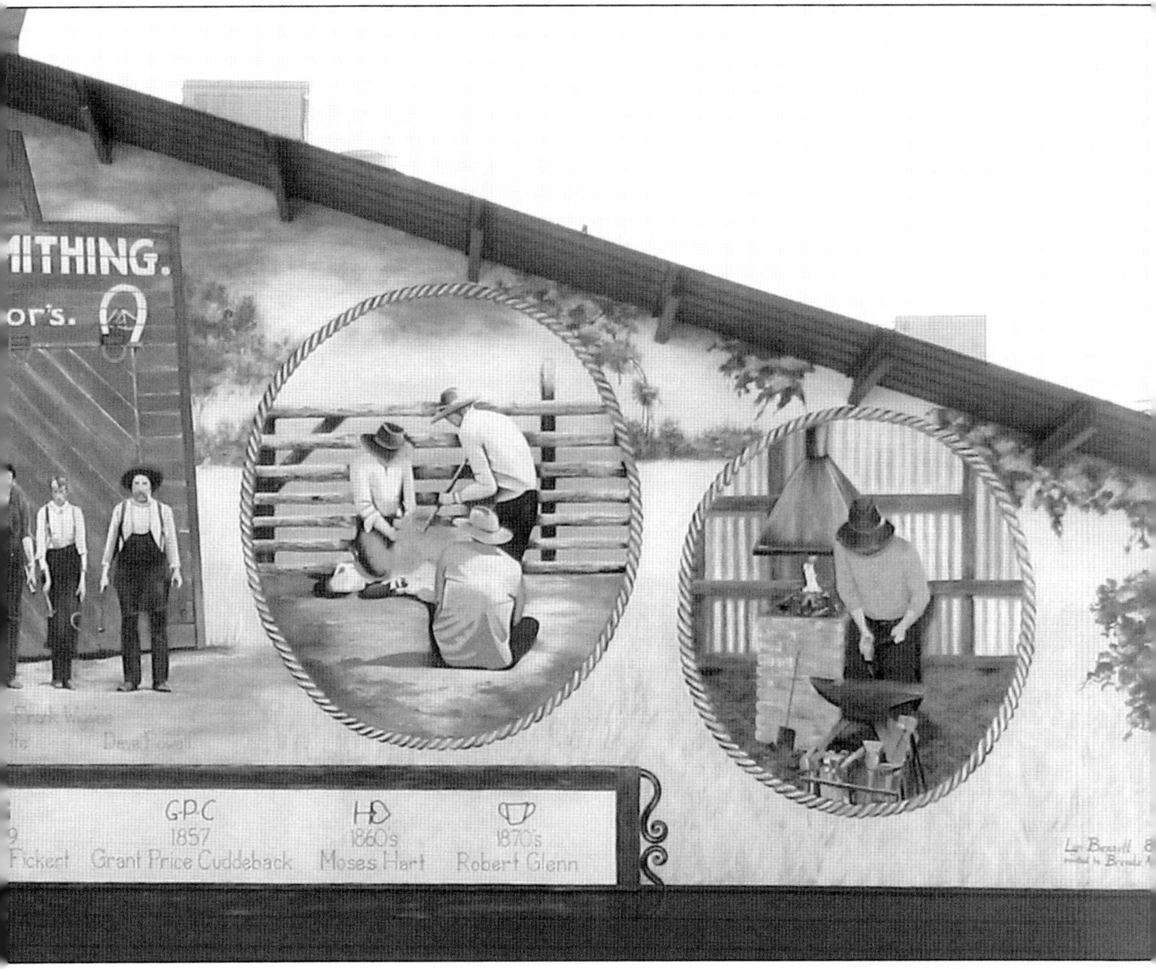

of John Brite and William Wiggins, who arrived here in 1854–1855. Bennett depicts these men and other early settlers who became prominent in local history. The mural was finished in 2005. (Main Street Tehachapi.)

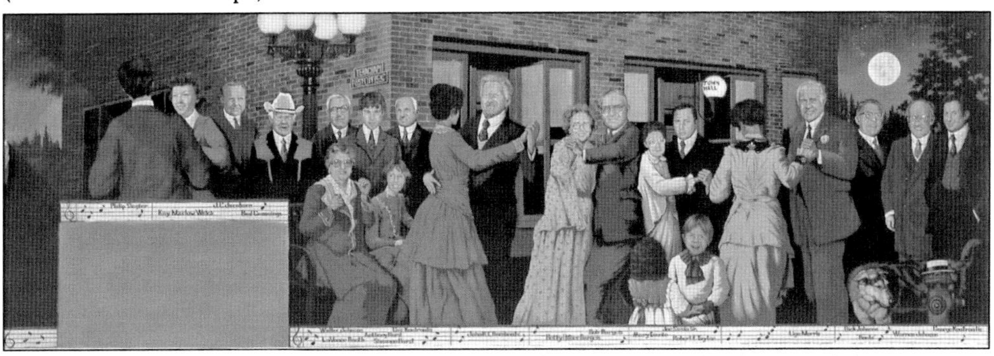

Public response to the first mural prompted more depictions of Tehachapi's rich history. *Street Dance* was taken from a 1915 photograph of residents celebrating the installation of the first streetlights in town. Artist Phil Slagter incorporated the faces of past and current residents (including five former mayors, one child, and a dog) into the scene. The mural was completed in 2004. (Main Street Tehachapi.)

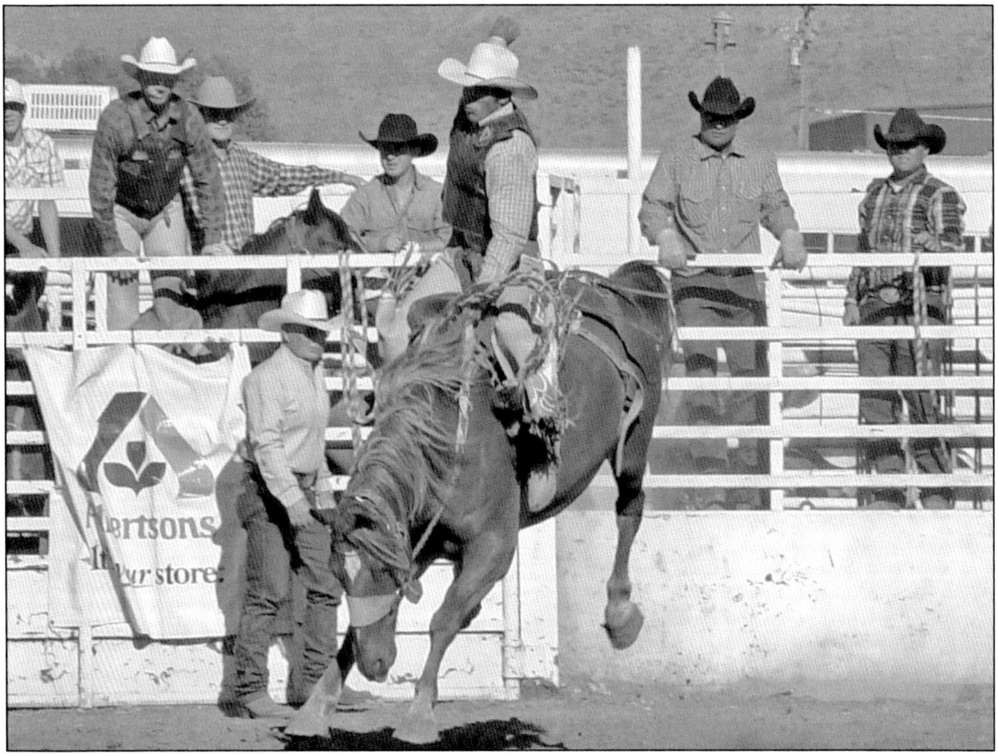

Saddle bronc-riding is but one of the skills of the old *vaqueros* and working cowboys that are showcased each August during the annual Tehachapi Mountain Festival Rodeo. It is a modern rendition of the inter-ranch competitions held on the last day of the old fall roundups. The first recorded Tehachapi Mountain Rodeo was held between Tehachapi and San Joaquin Valley cowboys in 1873. (Diane Wilder.)

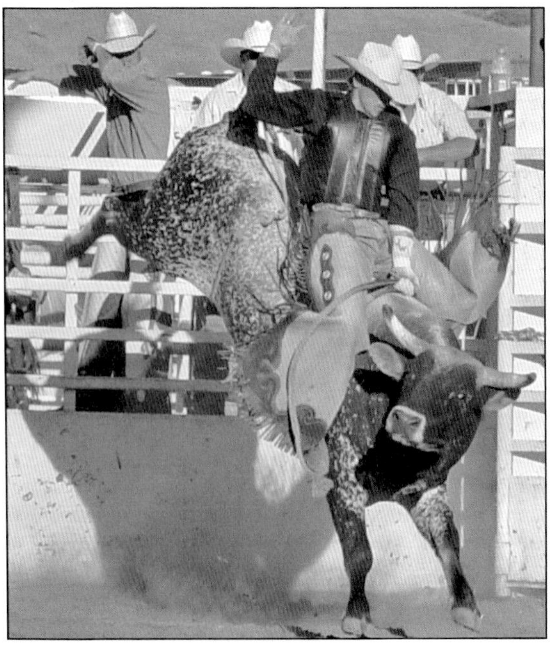

Rodeos, though still wild and woolly, are much safer today than in the past. Now they are held under the auspices of the Professional Rodeo Cowboy's Association (PRCA) and the Professional Bull Rider's Association (PBRA). In 1968, the City of Tehachapi constructed an approved rodeo arena. Previously, all events had been held in a wire-enclosed arena; there, bulls often jumped over the wire and ran amongst the spectators. (Diane Wilder.)

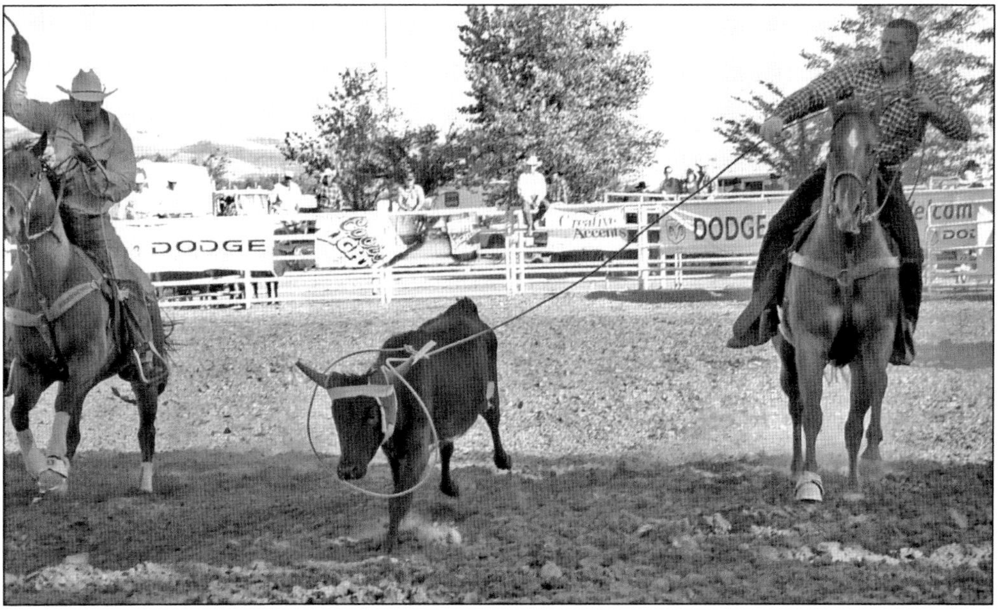

Team roping is an event requiring a good eye, roping skill, and coordination between partners and their horses. The process was originally used to catch and immobilize cows that were to be doctored or branded. Teams may consist of a father and son, father and daughter, husband and wife, or two friends. Team roping competitions are often held on local ranches throughout the year. (Diane Wilder.)

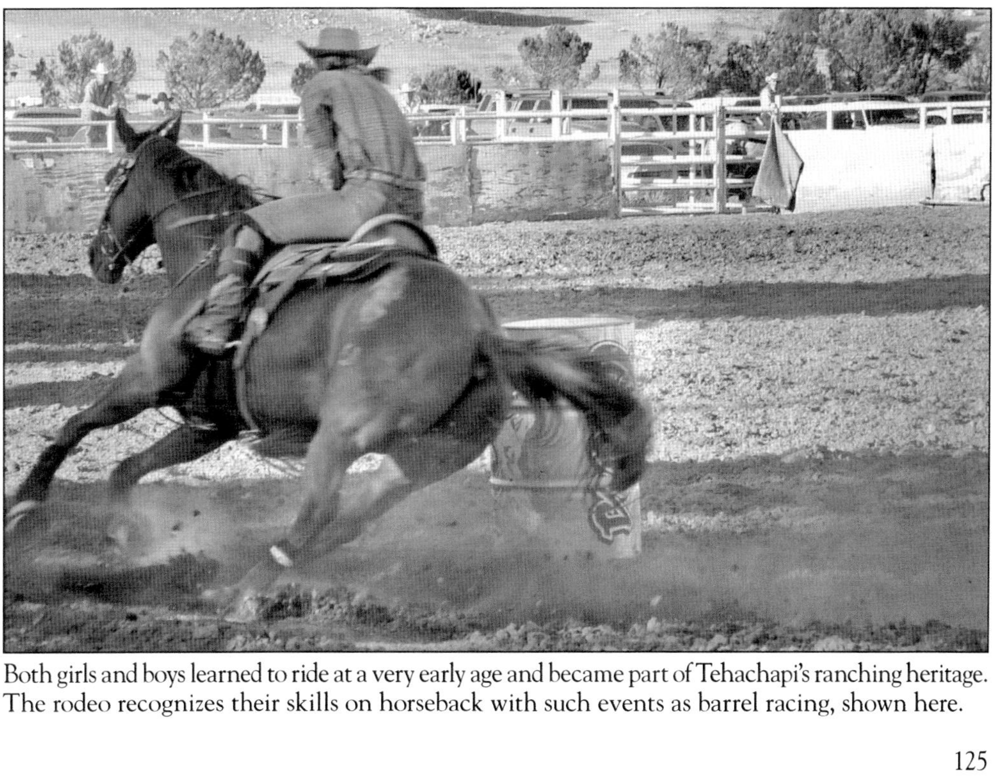

Both girls and boys learned to ride at a very early age and became part of Tehachapi's ranching heritage. The rodeo recognizes their skills on horseback with such events as barrel racing, shown here.

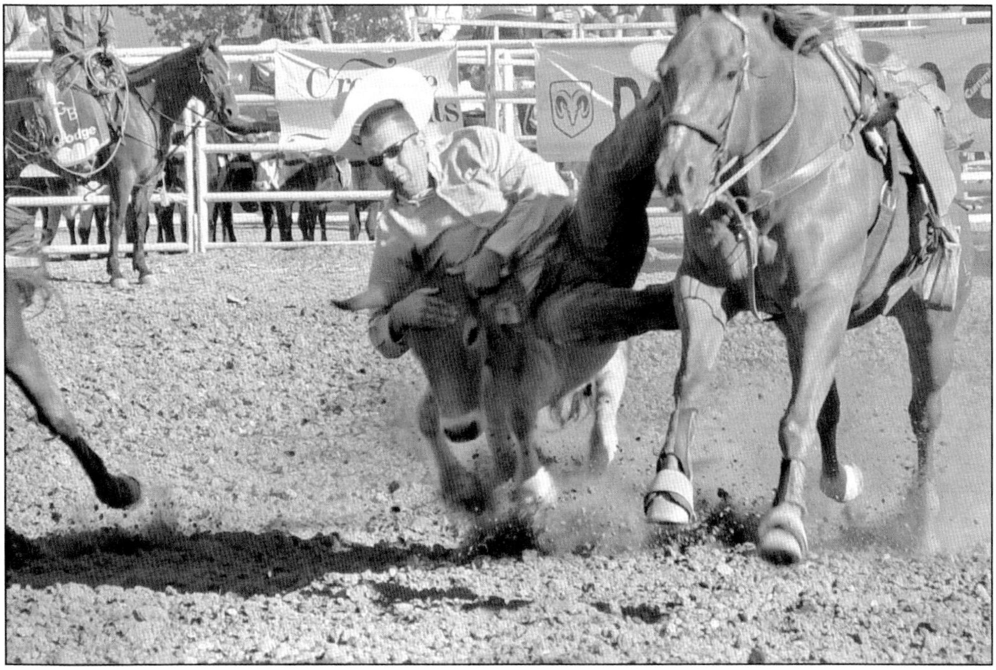

It is called steer wrestling, and the name fits the sport. The rider brings his horse up next to a running steer, then leaps from the saddle, grabs the steer's horns, and wrestles it to the ground.

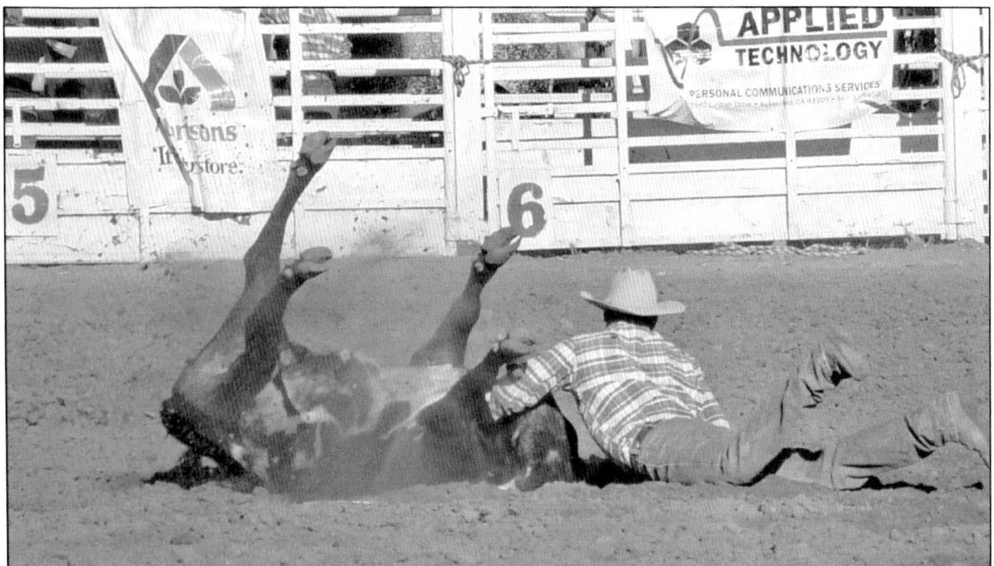

Sometimes the outcome is a draw—both steer and man end up on the ground. It is rough-and-tumble, just like a cowboy's life, and is all part of the tradition of rodeo.

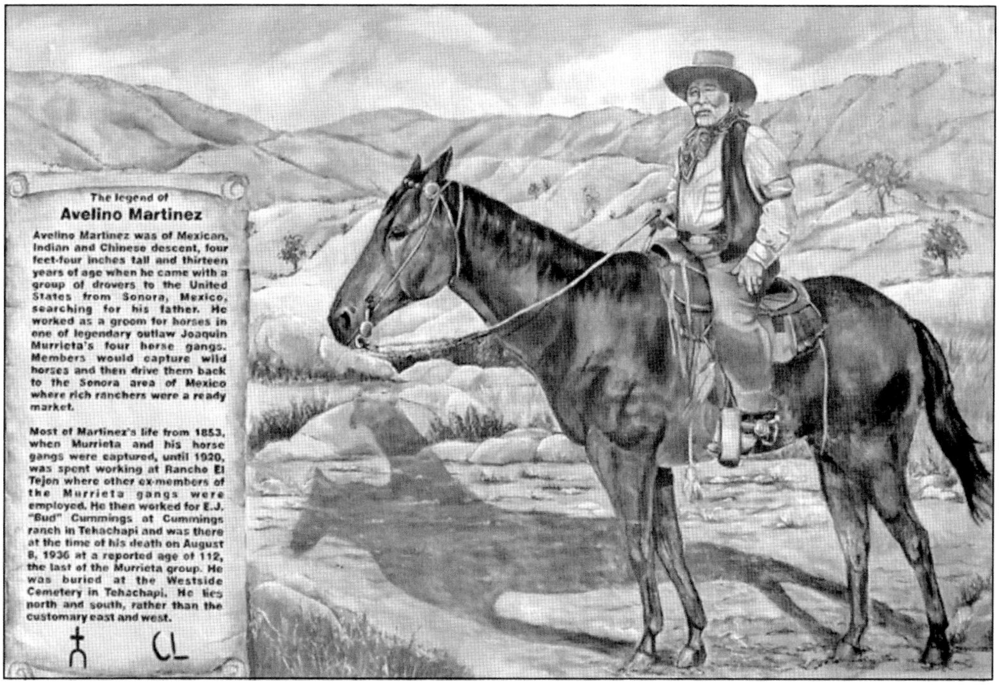

Patti Doolittle won the 2006 competition to paint this mural of Abelino Martinez. The image was taken from a 1940 photograph of the old *vaquero* when he was 110 and still riding horses. Raised in the Tehachapi Mountains, as a youngster Martinez served as a courier for the bandit Tiburcio Vasquez and later worked for both the Cummings and Tejon Ranches. (Main Street Tehachapi.)

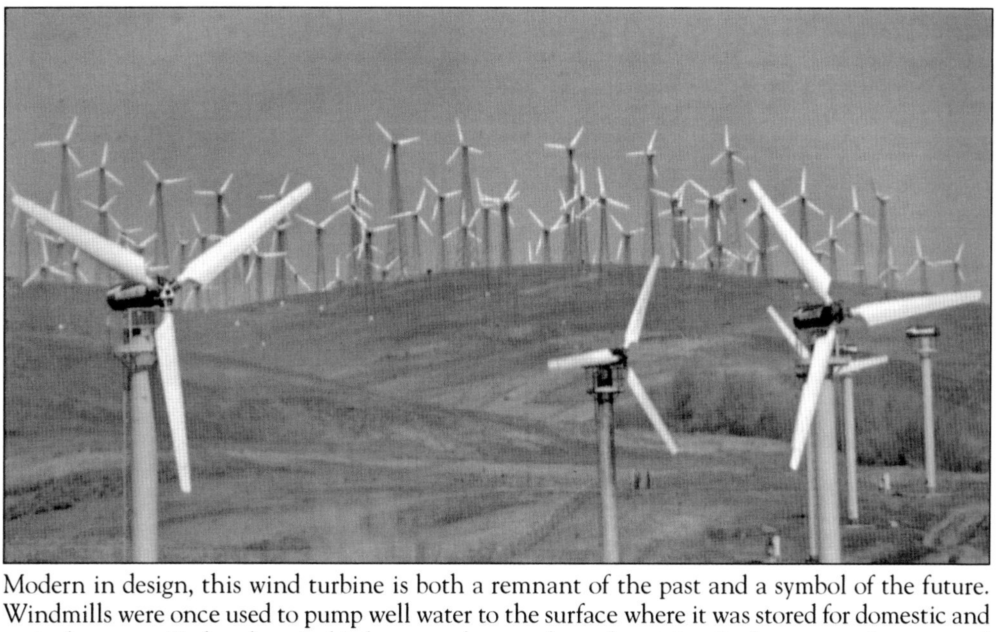

Modern in design, this wind turbine is both a remnant of the past and a symbol of the future. Windmills were once used to pump well water to the surface where it was stored for domestic and agriculture use. Today the wind is harnessed to produce electricity. Such roots to the past and their adaptation for the future may be why the original inhabitants called this area *Ta-chip-i*, or "the place." (Nick Smirnoff.)